# A ROAD TO NOWHERE

The Idea of Progress and Its Critics

Matthew W. Slaboch

**PENN**

UNIVERSITY OF PENNSYLVANIA PRESS

PHILADELPHIA

Published by
University of Pennsylvania Press
Philadelphia, Pennsylvania 19104-4112
www.upenn.edu/pennpress

Printed in the United States of America on acid-free paper
10  9  8  7  6  5  4  3  2  1

A Cataloging-in-Publication record is available
from the Library of Congress.
ISBN 978-0-8122-4980-4

*For my family*
*and to the memory of my father, Ronald W. Slaboch (1946–2016)*

# CONTENTS

Introduction                                                                    1

Chapter 1. "The Same, But Otherwise": Arthur Schopenhauer
as a Critic of "Progress"                                                        9

Chapter 2. The Autocrat and the Anarchist: Nicholas I, Leo Tolstoy,
and the Problem of "Progress"                                                   34

Chapter 3. "The Path to Hell": Henry (and Brooks) Adams
on History and Politics                                                         66

Chapter 4. Critics of the Idea of Progress in an Age of Extremes:
Three Twentieth-Century Voices                                                 89

Conclusion                                                                     110

Notes                                                                          121

Bibliography                                                                    165

Index                                                                          183

Acknowledgments                                                               193

# A Road to Nowhere

# INTRODUCTION

In 2008, Barack Obama campaigned for the American presidency on a message of "hope" and "change." Decades earlier, Ronald Reagan conveyed the same sort of optimism, envisioning for citizens a bright and sunny future: it was "morning in America." No doubt Obama, Reagan, and the countless other politicians who have promised better days ahead believed sincerely that the future looked bright. And why shouldn't they? Americans, living in a country that was founded at the height of the Enlightenment, are conditioned to accept certain principles, not the least of which is a belief in progress. This idea was put forth eloquently in a Fourth of July oration by James Wilson, a signatory of the Declaration of Independence and one of the original justices of the U.S. Supreme Court: "A progressive state is necessary to the happiness and perfection of man. Whatever attainments are already reached, attainments still higher should be pursued. Let us, therefore, strive with noble emulation. Let us suppose we have done nothing, while any thing yet remains to be done. Let us, with fervent zeal, press forward, and make unceasing advances in every thing that can support, improve, refine or embellish society."[1] Wilson concludes his speech by predicting "unceasing advances" not only in agriculture, commerce, and industry, but also in the arts, virtue, and liberty. As a piece of oratory, Wilson's speech is outstanding, with few to rival it. But the message of that speech is hardly unique: from the founding moment to the election and subsequent reelection of President Obama, the idea of progress has found common currency in American politics and society.

Obama's successful presidential bids are not the only testament to the fact that "progress" retains strong rhetorical and political appeal in the twenty-first century. Hillary Clinton and Bernie Sanders, seeking to capture the Democratic Party's nomination to succeed Obama as president, largely eschewed the term "liberal," battling instead over which candidate was the true "progressive." And on both the left and the right, proponents of this or that policy routinely accuse their opposition of being on the "wrong side of history," implying that historical change is unidirectional, a move from worse to better.

At the same time, public discourse and recent polls suggest that ordinary Americans' confidence in the future of their country has been shaken.[2] In June 2016, Obama declared at a town hall meeting in Elkhart, Indiana, that "the notion that somehow America is in decline is just not borne out by the facts." He offered an impassioned defense of his time in office and painted a rosy picture of the state of the union as his tenure wound down. In spite of the president's repeated efforts to reassure them about the prospects for their country, though, American citizens remained unmoved. Gwen Ifill, moderator of the Indiana event, noted with respect to the rhetoric of decline that "it resonates."[3] *New York Times* columnist David Brooks, too, observed that "pessimism is just en vogue . . . the country is not in a mood to think it's heading in the right track. There is almost a near consensus that we are not."[4]

Although not on the ballot, Obama made the 2016 presidential election a referendum on himself and his reforms. On election eve, he told a crowd in Michigan that "tomorrow, you will choose whether we continue this journey of progress, or whether it all goes out the window."[5] And on election day, a plurality of Michigan voters went to the polls to do precisely what Obama had asked them not to do: help ensure that Donald Trump became the forty-fifth president of the United States of America.

In elevating Trump to the presidency, voters repudiated a "third Obama term." Whether they likewise rejected the idea of progress—or merely Obama's vision of progress—is a matter for contestation. Candidate Trump made waves during the 2016 election with his gloomy portrayals of the everyday lives of Joe and Jane Q. Citizen; Hillary Clinton, his chief opponent in the general election campaign, derided him for painting a picture of "midnight in America" rather than "morning in America."[6] In his inaugural address, President Trump retained the somber rhetoric he had used in earlier stump speeches. He spoke of "American carnage" and observed that "the wealth, strength and confidence of our country has dissipated over the horizon." He lamented the "mothers and children trapped in poverty in our inner cities" and the "rusted-out factories scattered like tombstones across the landscape of our nation." But his address was hardly a dirge; Trump coupled his grim portrayal of the present with a lofty vision of the future. Americans may have lost their characteristic optimism, but the new president suggested he would do his part to help restore their faith: "we are looking only to the future," he said, and "stand at the birth of a new millennium." Indeed, rather than tamp down the expectations of an already forlorn citizenry, Trump exhorted his listeners to "think big and dream even bigger" and proclaimed that now was the time to "unlock the mysteries of space, to free the Earth from the miseries of disease, and to harness the energies, industries and technologies of tomorrow."[7]

If pessimism is "en vogue" in the United States, it is no less so in Europe. To its many defenders, the European Union (EU) is a post–World War II success story, an enterprise responsible for bringing peace and prosperity to a conflict-ridden region. But in a 2015 survey of citizens from nine EU member states, nearly three-quarters of respondents felt that the Union is moving in the wrong direction.[8] The ambition of "ever closer union" is uncertain. In place of widening, the process by which the EU's borders are expanded to include new member states, we see contraction, following the UK's June 2016 plebiscite on EU membership. In response to deepening, the process by which an increasing number of decisions are decided at the EU level rather than left to individual states, we see a resurgent nationalism.

Europeans, however, are not merely dissatisfied with the EU; they are also dismayed with the directions their respective countries are taking. A 2016 survey showed that more than 60 percent of citizens in the UK, nearly 70 percent of Germans, more than 80 percent of Spaniards, Italians, and Hungarians, and almost 90 percent of Frenchmen felt that their countries were on the wrong track.[9]

Even if Americans and Europeans were more bullish in forecasts of the future for their homelands, events of the preceding century should force us to reconsider our faith in the continued improvement of humankind as a whole. World War I, early in the century, was soon followed by the rise of fascism in Germany and Italy and communism in Russia. World War II was followed by conflicts in Korea and Vietnam, genocide in Cambodia, and the spread of communism across Eastern Europe and parts of Asia. To cap off the century, violent nationalism tore the Balkans asunder and genocides ravaged Rwanda and Sudan. The possibility that long-term, continued progress might be merely a dream is something people in general and political theorists in particular must consider.

If we look to the canon of political theory, we see that it is filled with historical optimists; skeptics, pessimists, and theorists of decline are exceptional. Modern political thought, in particular, is dominated by thinkers who believe that history tells a tale of progress; such thinkers may not share Gottfried Leibniz's view that ours is the "best of all possible worlds," but they do think the world can become better. Among such theorists was the Marquis de Condorcet, who, having surveyed past developments, predicted for the future "the progress of knowledge and the progress of liberty, of virtue, of respect for the natural rights of man."[10] Figures as distinct as Adam Smith, Immanuel Kant, John Stuart Mill, G. W. F. Hegel, Karl Marx, and the American founders likewise found cause to trust in future progress. The belief that humans are capable of making lasting improvements—intellectual and scientific, material, moral, and cultural—is a commonplace of our age.

To be sure, some brave souls have dared to consider the possibility that progress is more fiction than reality. I contend in this book that we can learn from such thinkers. The figures I have in mind come from the worlds of philosophy (Arthur Schopenhauer, Oswald Spengler), fiction (Leo Tolstoy, Aleksandr Solzhenitsyn), and professional history (Henry Adams, Christopher Lasch). These thinkers are hardly marginal—numbered among them are indisputable masters of their respective crafts, including a Pulitzer Prize winner (Adams) and a Nobel laureate (Solzhenitsyn)—but they are generally relegated to the margins in works by political theorists. Convinced that they are of more worth to political theory than a passing mention or a footnote, I bring them to the forefront by presenting their arguments against historical optimism. To show that these naysayers were not mere defeatists, I also highlight their varied prescriptions for individual and social action.

This book addresses several questions: What do political theorists and political leaders mean when they speak of "progress"? To what end or ends are we supposed to be progressing? What evidence of progress do we have, and, more important (for this project), what are the arguments against its existence? For those who believe in it, is progress to occur organically, or are governments supposed somehow to push it along? For those who deny that progress exists or feel it is not something with which we should concern ourselves, how are we to structure our lives? What is the purpose of politics if not to help make society better and to create lasting improvements?

### Approach and Organization

The idea of progress is commonly associated with Europe's eighteenth-century Age of Enlightenment. Although there are notable thinkers from the eighteenth century who questioned this idea or rejected it outright (Edmund Burke, Joseph de Maistre, and others), stronger critics emerged in the following century. I believe that we can learn from these later critics, who lived in a century that was less violent and destructive than the twentieth, but who nevertheless saw reason to reject the notion that humankind or their own particular societies were improving. What was transpiring in the nineteenth century that made progress seem illusory? And what individual or social action did critics of the idea of progress propose in response? Against whom were these critics arguing? I aim in this book to analyze the main arguments made by important figures, while simultaneously situating those thinkers in their social and historical environments. In the background will be the question why these issues should matter to us today.

Such a book is not only timely, in light of a changing political atmosphere, but in my view necessary as well. For if there is a relative paucity of thinkers critical of the idea of progress, there is likewise a dearth of secondary literature sympathetic to these critics. By contrast, works celebrating the idea of progress and its progenitors are legion. Early in the twentieth century, the Irish historian J. B. Bury penned one of the most famous works of this latter sort, *The Idea of Progress*, which is notable for its contention that "progress" is a modern concept, unknown to the ancients, who thought in terms of historical cycles. Bury, who dedicated his work to "Condorcet, Auguste Comte, Herbert Spencer, and other optimists,"[11] wrote before World War II, a period of unsurpassed barbarism. But even writers who lived through the horrors of that war continued to sing the praises of "progress." Robert Nisbet, who served in the U.S. army during the war and later became a noted sociologist and conservative commentator, contends in his *History of the Idea of Progress* that the "idea of progress has done more good over a twenty-five-hundred-year period . . . than any other single idea in Western history."[12] A strong claim, to be sure, but Nisbet's high estimation of the idea of progress is far from unique in contemporary scholarly circles.

In what follows, I do not attempt to create a genealogy of critics on par with what Bury and Nisbet achieved for champions of the idea of progress. Instead, I aim to understand the conditions that give rise to historical pessimism and to assess the political implications of such pessimism by looking at three particular cultures. I begin in Chapter 1 with a look at German culture. The German lands produced both Leibniz and Hegel, the former a metaphysical optimist and the latter a historical one. However, German culture also gave us Schopenhauer, a deeply severe critic of any sort of optimism. Schopenhauer had as intellectual heirs Friedrich Nietzsche and the German-Swiss historian Jacob Burckhardt, both of whom are considered in their own right.

After exploring German challenges to the idea of progress, I turn in Chapter 2 to the Russian context. Throughout most of its history, Russia has been influenced by, but stood apart from, the West. Nineteenth-century Russia was home to both thinkers who defined progress differently from their counterparts in other countries (for example, the Slavophiles) and those who rejected the concept of progress altogether (for example, Leo Tolstoy). I focus on both types of critic, paying special attention to the latter.

Turning from a society that remained distant from Enlightenment ideals to one founded on such principles, including faith in progress, I look next to the American context. Through much of the country's history, many politicians, writers, and members of the general public have contended that the United States has an obligation to lead the rest of the world to progress. However, such a view has not gone unchallenged. In Chapter 3, I consider as opponents of the predominant narrative two brothers, Henry and Brooks Adams, historians and scions of an important political family.

The comparative focus this project employs has some advantages. It allows us to consider how people in different social contexts defined progress, and also to consider their reasons for doubting that their cultures (or the world) were progressing. Moreover, this approach allows us to see whether the proposals for action differed at all, given different institutional and social constraints. Since its founding, the United States has been a democratic republic. Nineteenth-century Russia, by contrast, was an autocracy. The idea of the "end of history" notwithstanding, the contemporary world is still divided into democratic and nondemocratic regimes, and we may better understand the importance of the idea of progress if we consider its role in multiple social and political contexts. The cases of Germany, Russia, and the United States are particularly illustrative because these countries would become synonymous with the twentieth century's three leading ideologies: fascism, communism, and democratic capitalism, respectively. In this book, I consider the ways in which nineteenth-century proponents and critics of the idea of progress contributed to or helped forestall the emergence of various twentieth-century regime types.

To maximize the benefits of employing a comparative approach, this book engages in not only cross-cultural but also cross-temporal comparisons. In Chapter 4 I turn to prominent twentieth-century critics of the idea of progress—Spengler, Solzhenitsyn, and Lasch. In my Conclusion I explore the contemporary relevance of the ideas explored in preceding chapters; here, I wish to show that nineteenth- and twentieth-century critics of the idea of progress are not mere curiosities who dared challenge one of the dominant paradigms of their day, but thinkers who challenge us even in the present.

In Chapters 1 through 4, the questions asked with respect to critics of the idea of progress are the same: What kind of progress is being denied? Universal? Western? National? What is the argument against progress, that is, how is the argument made? Is it made using historical examples? Is it shown "scientifically"? Or is the idea of progress simply dismissed as self-evidently wrong? Do the authors in question focus on any particular facet of life to show that there has been no progress—cultural and aesthetic, moral, intellectual, and so forth? What are the solutions to the problems of stagnation or decay, that is, how do we reform those facets of society in need of rejuvenation? What should we do as individuals? What should we ask of our fellows? What should we expect from the state? This approach may be formulaic, but it allows me to assess whether and how the social and political context shapes the responses of thinkers who grapple with similar questions in different nations and times.

In my investigation, I seek both to reconstruct the arguments made by the authors in question and to comment upon their ideas. To do so, I select representative passages from main (and sometimes secondary) texts by these authors, which I discuss at length. I find that, when speaking of critics of the idea of progress, one must distinguish between, on the one hand, thinkers who posit that history has no discernable pattern or points straight to decline, and on the other hand, thinkers who believe that history unfolds in a series of predictable cycles. I argue that thinkers of the former type tend to be antipolitical thinkers; they believe that achievements brought about by politics are no more permanent against the tides of history than are sand castles against the tides of the ocean. Cyclical theorists, by contrast, tend to place a higher priority on political engagement; they find in history periods of both progress and decline, and they focus on the ways in which political activity can help prolong advancement or retard decay.

This book looks first at Schopenhauer, who deserves pride of place in a work about critics of the idea of progress for several reasons. First, the term "pessimism" is more closely associated with Schopenhauer and his writings than with any other philosopher or work. Moreover, several of the other authors discussed in this book regarded themselves as intellectual heirs of Schopenhauer. Nietzsche was not alone in seeing Schopenhauer as an "educator."[13] In correspondences with Nietzsche, Burckhardt referred

to Schopenhauer as "our philosopher."[14] Tolstoy asked, "are we two—
Schopenhauer and I—the only two men wise enough to have insight into the
meaning of life?"[15] And Henry Adams paradoxically claimed that he "drew
life from Hegel and Schopenhauer rightly understood."[16] Schopenhauer's
exerting such an influence on these later writers justifies an in-depth treatment of his ideas. And so it is with Schopenhauer that this book begins.

# CHAPTER 1

# "The Same, But Otherwise": Arthur Schopenhauer as a Critic of "Progress"

## Introduction

Scholars have tended to overlook the political import of the ideas of Arthur Schopenhauer (1788–1860). This is perhaps unsurprising, since Schopenhauer himself was not a political philosopher and in fact wrote relatively little about political matters. But his near silence on political topics should warrant our attention: why would a systematic philosopher, who made lasting contributions in metaphysics, ethics, and aesthetics, devote so little of his attention to politics? Surveying the extant literature on Schopenhauer's philosophy, we are hard pressed to find an answer, which this chapter aims in part to provide.

For Schopenhauer specialists, the political dimension of the Prussian philosopher's work has hardly seemed worth addressing. In his impressive intellectual biography of Schopenhauer, David Cartwright contends that his subject approached political affairs with "relative indifference" and that whatever he wrote on the matter was "simply an afterthought."[1] Bryan Magee disagrees on the personal importance of politics to Schopenhauer, arguing that he held his political views "with passionate conviction, and acted on them whenever it was appropriate to do so."[2] But Magee, too, sees fit to offer in his monumental work on Schopenhauer merely a "sketch" (his words) of Schopenhauer's political ideas.[3] Major works by Patrick Gardiner, Christopher Janaway, Dale Jacquette, and Julian Young similarly downplay or outright ignore Schopenhauer's thoughts on politics.[4]

When political theorists bring Schopenhauer into their conversations, they tend to highlight his affinity with or influence on other thinkers, thus minimizing the importance of his ideas in their own right. Joshua Foa Dienstag, for instance, draws parallels between Schopenhauer and Sigmund Freud (1856–1939), contrasting the former's metaphysics with the latter's psychology.[5] Yannis Constantinidès identifies Schopenhauer and the Savoyard conservative Joseph de Maistre (1753–1821) as intellectual allies in the fight against Enlightenment rationalism.[6] The name most readily linked with Schopenhauer's, however, is Friedrich Nietzsche (1844–1900). Schopenhauer's impact on Nietzsche is well known, and it is primarily in Nietzsche studies that one will find political theorists engaging with Schopenhauer.[7]

Only rarely has Schopenhauer's political philosophy been discussed in its own right. The exceptions include a chapter in Raymond Marcin's *In Search of Schopenhauer's Cat*, which focuses on Schopenhauer's theory of justice. Marcin contends that "the implications of Schopenhauer's theory of eternal justice for contemporary political and jurisprudential thought are as sweeping as they are profound."[8] Such a claim might well be defended, but the short (six-page) chapter Marcin offers in support is hardly satisfactory. Neil Jordan offers a more insightful look at Schopenhauer's political thought, elucidating the connection between Schopenhauer's ethical views and his political reflections.[9] Illuminating though his work may be, Jordan is no more likely than Marcin to convince readers that Schopenhauer's ideas have "profound" or "sweeping" implications. The best defense of Schopenhauer's value to those interested in the history of political thought perhaps comes from Robin Winkler, who argues that "Schopenhauer's philosophy is not apolitical but anti-political."[10] Schopenhauer's propounding an antipolitical theory is not in and of itself exceptional; what is so unusual is his antipolitical stance at a time when so much other thought *was* politicized.

I am sympathetic to Winkler's portrayal of Schopenhauer as an antipolitical thinker, but I wish to offer a different take on Schopenhauer's thought, focusing particularly on the relationship between his philosophy of history and his political ideas. I argue that Schopenhauer can best be regarded as a critic of the idea of progress, particularly "progress" conceived of as national development or the growth of the state. His articulation of ideas, strongly at odds with those of Johann Fichte (1762–1814) and Georg Hegel (1770–1831), made Schopenhauer a countervailing force in nineteenth-century German thought. As John Gray says, "few great modern thinkers have gone so much against the spirit of their time."[11]

This chapter proceeds as follows. First, I provide a brief biographical sketch of Schopenhauer. To better explain what makes him novel in intellectual history, I then discuss the idea of progress as it was articulated by four major predecessors in German thought: Immanuel Kant (1724–1804), Johann Gottfried Herder (1744–1803), Fichte, and Hegel. Following this, I re-create Schopenhauer's arguments against the idea of progress, focusing particularly on his attacks on philosophies of history that glorify nation or state. The chapter concludes with a short discussion of Schopenhauer's legacy—which includes his influence on Nietzsche and on German-Swiss historian Jacob Burckhardt (1818–1897)—and his importance for contemporary political thought.

## The Life and Times of Arthur Schopenhauer

For the antinatalist Arthur Schopenhauer, not having been born would have been preferable to existence.[12] But born he was, with February 22, 1788, marking the start of a life full of disappointments. He spent his first five years in Danzig; thereafter, his family called Hamburg home. His father was a successful merchant, and as a youth Schopenhauer apprenticed in this trade. Unsuited for commercial activity, however, he would later quit this pursuit to embark on university studies.

Schopenhauer began his university education at the University of Göttingen (from 1809 to 1811) and later studied at the University of Berlin (from 1811 to 1813). At Berlin, he attended lectures by such prominent philosophical figures (and objects of scorn, for Schopenhauer) as Johann Fichte and Friedrich Schleiermacher (1768–1834). In 1813, the University of Jena awarded him a doctorate in philosophy for his dissertation *On the Fourfold Root of the Principle of Sufficient Reason*. Shortly thereafter, Schopenhauer began writing his masterwork, *The World as Will and Representation*, which was completed in 1818 and published in January 1819.

In the preface to his chief work, Schopenhauer acknowledges Immanuel Kant and Plato as key influences. "I start in large measure from what was achieved by the great Kant," he writes. Indeed, Schopenhauer assumes from his readers a background in Kant's philosophy, regarding familiarity with Kant's ideas as requisite for understanding his own work. He adds, however, that, "if in addition to this the reader has dwelt for a while in the school of the divine Plato, he will be better prepared to hear me."[13] For the introduction to Plato and Kant, Schopenhauer was indebted to Gottlob Ernst Schulze (1761–1833).

To his other, more renowned teachers, Schopenhauer offered less gratitude. In his notes from Fichte's lectures, he remarked that his professor had "said things which made me wish to place a pistol to his chest and say to him: You must now die without mercy, but for your poor soul's sake tell me whether with all that gallimaufry you had anything precise in mind or whether you were merely making fools of us?"[14] Schleiermacher's lectures were hardly an improvement: he "bored the Berlin Academy for a number of years" with his moral discourses.[15]

Schopenhauer's greatest target, however, was not Fichte, Schleiermacher, or any of his teachers, but Georg Hegel. To Schopenhauer, Hegel was a "common mind"[16] and a "repulsive and dull charlatan and an unparalleled scribbler of nonsense."[17] Hegel's philosophy was nothing short of "mind-destroying."[18] Indeed, calling Hegelian ideas "philosophy" would be misleading, for Hegelianism amounts at best to "pseudo-philosophy."[19] Hegel was guilty of "the greatest effrontery in serving up sheer nonsense, in scrabbling together senseless and maddening webs of words, such as had previously been heard only in madhouses."[20] Should we find Schopenhauer's invectives against Hegel in the *World as Will and Representation* too subtle and restrained, the author also offers this in *On the Basis of Morality*:

> Now if . . . I were to say that the so-called philosophy of this fellow Hegel is a colossal piece of mystification which will yet provide posterity with an inexhaustible theme for laughter at our times, that it is a pseudo-philosophy paralyzing all mental powers, stifling all real thinking, and, by the most outrageous misuse of language, putting in its place the hollowest, most senseless, thoughtless, and, as is confirmed by its success, most stupefying verbiage, I should be quite right. . . .
>
> Further, if I were to say that this *summus philosophus* . . . scribbled nonsense quite unlike any mortal before him, so that whoever could read his most eulogized work, the so-called *Phenomenology of the Mind*, without feeling as if he were in a madhouse, would qualify as an inmate for Bedlam, I should be no less right.[21]

To Schopenhauer, anyone who could challenge Hegel's influence had an obligation to do so.[22] He issued this demand with the utmost sincerity, and he himself made an earnest attempt to stem the tide of Hegel's waxing popularity. Having in 1820 secured a teaching appointment at the University of Berlin, where Hegel was then teaching, Schopenhauer scheduled his own lectures against his bête noire's. Hegel's lectures were wildly popular; Schopenhauer's were scarcely attended.

Socrates was sentenced to death by his fellow citizens for having corrupted the youth with his ideas. Hegel, Schopenhauer believed, was actually guilty of such corruption: Schopenhauer lamented the "minds strained and ruined in the freshness of youth by the nonsense of Hegelism."[23] But Schopenhauer's contemporaries failed to condemn Hegel for his "extremely pernicious, really stupefying, one might say pestilential, influence."[24] Instead, they chose to place laurels around his neck and grant him free meals in the prytaneum. Schopenhauer's attempt to counteract Hegel's influence with his own ideas was mostly futile: his teaching career was short-lived, and he would not achieve a literary reputation until late in life.[25]

## The Idea of Progress in German Thought

His ad hominems notwithstanding,[26] Schopenhauer took issue with more than merely the personalities and writing styles of Fichte, Hegel, and other contemporaries; he chafed also at their ideas. Among the ideas en vogue in late eighteenth- and early nineteenth-century Europe, and one with which Schopenhauer took the strongest possible exception, was that of mankind's continual and sustained progress through history. In German-speaking Europe, several marquee names in philosophy, from Herder to Hegel, helped promulgate the idea of progress. As will be shown, the definitions and proposed means of achieving progress varied from thinker to thinker.[27] What I will stress is the shift from the cosmopolitan philosophies of Herder and Kant in the eighteenth century to the nationalistic and state-centric doctrines of Fichte and Hegel in the nineteenth.

Several years before Immanuel Kant offered his musings on universal history, Johann Gottfried von Herder, his one-time student and later rival, propounded his own unique historical vision. Notoriously unsystematic in his thought, the ideas Herder expresses in *This Too a Philosophy of History for the Formation of Humanity* (1774) and *Reflections on the Philosophy of the History of Mankind* (1784–1791) often seem at odds with one another. In the former work, Herder shows an ambivalence toward the idea of progress.

He rejects outright the notion of linear progress, mocking philosophers who espouse that idea: "if only it were true that everything proceeded prettily in a straight line and that every succeeding human being and every succeeding race got perfected according to his [the philosopher's] ideal in a beautiful progression."[28] Instead, Herder argues that with progress in some fields comes regress in others: "the human container is capable of no full perfection all at once; it must always leave behind in moving further on." Thus, for instance, Herder claims that the ancient Greeks built upon Egyptian culture but at the same time neglected and lost certain attributes that had made the Egyptians successful.[29]

In *Reflections on the Philosophy of the History of Mankind*, Herder sounds a more positive note on the idea of progress. Granting that advances in technology, agriculture, and navigation are readily apparent in the course of history, Herder asks: "how have all these arts and inventions been applied? Have practical reason and justice, and consequently the true improvement and happiness of the human species, been promoted by them?"[30] He answers the second question in the affirmative. Certain "rude powers" led mankind out of chaos, and from these powers developed true understanding, which will in turn lead to goodness.[31] Thus, Herder maintains that "there is nothing enthusiastical in the hope, that, wherever men dwell, at some future period will dwell men rational, just, and happy: happy, not through the means of their own reason alone, but of the common reason of their whole fraternal race."[32] The wisdom of the ages contributes to the development of *humanität*, humanity, in whose progress Herder stakes his faith.

One of the major critiques of Herder's philosophy of history came from none other than Kant, who reviewed Parts One and Two of the *Reflections*. The review of Part One, published anonymously in 1785, led to a lasting rivalry between the Königsberg sage and his slighted former pupil. Allen Wood argues that posterity has exaggerated this rivalry between Kant and Herder, whose thoughts on history, he claims, were not terribly dissimilar. However, I would like to point to two important distinctions between Kant and Herder. The first distinction, which Wood himself grants, is that the state plays more of a role in Kant's philosophy than it does in Herder's.[33] Second, I concur with Michael Forster's suggestion that Herder's cosmopolitanism is "more attractive," or at least more sincere, than Kant's.[34]

For Kant, progress comes concomitant with advancement toward a global peace, a peace that can be achieved only through state action. He laments that "Nowhere does human nature appear less lovable than in the relations of entire peoples to one another."[35] However, he foresees a time when international conflict will cease and states will be able to coexist peacefully. He maintains that "wars by which states in turn try to encroach upon or subjugate one another [must] at last bring them, even against their will, to enter into a *cosmopolitan constitution*" (Kant's emphasis).[36] Just as individuals establish civil constitutions to escape the *bellum omnium contra omnes*, states will come together under international law to end conflict among themselves.

Kant argues that *republican* governments will effect the desired change and bring about perpetual peace, and he posits that, having attained such a peace, "progress toward the better is assured humanity."[37] For governments that do not rely on citizen approval, entering into war is "the easiest thing in the world." Ordinary citizens treat war as a serious matter, however, and governments that allow for citizen participation will seek to avoid conflict.[38] Thus, as the prospects for republican government grow, so do the prospects for peace. And, since war is the "greatest obstacle to morality,"[39] the advance of republicanism allows for moral progress: "the good moral education of a people is to be expected from a good state constitution"—that is, a republican constitution.[40]

Kant's vision of political progress leading to moral progress is problematic, specifically with regard to the "cosmopolitan aim" of his universal history. On the one hand, he proclaims his belief in a time when "all the peoples on earth . . . will gradually come to participate in progress."[41] On the other hand, he seems to dismiss the notion that all peoples will play an equal and active role in this progress: he argues that one can discover in *Europe*'s history "a regular course of improvement of state constitutions," and that *European* states will "probably someday give laws to all the others."[42] Such eurocentrism undermines Kant's professed cosmopolitan intent, and it marks a departure from Herder, whose humanism was sincere and consistent.[43]

We see an even more marked change in German philosophies of history as we move from Kant to Fichte, who made no pretensions about offering a cosmopolitan history: Fichte was the German linguistic nationalist scholars so often purport Herder to have been.[44] In place of Herder's pluralistic cultural nationalism, Fichte offered a chauvinistic political nationalism. He articulates his philosophy of world history in *The Characteristics of the Present Age* (1806), and in the later *Addresses to the German Nation* (1808) he pronounces a special role for Germans in that history.

According to the schema Fichte presents in *Characteristics*, humankind progresses through five epochs, from a time during which societies organize themselves through instinct to a point at which they organize themselves according to reason. Fichte characterizes his own age as part of the third epoch, which he regards as a revolutionary moment in history. The third epoch is "the declared foe of all blind Instinct and of all Authority" and has pledged to "accept nothing but what is understood."[45] The ruling powers can no longer expect mere obedience from their subjects; people are questioning the established institutions. However, humans are not meant to remain in this time of tumult and questioning. Rather, Fichte expects humanity to discover what is true and to organize itself in light of this knowledge. What is the life of reason? Fichte explains that it "consists herein,—that the Individual forget himself in the Race, place his own life in the life of the Race and dedicate it thereto."[46]

Fichte guarantees mankind's progress toward the life of reason, insisting that history "proceeds and moves onward according to a settled plan which must necessarily be fulfilled."[47] His philosophy is not strictly deterministic, however, since fulfillment of the great "world-plan" depends on the decisions that humans make.[48] In the *Addresses*, Fichte exhorts his fellow Germans to make the right choices. He gives them an almost divine mission, insisting that "it is the Germans above all who can be expected to begin the new era, leading the way and serving as an example for the rest."[49] He tells his compatriots that "among all modern peoples it is in you that the seed of human perfectibility most decidedly lies, and to whom the lead in its development is assigned."[50] But Fichte recognizes that the German nation cannot achieve its glorious ends without political backing, and thus he declares that "it is therefore to the state that we should first look in expectation."[51]

The state plays no less a role in Hegel's philosophy of history than it does in Fichte's, but Hegel's nationalism is a matter of continual debate. Karl Popper argues in *The Open Society and Its Enemies* that Hegel "developed the historical and totalitarian theory of nationalism,"[52] helping shed German nationalism of any liberal and democratic features and "transforming it into a well-disciplined Prussian authoritarianism."[53] Shlomo Avineri attacks this view, contending that "the Germans of the nineteenth century, who knew Hegel in the context of the German political reality of his period, saw him as utterly hostile to nationalism."[54] However, at least one prominent nineteenth-century critic saw Hegel's philosophy as privileging his place and time:

Nietzsche wryly observes of Hegel that for him "the apex and culmination of the world process coincided with his own existence in Berlin."[55] More recent commentators remain divided as to whether Hegel's division of history into Oriental, Greco-Roman, and Germanic periods constitutes a nationalistic philosophy that glorified the German people.[56]

Less a matter for contention than Hegel's nationalism is the degree to which the state figures in his interpretation of history. For Hegel, the development of the state is the supreme goal of a rational historical process; history is nothing other than the progressive development of mankind from lesser to greater consciousness of freedom, a freedom that can be realized only through the state.[57] Rather than regard the state as something that limits individual freedoms, as people often do, we should recognize it as "the reality within which the individual has and enjoys his freedom, but only in so far as he knows, believes in and wills the universal."[58] At the same time, the state's existence is requisite for a person's showcasing his or her moral nature. "Ethical life is duty," that is, duty to the "whole" or the state, and thus only as part of a state does the human being possess any moral worth.[59]

The gulf between the philosophies of Herder and Kant on the one side and Fichte and Hegel on the other might appear to us as unbridgeable. Herder questions "how man should be made for the state";[60] Hegel questions how a man could matter apart from the state. Kant formulates a universal moral imperative[61] and anticipates a cosmopolitan political order; Fichte stresses national glory and the supremacy of the German people. But while the shift from Herder and Kant to Fichte and Hegel perhaps seems radical to us, Schopenhauer's writings suggest that we ought not to be surprised by the change in tenor as the eighteenth century gave way to the nineteenth. He argues that "constructive histories, guided by a shallow optimism, always ultimately end in a comfortable, substantial, fat State."[62] Whatever their differences, Herder, Kant, Fichte, and Hegel each offered optimistic philosophies of history. Having provided visions of a better future, these philosophers—or their popularizers—naturally desired some entity to bring about that earthly Elysium; almost inevitably, the deity to which the worshippers of progress prostrated themselves was the state. Georg Iggers argues that, throughout the nineteenth and twentieth centuries, we find one dominant tradition of historical thinking among Germans: "conservatives, liberals, democrats, and socialists of every description" were united by "the central role they assigned to the state and in their confidence of its beneficial effects."[63] To Schopenhauer, both belief in progress and faith in the national state to achieve that progress are misguided.

## Schopenhauer on History and Politics: Eadem, Sed Aliter

A true philosophy of history, Schopenhauer insists, amounts to the recognition that in spite of all the upsets and upheavals historians have recorded, "we yet always have before us only the same, identical, unchangeable essence."[64] That essence is the will, the guiding force of the world. In nature, the will manifests itself as magnetism, gravity, and other such scientific occurrences. Among people, the will shows itself in each action an individual takes. Even life itself—the act of existing—is an instance of the will's asserting itself in the world. But the will is unceasing and, ultimately, purposeless: while "every individual act has a purpose or end," the will itself "has no end in view."[65]

Lacking a final end and the possibility of being satisfied, the will makes a Sisyphus of each of us: we traipse through life looking for a contentment we will never find. The will underlies each of our actions; we can do as we want, but we want what we do because of the will. When our desires are not satisfied, we feel deprived. But even when they are fulfilled, the happiness that comes from such fulfillment is fleeting: almost as soon as a desire is met, boredom arises, and it remains until we have some new end to pursue. The pursuit of a new end, however, brings with it new suffering. Thus, Schopenhauer claims, "life swings like a pendulum to and fro between pain and boredom."[66] There is a constant transition from desire, pursuit, and attainment to new desires and pursuits; each fulfilled need or want marks the transition to a new course. And because "there is no ultimate aim of striving," we can likewise say that "there is no measure or end of suffering."[67]

Suffering is a universal problem which optimistic philosophies downplay. Such philosophies are not merely "absurd" but "*wicked*," making a "bitter mockery" of the real and significant pains humanity must endure.[68] Chief among the optimistic philosophers was Leibniz, against whom Schopenhauer takes direct aim:

But against the palpably sophistical proofs of Leibniz that this is the best of all possible worlds, we may even oppose seriously and honestly the proof that it is the worst of all possible worlds. For possible means not what we may picture in our imagination, but what can actually exist and last. Now this world is arranged as it had to be if it were to be capable of continuing with great difficulty to exist; if it were a little worse, it would be no longer capable of continuing to exist. Consequently, since a worse world could not continue to exist, it is absolutely impossible; and so this world itself is the worst of all possible worlds.[69]

Schopenhauer, then, explicitly rejects metaphysical optimism. In its place he proposes a metaphysical pessimism in which an aimless and unquenchable will directs both the natural world and human existence.

Unsparing in his criticism of Leibniz's metaphysical optimism, Schopenhauer even more bluntly condemns historical optimism. Leibniz's theodicy may have been "sophistical," but at least it was not "pernicious" and "pestilential" in the way Hegel's was. Real harm comes less from the belief that ours is the best of all possible worlds than from the belief that our world could become measurably better. Progress-minded historians and philosophers imagine that something new and grand will emerge in the future, and so they look to history for clues as to what might unfold. But only "fools" would "concede to history a principal place in their philosophy," and the belief that the future has something new in store is ill-founded.[70] In the nineteenth century, this naïve belief fostered the growth of the state and the rise of nationalism, two developments Schopenhauer attempted in vain to counteract.

Schopenhauer's expectations of the state are modest: he plainly denies it a grand purpose, claiming that its "sole purpose is to protect individuals from one another and the whole from external foes."[71] Even in this limited capacity, however, the state will fail: internal dissent can never be entirely eliminated, and where it is stifled, the threat of cross-border conflict is never far off.[72] Despite its limitations, the state should nevertheless do its best to provide security. In a manner reminiscent of Thomas Hobbes (1588–1679), Schopenhauer asks us to consider what would happen if the coercive power of the state was cast aside, insisting that "every thinking man will recoil at the expected scene."[73] But beyond providing some order and stability, there is not much that the state can or should do.

Indeed, Schopenhauer seems to concur with Edmund Burke (1729–1797), who declares that "it is in the power of government to prevent much evil," but maintains that "it can do very little positive good."[74] He takes to task eudemonistic optimists who believe that the state exists to foster happiness.

The government's job is not, contrary to some doctrines, to bring about heaven on earth or to arrange society so that all men "could gorge, guzzle, propagate, and die, without effort and anxiety." The belief that the state is capable of bringing about such an arrangement is misguided. People often make this error in judgment, however: "everywhere and at all times, there has been much discontent with governments, laws, and public institutions, but for the most part only because we are always ready to make these responsible for the misery that is inseparably bound up with human existence itself."[75]

But attempts to remake the world through the rejiggering of institutions are futile, Schopenhauer insists: "the ceaseless efforts to banish suffering achieve nothing more than a change in its form."[76] He does acknowledge that "things which in former times one could hardly afford are now obtainable at a low price and in quantities, and even the life of the humblest classes has greatly gained in comfort."[77] However, the abundance of inexpensive goods cannot make people happy: people will always desire more, no matter how much is already available to them. If the government successfully alleviates one misery, new desires and new pains will emerge to take the place of the old. In other words, the state can never eliminate the misery of existence. Even if the state could diminish the suffering that stems from need and want, boredom would simply arise to take the place of this other evil.[78] The "happiness" that we do see in the world is superficial: this so-called happiness is a "hollow, deceptive, frail, and wretched thing, out of which neither constitutions, legal systems, steam-engines, nor telegraphs can ever make anything that is essentially better."[79]

Just as we are wrong if we think that governments can make the world something other than it naturally is, we are misguided if we assume that the state can make man something other than nature makes him. Schopenhauer recognizes that "a few German philosophasters of this mercenary age would like to distort the State into an institution for spreading morality and edifying instruction."[80] However, contra Fichte, Hegel, and their disciples, he maintains that the state is not an institution that exists to promote morality.[81] The wish to make it such is problematic, for several reasons. The first problem, again, is that the goal itself is unattainable; the state cannot succeed at improving man's character. Education or instruction will not change a person's innermost nature, which remains fixed throughout life.[82]

Moreover, if we regard the state as a vehicle to promote morality, then we conflate political goals with ethical aims, lawfulness with morality. Even if some perfect state arose with the capacity to prevent every crime, this state would still be unable to shape morality. The state, with its threats of punishment and rewards, is able merely to shape behavior; it lacks the ability to change people's dispositions.[83] Thus, perhaps the state can mold us as citizens and subjects. But we are more than mere instruments of the state—we are individuals with moral worth, and moral worth is "the principal thing in a man's life."[84] This being so, the working out of his salvation is something that should be left to the individual alone, rather than dictated by the state.

State-led attempts to bring about the moral improvement of mankind are not only ineffectual but dangerous. Behind the seemingly noble objective of inculcating good character lies the more sinister goal of robbing people of their personal freedom and capacity for self-development. Schopenhauer argues that, rather than having a beneficent effect, the state actually harms society when it seeks to make people moral. The state makes men "mere wheels of a Chinese machine of State and Religion" when it tries to edify its citizenry. State-led projects to improve morality lead not to such improvement, but along the road to inquisitions and wars of religion.[85]

Because he believes that individuals should work out their own salvation, Schopenhauer opposes state-sponsored activities that would prevent them from doing so. However, he sees such activity taking place on a grand scale: each of the governments with which he is familiar has taken upon itself "the provision for the metaphysical needs of its members."[86]

One example of overreach might be the state's imposing itself in the sphere of education. Thomas Nipperdey remarks on the establishment of compulsory education in the German-speaking lands: "Nineteenth-century Germany became a land of schools. Alongside compulsory military service and compulsory taxation, compulsory education became one of the basic duties for the modern citizen. It was the state which had established this duty. It organised the schools, thereby intervening in the life of the individual and a person's journey through life, as it had never done before."[87] With compulsory education came increased governmental regulation of the schools and the citizenry. German state governments supervised the curricula of the gymnasia and established approved paths to higher education. Consequently, "by the age of nine or ten . . . the most important decisions about a young person's educational future had been made." But compulsory education was established not merely so that the German governments could control people. Rather, reforms were enacted in part because "many educational innovators had cherished the ideal of universal education as a source of social progress and equality."[88] That is, educational reformers cared about certain "metaphysical needs" of people, and the states took up their cause.

States had certainly placed demands on citizens prior to the nineteenth century, and the Europe of the 1800s cannot be regarded as unique in that regard. However, a movement unique in world history did gain traction in the nineteenth century, and this movement provided a novel challenge to individual self-development. Nationalism, often traced back to the French Revolution of 1789,[89] was one of the chief political concerns of Schopenhauer's day. Nationalist revolutions broke out across Europe in 1848, four years after the second edition of *The World as Will and Representation* appeared and three years before the publication of *Parerga and Paralipomena*.

Just as he was wont to defend the individual against an overreaching state, so too did Schopenhauer defend the individual against the demands of the nation. In one of his essays, he says forthrightly that "individuality far outweighs nationality." For an individual to take pride in his own nation, that individual would be admitting his own inferiority: if he had unique and estimable qualities, he would take pride in those traits rather than in characteristics he shares with millions of other countrymen.[90]

Such antinationalism was in part a legacy of Schopenhauer's upbringing. Brian Magee recounts that Schopenhauer's father selected the name "Arthur" because the name is the same in German, French, and English. Both Schopenhauer's parents were cosmopolitans who traveled widely and took their children on extended trips outside the German-speaking lands. Schopenhauer spent much of his youth in France and England.[91] According to David Cartwright, Heinrich Floris Schopenhauer aimed to instill "liberal and cosmopolitan attitudes in a son [Arthur] who would be well connected to various trading partners."[92] Whether Heinrich successfully implanted liberal ideas in his son's mind is debatable. (I will argue in the next section of this chapter that he did not.) Less debatable is the younger Schopenhauer's cosmopolitanism and lack of attachment to the German nation.

Schopenhauer freely and frequently expresses an aversion to nationalism in several of his works. He manifests his lack of a national pride in several quips about his fellow German-speakers. In *The World as Will and Representation*, for instance, he writes that "for a German it is even good to have somewhat lengthy words in his mouth, for he thinks slowly, and they give him time to reflect."[93] In an essay on government, he maintains that "it is a characteristic failing of the Germans to look in the clouds for what lies at their feet."[94] In no wise could Schopenhauer be proud of a nation that revered Hegel, whose philosophy would serve as "a lasting monument of German stupidity."[95]

But Schopenhauer did not single out the Germans as the only nation with faults. Herder had posed the rhetorical question: "Is not the good on the earth strewn about?"[96] Schopenhauer might have turned this question around and asked whether the bad on earth is limited to one particular group. We know what his answer to such a question would have been: "every nation ridicules the rest and all are right."[97]

Behind his caustic remarks about his own and other nationalities, Schopenhauer harbored real concerns about history and society. Anticipating Benedict Anderson's *Imagined Communities*[98] by more than a century, he refers to nations as "mere abstractions," and argues that "only the individuals and their course of life are real."[99] Histories, focused as they are on national development, may be effective in teaching us about particular groups of *men*, but they reveal less about *man*, that is, about human nature.[100] If we truly wished to understand mankind, we would do well to consult biographies instead of histories, since they are richer in detail and allow us to understand multiple facets of a man's existence.[101] And, where histories pave the way for "comfortable, substantial, fat" states, which devise purely national, political solutions to problems that are universal and moral, proper biographies show us the true route to salvation. That path, according to Schopenhauer is a life of compassion and asceticism, which is an individual's surest way of escaping the torments of the will.[102]

## Schopenhauer and the Twentieth Century

Candide, the titular hero of Voltaire's renowned novella, clings desperately to the optimistic doctrine of his mentor, Pangloss, for as long as he can. But the course of his life causes Candide to lose faith. Having experienced suffering of his own and seen the people he cares about tormented, he begins to question the blithe declaration that "all is for the best." Ultimately, he rejects Panglossianism, and adopts instead the position of his neighbor, a simple Turkish farmer, who, rather than try to rationalize the miseries of the world, turns to his work as an escape from such misery. Candide's takeaway from this lesson is that "we must cultivate our garden," that is, focus on the task at hand, rather than get wrapped up in tortuous philosophizing.[103]

In many respects, Voltaire's Turk represents the Schopenhauerian ideal. Schopenhauer writes that "the most significant phenomenon that the world can show is not the conqueror of the world, but the overcomer of the world."[104] For Schopenhauer, permanent overcoming of the world means denying the will, turning the will against itself—this is the life of the saint who is not beholden to his desires.[105] But there are other, temporary ways of escaping the world. Schopenhauer identifies aesthetic contemplation and the experience of the beautiful and sublime, prompted alike by art and natural phenomena, as something that would allow us to forget our wants, our cares, and our self-interest.[106] The Turk finds his own type of escape, telling Candide that "our work keeps us free of three great evils: boredom, vice, and poverty."[107] Like the Turk, Schopenhauer seeks an "out" from the vacillation between boredom and poverty (or want more generally).

Schopenhauer resembles the Turk in another respect as well. The Turk tells Candide: "I assume that, in general, those who take part in public affairs sometimes perish miserably, and that they deserve it; but I never pay attention to what goes on in Constantinople."[108] I hope to have shown that Schopenhauer held politics in similar low regard. For Schopenhauer and the Turk alike, the onus falls on the individual to find peace for himself; the goings-on of the state are not a matter of top concern, and we should certainly not expect the state to eradicate all evil.

Though I have presented Schopenhauer as an individualist and a skeptic of the state, I do not wish to portray him as a liberal or an anarchist. He does offer, as Neil Jordan observes, what is essentially a Lockean argument in defense of property rights.[109] But in his later manuscripts he writes that "every constitution should be a much nearer approach to despotism than to anarchy."[110] Elsewhere he rejects popular participation in politics, fearing that "all those with narrow, feeble, and vulgar minds are at once in league or instinctively united" and will somehow conspire to suppress men of talent and worth.[111] He argues against trial by jury, fearing not what the masses will do to their superiors, but what they will do to one another: if given the chance, members of the same class would do each other harm, and only judges can rule cases impartially.[112] And, though he stops short of endorsing strict censorship, he decides that he is "very much afraid that the dangers of a free press outweigh its advantages."[113] Schopenhauer's views hardly show the imprint of liberalism.

But if we cannot defend the view that Schopenhauer advocated a liberal politics, nor can we endorse the view that Schopenhauer's system justified or enabled totalitarianism. Other authors have tried to make that case. In his seminal *History of Political Thought*, George Sabine argues that "the intellectual affinities of fascism and national socialism were with philosophic irrationalism," a mode of thinking pioneered by Schopenhauer and Nietzsche.[114] György Lukács, in *The Destruction of Reason*, makes a similar argument, averring that "it is with Schopenhauer that German philosophy starts to play its fateful role as the ideological leader of reactionary extremism."[115]

Sabine and Lukács are correct in that the world Schopenhauer describes is not rational and in that Schopenhauer critiques abstract reason as a basis for constitutions.[116] Sabine and Lukács are also correct in that the foundations for the totalitarian regimes of Hitler and Mussolini were far from rational. But the attempt to link Schopenhauer with fascism or Nazism is more than uncharitable, and to jump from Schopenhauer to the Axis powers, we ourselves must dispense with reason. Only through the betrayal of reason can we make an ardent statist of someone who mocks the "narrow-mindedness and shallowness of the philosophasters who in pompous phrases represent the State as the highest purpose and the flower of human existence."[117] With only the greatest difficulty can we make a militarist of a man whose model is the saintly overcomer-of-the-world rather than the global conqueror. And but by the most convoluted logic can we make an extreme nationalist of someone who declares that "the cheapest form of pride is national pride."[118] Hajo Holborn hits the mark when he writes that "Hitler's whole thinking did not show the slightest impress of Schopenhauer; it was indeed a world apart from a philosophy strongly opposed to man's being submerged in the state and looking for salvation from the ills and sufferings in the negation of the will for life."[119]

If Schopenhauer would have rejected fascism and Nazism, we can be as certain that he would have objected to the communist dictatorships of the twentieth century. He had supported efforts to quash the revolutions of 1848 not solely, as Max Horkheimer argues, because he was concerned about protecting his own privileged place in society and viewed the revolutions as threatening his station.[120] Nor did he reject the revolutions simply because of their nationalist character, although Karl Popper rightly suggests this might have been one of his motivations.[121] Rather, Schopenhauer opposed the revolutions because he was conservative: he praised the English for demonstrating "great judgement" by "sticking firmly and religiously to their ancient institutions, customs, and usages, even at the risk of carrying such tenacity to excess and making it ridiculous."[122] If, during the revolutionary upheaval, his conservatism bordered on *authoritarianism*, this was because he feared "left-oriented Hegelianism" and the possibility of *totalitarianism*.[123]

Schopenhauer, then, was no forerunner of twentieth-century totalitarian movements: his is a philosophy that challenges rather than initiates chauvinist nationalism, party-led communism, or any other totalizing ideology. He feared the state's making us cogs in some great machine, and he warned that the progressive philosophies of his day were leading to just such an outcome. Popper writes that "too many philosophers have neglected Schopenhauer's incessantly repeated warnings; they neglected them not so much at their own peril . . . as at the peril of those whom they taught, and at the peril of mankind."[124] Whether the horrors of the twentieth century could have been averted if Schopenhauer had been better appreciated during the previous century is a matter for contention (to say the least). A more defensible claim, which I have made, is that Schopenhauer was an important intellectual figure who encouraged people to cultivate their own gardens rather than look to the nation-state to bring about the millennium.

## Schopenhauer's Heirs: Jacob Burckhardt and Friedrich Nietzsche

In this chapter, I have stressed Schopenhauer's originality and his attack on the prevailing ethos of his day. Here I will conclude by acknowledging strong similarities between Schopenhauer and two of his successors, Jacob Burckhardt and Friedrich Nietzsche. I will comment, as well, on the relationship between Burckhardt and Nietzsche, noting the influence of the former on the latter. In this short discussion, I by no means attempt a full appraisal of the political ideas of either, which, especially with respect to the voluminous Nietzsche, would be an impossible task for a chapter of this brevity. Instead, I pay special attention to the ideas of Burckhardt and Nietzsche that most bear the imprint of Schopenhauer and most clearly reveal a connection between the philosophy of history and political theory. In the case of Nietzsche, I have chosen to focus on the writings of the great philologist-philosopher's early phase, that is, the period during which he regarded Schopenhauer as his "educator." But I turn first to Burckhardt, who stood in a singularly odd position: as a professional historian who found himself in agreement with Schopenhauer regarding the limits of historical thinking.[125]

Echoes of Schopenhauer abound in Burckhardt's lectures at the University of Basel,[126] published as *Judgments on History and Historians* and *Reflections on History*. The similarities between Burckhardt and Schopenhauer are so striking that Erich Heller goes so far as to say that, by looking to the passages from *The World as Will and Representation* that Burckhardt cites in his lectures, readers may gain an almost complete understanding of Burckhardt's philosophy.[127] And Richard Sigurdson suggests that, in spite of Burckhardt's oft-repeated claims that he lacked a philosophy of history, "Burckhardt perhaps ingested uncritically all that Schopenhauer wrote about the matter."[128] Burckhardt himself noted his affinity for Schopenhauer: to him, his German predecessor was "the" philosopher.[129]

The trait for which Schopenhauer is best known—his pessimism—is also readily apparent in the thought of Burckhardt, for whom there is no rhyme or reason in the world—past, present, or future.[130] Looking to bygone eras, Burckhardt asks us to "regard antiquity as merely the first act of the drama of man, to our eyes a tragedy with immeasurable exertion, guilt, and sorrow."[131] The tragic nature of the human experience, he explains, becomes more readily apparent over time, "the struggle for existence" increasingly manifesting itself in "national wars and deadly industrial competition."[132] There is no cause to believe that this is a struggle with an end, he adds. The Enlightenment's defenders look to the gradual spread of reason as hope for humanity, but they should not: "*The Heightening of Consciousness* in modern times is probably a sort of intellectual freedom, but [it is] at the same time a heightening of suffering. The consequences of reflective thought are postulates which can set whole masses in motion, but, [which] even when fulfilled themselves, will only produce new postulates, i.e., renewed desperate and consuming struggles."[133] The Enlightenment encouraged competing camps to pursue seemingly high-minded ideals; in truth, rival groups sought the same end—"happiness," which really boiled down to material comfort—but disagreed on the best way to achieve that end. To Burckhardt, partisans of all stripes, past and present, have engaged in battles they could not win, for "material desires are in themselves absolutely insatiable, and even if they were continually gratified, then they would be all the more insatiable."[134] Because he cannot countenance a time when humankind would see all its wants satisfied, Burckhardt concludes that he must "reject the eudemonic, the so-called progressive, way of thinking."[135]

Burckhardt's idea of eternal struggle in history closely mirrors Schopenhauer's doctrine of the unceasing will. And, just as Schopenhauer came to

regard political endeavors as, at best, futile efforts to keep privation at bay,
so too did Burckhardt. Burckhardt observes that "the theory prevalent in
modern times claims absolute and universal power of the state as a major
aim of all existence." He cautions against the prevailing view, however, insisting that "power usually does not make men better and scarcely ever
happier, because of their inner insatiability."[136] Burckhardt did not regard
state-sponsored programs as merely ineffective, though; like Schopenhauer,
he viewed the state askance, wary of potential abuses of power. To his
eyes, "power is in its nature evil, whoever wields it."[137] He lamented, for
instance, the fact that citizens and subjects are forced to open their
pocketbooks for the state, an entity that in turn squanders any chance of
present contentment in its pursuit of a greater future bliss: "the state in-
curs those well-known debts for politics, wars, and other higher causes
and 'progress.' "[138] State policies are not simply well-meant endeavors
that fail in their execution; frequently they are ruinous (financially and
otherwise).

While Burckhardt traced increased state profligacy to modern theories
of credit,[139] he attributed another recent scourge—nationalism—to the
French Revolution. The Revolution and the wars that followed, he observed,
cemented links between members of already unified groups and sparked nationalist sentiments where they had not previously existed. In France, the
revolutionaries embarked on a campaign of "*lawless centralization*." The republic they created was fit to "serve as a model for all despotisms for all eternity." And, indeed, the states of Europe were quick to model themselves
after France; "even in the monarchies," Burckhardt writes, "this centralization has existed in complete form . . . only since the revolution, having been
created partly for purposes of defense, partly as an imitation."[140] One aspect
of this ongoing process of centralization is the melding of state and nation,
which in the postrevolutionary period are to be "coterminous." The state is
to "expand until it encompasses all who speak the same language." As a
matter of domestic policy, "foreign elements already within the state are
crushed." With respect to external affairs, "the nationalistic state can never
be too powerful or can hardly be powerful enough."[141] For Burckhardt, the
logical implications of linguistic nationalism and further state centralization
and expansion were unwelcome, for they spelled the demise of his multilin-
gual Helvetic homeland.[142]

In much of his political thinking, Burckhardt was unremarkable, advocating positions typical of conservatives of his day (though describing his

stances with incomparable elegance).[143] But his novel approach to the writing of history did have some unique and important implications for the way that we think about politics. With a mockery fitting for a disciple of Schopenhauer, Burckhardt dismisses "the philosophical concept (Hegel!) which would pass the state off as the realization of morality on earth."[144] As propagandists of the Hegelian idea, the historians of Burckhardt's day viewed themselves as midwives in service to the state; the state would deliver progress, while the historians would show the way. But Burckhardt did not share his brother historians' view of progress, and he did not see himself as a servant of the state. Instead, he regarded himself as a guardian of *culture*. Defining history as *"the record of what one age finds worthy of note in another,"*[145] Burckhardt would draw attention to noteworthy works of art and poetry, and he himself would approach his craft with "the sensibility and intuition of the artist."[146] *The Civilization of the Renaissance in Italy* is Burckhardt's best-known work, and it represents an attempt to move historiography beyond its myopic focus on states, nations, battles, and diplomacy by incorporating a discussion of mores, morals, and the arts.

A challenge to historians to reconsider how they practice their discipline, *The Civilization of the Renaissance in Italy* is at the same time a challenge to members of a wider audience to reconsider how to view politics. In this piece, Burckhardt writes of the "State as a Work of Art,"[147] a work of art in the sense that it is "the outcome of reflection and calculation." The state as a work of art emerged as a "new fact" in world history during the Renaissance;[148] Florence, in particular, "deserves the name of the first modern State in the world." In Florentine history, "the most elevated political thought and the most varied forms of human development are found united."[149] Florence, too, produced—"of all who thought it possible to construct a State, the greatest beyond all comparison"—Niccolò Machiavelli. Granting that "the objectivity of his political judgement is sometimes appalling in its sincerity," Burckhardt admires Machiavelli precisely for this objectivity, and he commends the fact that "Machiavelli was at all events able to forget himself in his cause."[150] The aspiration to objectivity and the delineation of paths that would allow one to forget oneself are, as noted earlier, hallmarks of Schopenhauer's thought. For Schopenhauer, aesthetic appreciation was one way by which the ego might be overcome, which, in the context of the present discussion, raises an interesting question. If the state is regarded as a work of art, might one lose oneself through the disinterested admiration of it? Burckhardt's thought seems to offer an answer in the affirmative.[151]

Burckhardt's advocacy of an aesthetic understanding of the world and for deeper commitment to culture has important political consequences. Through his investigations, Burckhardt notes in history a peculiar tendency: "It cannot stand variety. Clerics of all denominations, fanatics of all denominations and non-denominations, popular philosophers, dynasts, and radical politicians who in history cannot stand the sight of rival forces and their fights demand one thing, completely and immediately, too, although this would make the world dead and colorless until those concerned killed one another out of sheer boredom or produced a new conflict."[152]

A "dead and colorless" world is precisely what Burckhardt fears. In our own day, nationalism might be regarded as a response to the homogenizing effects of globalization. But in Burckhardt's time, nationalism could be considered a threat to the world's variety. Burckhardt's fear of the pernicious effects of nationalism and the development of the unitary state led him to defend localism, federalism, and the numerically smaller peoples of Europe. This fear also led to the conclusion that "the savior of Europe is, above all, he who saves it from the danger of an imposed politico-religious-social unity and forced leveling which threaten its special character, the varied richness of its spirit."[153]

Burckhardt prophesied dark days ahead for Europe. And while he knew that he was in no position to serve as the admiral who would lead the continent through stormy times, he pledged to do his small part to keep the ship afloat. "We may all perish," he wrote to a friend, "but I for one shall choose the cause for which I am going to perish: the culture of old Europe."[154] Burckhardt would serve this cause by doing what he had been doing: delivering lectures on European cultural history. Alan Kahan writes that Burckhardt viewed educating the public as necessary if Europeans were to preserve their cultural heritage and traditional values. While Burckhardt harbored no high hopes for the masses, an elect minority would surely hear his pleas and guard the art, artifacts, and customs of their forebears. But, Kahan adds, Burckhardt thought this was the best that could be hoped for—mere preservation of older culture, because the nineteenth century was not a time ripe for the creation of anything new and worthy.[155] If new culture is to emerge, "great individuals are needed, and they need success."[156] The question of how to cultivate the conditions needed for great individuals to flourish would fall to Burckhardt's junior colleague at the University of Basel, Friedrich Nietzsche.

Nietzsche taught classical philology at Basel from 1869 to 1878. While there, the young professor gained the acquaintance of Burckhardt, and the two struck up a professional relationship that remained long after Nietzsche vacated his teaching position. The two men shared above all an interest in Schopenhauer. In his writings to Nietzsche, Burckhardt referred to Schopenhauer as "our philosopher."[157] And Nietzsche, during his Basel days, spoke of "Schopenhauer as educator," the title of one of his *Unfashionable Observations*.[158] But Schopenhauer was not Nietzsche's only educator—Burckhardt himself taught Nietzsche a great deal. In an 1870 letter to a former classmate, Nietzsche wrote of sitting in on Burckhardt's weekly lectures. Of his elder colleague, Nietzsche writes: "I believe I am the only one of his 60 listeners who understands his profound train of thought with all its strange twists and breaks wherever the matter fringes on the questionable. For the first time I have enjoyed a lecture."[159] Nietzsche was not only fascinated by, but also eager to please his new mentor. Sigurdson writes that "Nietzsche would send Burckhardt a copy of each new book that he published, and just as dutifully. . . . Burckhardt would respond coolly but politely, that he could not comment on the subject because it went far above his poor old head, and then he would ask about Nietzsche's health or some such thing."[160] Despite these rebuffs, Nietzsche remained fond of Burckhardt, to whom he would address his final letter.[161] Although his thought changed in a dramatic fashion as he aged, there would remain for Nietzsche, in the words of Heller, two men "whom he continued to love, respect and admire: Schopenhauer and Burckhardt."[162]

The parallels between the thought of Nietzsche and that of his predecessors are multiple. First, there is the rejection of optimistic philosophies of history. Nietzsche writes of his age as a world "shrouded in lies," false doctrines that "do not necessarily have to be religious dogmas, but only such misguided notions as 'progress.'"[163] And he speaks critically of Hegel for spreading the idea of a "world process" and for trumpeting his age as the telos toward which all prior history had been moving.[164] The second aspect of his thought that Nietzsche shares with Burckhardt and Schopenhauer is his antipolitical stance. He writes: "any philosophy that believes that the problem of existence can be altered or solved by a political event is a sham and pseudophilosophy. . . . How could a political innovation possibly be sufficient to make human beings once and for all contented dwellers on this earth?"[165] As Tamsin Shaw argues, the "principled stand against political power" that Nietzsche takes is possible *because* he rejects "the theological or quasi-theological attitude to history" shared by his contemporaries.[166] In rejecting the very idea of a goal in history, Nietzsche simultaneously casts aside the notion that there is a trend toward some ideal political framework and dismisses state-led efforts to bring about "progress."

Nietzsche, like Schopenhauer and Burckhardt before him, matched his disdain toward the realm of politics with a high valuation of the realm of art and culture.[167] In *The Birth of Tragedy* he famously celebrates the pre-Socratic period in Greece, hailing ancient Greeks for their ability to harness both "Dionysian" and "Apollonian" energies. From Burckhardt's *Civilization of the Renaissance in Italy,* he learned to appreciate the Renaissance as another worthy era.[168] His own age, however, he held in low regard, noting "how wretched we modern human beings are when compared to the Greeks and Romans."[169] He recognized state-led efforts to revive culture, but he lamented the fact that "everywhere where culture now seems to be promoted most energetically the goal of culture remains unknown." In fact, there was an antagonism between state and culture, since "no matter how loudly the state proclaims all that it has done for culture, it promotes culture only in order to promote itself."[170] The idea that the state poses as a threat to true culture is Burckhardtian; the Swiss sage speaks derisively of "the modern centralized State, dominating and determining culture, worshipped as a god and ruling like a sultan,"[171] noting too that "powerful governments have a repugnance to genius."[172] Here is not simply an issue of common ideas between two thinkers, but one of the influence of one scholar on the other. Shaw writes of Nietzsche that it was Burckhardt who "provided him with a view of politics that emphasized the perpetual potential conflict between coercive political power and the realm of culture, governed by the noncoercive authority of norms."[173]

Burckhardt and Nietzsche agreed in their diagnoses of threats to culture, but they parted ways with respect to what could be done to preserve or promote it. Burckhardt, we have seen, expanded Schopenhauer's definition of the aesthetic to include history. Prone to resignation from his youth,[174] he would content himself with teaching about the great works of the past and contemplating history's strange and beautiful course. Nietzsche, too, went beyond Schopenhauer in his understanding of the aesthetic, declaring in *The Birth of Tragedy* that "it is only as *an aesthetic phenomenon* that existence and the world are eternally *justified.*"[175] If life itself is art, an act of creation, then Burckhardt's resigned approach would not do for Nietzsche. Nietzsche writes that "we possess nothing but this brief today in which to show why and what purpose we have come into being precisely at this moment." He adds that "we have to approach existence with a certain boldness and willingness to take risks."[176] Dienstag rightly argues that Nietzsche's advocating such boldness marks a key distinction between Nietzsche and his predecessors, a difference Nietzsche recognized all too well.[177]

Nietzsche departed from Burckhardt in another way, too. His older colleague had spoken of the need for great individuals, but let the matter drop. Nietzsche picked up that issue and, as Sigurdson suggests, "went well beyond Burckhardt's intentions."[178] Nietzsche questioned, "given the dangers threatening our age, who . . . will pledge his services as sentinel and champion of humanity, to watch over the inalienable, sacred treasures amassed by such diverse generations?"[179] From Burckhardt's perspective, such a question was appropriate. But Nietzsche's answers gave him pause. In the period during which Nietzsche and Burckhardt had personal contact, the former had already begun speaking not only of humanity's *need for* but of its *need to produce* great individuals.[180] The individual, he said, could "obtain the highest value" and guarantee the "deepest significance" for his or her life by "living for the benefit of the rarest and most valuable specimens" of humanity.[181] The inegalitarianism implied here is as much a facet of Burckhardt's philosophy. But, over time, Nietzsche's philosophical lexicon changed. Nietzsche began writing not merely of humanity's "best specimens," but of a race of *supermen*.[182] He moved past the call to embrace the will to life, and began talking instead about a "will to power." This was not language that Burckhardt, who declared that power is inherently evil (and who could not look "beyond good and evil"), could endorse;[183] it was, however, a vocabulary that would appeal to Oswald Spengler (1888–1936). Thus Nietzsche might be regarded as the link between the pessimistic Schopenhauer and Spengler the same way that Fichte is the bridge between the optimistic Kant and Hegel.

# CHAPTER 2

# The Autocrat and the Anarchist: Nicholas I, Leo Tolstoy, and the Problem of "Progress"

Progress? What progress? This word must be deleted from official terminology.

—Tsar Nicholas I

Those who believe in progress are sincere in their belief, because that faith is advantageous to them. . . . I involuntarily recall the Chinese war, in which three great Powers quite sincerely introduced the belief in progress into China by means of powder and cannon-balls.

—Leo Tolstoy

## Introduction

The man credited with instigating Russia's autochthonous philosophical tradition is Grigory Skovoroda (1722–1794), known to his countrymen as the "Russian Socrates." That an entire millennium passed between the more renowned Athenian thinker's death and the birth of philosophy in Russia points to two things: first, the relative newness of academic philosophy in Russia; and second and more important for present purposes, the chasm that separated Russian and West European cultures until and, indeed, beyond the eighteenth century. On the first point, little changed in Russia after Skovoroda's appearance on the scene. As James Edie, James Scanlan, and Mary-

Barbara Zeldin note, "Russian philosophical thought has been uniquely non-academic and non-institutional,"[1] and it remained so after Skovoroda's death.[2] With respect to the second point, the situation in Russia did change dramatically in the nineteenth century; though Russia had long slumbered in a quiet corner of its own, in the nineteenth century it became a more noticeable player on the world stage, jolted wide awake by an existential crisis. The instigator of this crisis was not a grecophile Russian philosopher, but an expansionist Corsican emperor-general. The ill-fated incursion of Napoleon Bonaparte (1769–1821) into Russia prodded the Russian bear into action, with Russian forces under Tsar Alexander I (1777–1825) playing a pivotal role in bringing about the end of the Napoleonic Wars in Europe. Bonaparte's march on Moscow also stirred the collective conscience of the Russian intelligentsia, who, with the Grand Armée not merely at their doorsteps but actually quartered in their homes, were forced to confront Russia's relationship with Europe.

To be sure, the question of Russia's relationship with its western neighbors had been raised before. Indeed, during his tenure as tsar, Peter I (1672–1725) had sought to definitively answer the query whether Russia belonged to Europe; seeking to dispel any doubts, Peter embarked on a massive reform campaign that sought to reorganize Russian society in the mold of Western Europe. To underscore his country's connectedness with Europe, the tsar commissioned the building of St. Petersburg, a new capital that would serve as his "window to the West" and as a visual reminder of Russia's proximity to other European lands. Not merely symbolic, Peter's reforms also included modernization of the Russian army and navy, reorganization of the civil service such that it became more meritocratic, changes to the tax code, establishment of institutes of higher education, and secularization of the office of the tsar.[3]

Peter's greatness and the wisdom of his policies did not go unquestioned, however. Though Cynthia Whittaker suggests that each generation of Russians from Peter's reign onward "expected its own 'reforming tsar' to accommodate whatever was perceived as necessary for progress,"[4] Hugh Ragsdale argues that Peter's agenda was hardly endorsed in his own time, let alone held up as a model by subsequent generations.[5] Even if there had been a favorable consensus regarding the Petrine reforms, enthusiasts of Peter's policies would have found themselves disappointed by the tsar's successors: whereas Catherine II (1729–1796), German by birth and a correspondent of Voltaire, was a notable reformer and a proponent of the

Enlightenment,[6] other Russian rulers are more likely to see their tenures deemed "reactionary" than "progressive."[7] Indeed, under Nicholas I (1796–1855), the very concept of "progress" had become verboten, to say nothing else of other Enlightenment ideas.

But, although Nicholas I may have sought to stamp out the very term, "progress" was a watchword during his tenure as tsar. While historians typically describe the tsar's reign as conservative and even repressive, it was also a time of unmatched scholarly activity in Russia. Nicholas took the reins of power in 1825, just more than a decade after the expulsion of Napoleon's forces from Moscow. With the memory of the French invasion still fresh, Russian thinkers rekindled a debate that Peter had sought to stifle a century prior: did Russia's future lie with or apart from Europe's? Two main camps emerged with answers to this central question of the day: the Slavophiles, opponents of the Petrine reforms who believed that Russia's salvation lay in her return to native-born practices, and the Westernizers, who favored further reform and emulation of Europe. Different as their views were, the Slavophiles and the Westernizers found common cause in at least one area: the belief in progress. As Andrzej Walicki writes, "it is no exaggeration to say that in nineteenth-century Russian thought the idea of progress was even more central and pronounced than in West European or American thought of the Victorian Age."[8] To find prominent nineteenth-century Russian criticism of the idea of progress, we must look toward the end of that century in the works of Leo Tolstoy (1828–1910), the preeminent writer of his age and one of this chapter's main subjects.

At first blush, it might seem strange that Tolstoy, an anarchist and apostate, would hold any but the most superficial beliefs in common with Nicholas I, whose governing motto was "Orthodoxy, Autocracy, and Nationality." But both men had reasons to be skeptical of the belief in progress. Nicholas could equate calls for "progress" with far-reaching demands on his government. Tolstoy, in turn, had reason to fear that the Russian autocrat (or anyone in a similar position of power) could require great sacrifices from his subjects in the name of progress. This chapter argues that, despite their enormous differences, Nicholas and Tolstoy found common cause in their fear of the political implications of the idea of progress.

The chapter proceeds as follows: it begins by analyzing the ideas of Petr Chaadaev (1794–1856), whose writings sparked nineteenth-century Russia's great debate about the trajectory of history. It then presents the doctrines of the Slavophiles and the Westernizers, the two camps that emerged to answer

Chaadaev's principal questions. After highlighting what Nicholas I feared about Slavophile and Westernizing ideas of progress, I turn to the life and work of Leo Tolstoy, who waged an internal debate about meaning in history before he shared his conclusions with others. Finally, the chapter compares and contrasts Nicholas and Tolstoy as critics of the idea of progress.

### A Challenge Issued, a Challenge Accepted: Petr Chaadaev and the Slavophile-Westernizer Debate

Grigory Skovoroda may have laid the groundwork for academic philosophy in Russia, but Petr Chaadaev, a noble and former army officer, had a more pronounced and far-reaching impact on Russian thought. Chaadaev is particularly important for having instigated a discussion about Russia's place in world history. In his *Philosophical Letters* (begun in 1829), he threw down the gauntlet, telling his compatriots that "Historical experience does not exist for us; centuries and generations have passed without benefiting us. To behold us it would seem that the general law of mankind had been revoked in our case. Isolated in the world, we have given nothing to the world; we have not added a single idea to the mass of human ideas; we have contributed nothing to the progress of the human spirit. And we have disfigured everything we touched of that progress."[9] Chaadaev's denunciation of his country's place in the world of thought was bound to cause a reaction from his readers. The reaction he received was censure from Tsar Nicholas I, who had Chaadaev declared mad and placed under house arrest.[10] But the response he had hoped for was the discussion and development of "a wholly new philosophy of history."[11] His philosophical letters provided ample ammunition for both camps that emerged to accept his challenge in the 1840s.

Chaadaev shared numerous beliefs with the Westernizers who would follow him. The first, already alluded to, was the concern that throughout its history Russia had remained too distant from her Western neighbors. While admitting that Europe had its vices, Chaadaev nevertheless insisted that his countrymen could learn from Europeans by paying particular attention to the characteristics that were leading them along "the road to greater moral perfection and indefinite progress."[12] To become like "other civilized nations," that is, the West, Chaadaev lamented that it would be necessary for Russia "to repeat the whole education of mankind."[13] He warned, however, that such a lesson would not be learned overnight and without effort: "is it not absurd to suppose," he asked, "that we can appropriate in one stroke this progress of the peoples of Europe, made so slowly through the direct action of a unique moral force, and to suppose that we can do this without even trying to find out how it developed?"[14]

Westernizers could find common cause with Chaadaev, too, when it came to accepting the Enlightenment faith in reason. Chaadaev believed, first, that rational inquiry could help elucidate the forces that govern the natural world. Although generations had remained ignorant of these forces, mankind could be assured that "human reason should discover all that for itself, little by little."[15] But second, and more germane to the present discussion, Chaadaev believed that rational investigation could unlock the laws that shaped humanity's development over time. In his call for a new philosophy of history, Chaadaev maintained that the mere accumulation of facts would not suffice. Rather, it was necessary to ascertain "the features of each epoch according to the laws of practical reason."[16] If Russia were to emulate the West, understanding why Europe developed as it did would be more fruitful than merely surveying the events that had transpired during that region's long history.

While the *Philosophical Letters* certainly constituted an indictment of Russia, the Westernizers were not the only group whose members sympathized with its themes; indeed, the Slavophiles initially mistook Chaadaev for one of their own.[17] And there is much in Chaadaev's thought that would merit approval from the Slavophile camp. First, while Chaadaev decried Russia's isolation from the rest of the world, he objected in equal measure to the "blind, superficial, and often very awkward imitation of other nations" that he observed in most Europhiles.[18]

Second, Chaadaev bemoaned social atomism. Certain groups have been wracked by "moral individualism" and "the isolation of souls and minds."[19] Such fragmentation in society necessarily proves problematic. "Nations," Chaadaev claims, "are in fact like individuals"—both are "moral beings."[20] Moral perfection comes to nations and individuals alike as a benefit of time; nations inherit and augment the wisdom of prior eras, and individuals develop as they age. But Russia is a land of "lost souls,"[21] a place inhabited by individuals "without any links with people who lived on earth before us." Consequently, Russia has seen "no inward development, no natural progress."[22]

Finally, Chaadaev's embrace of rationalism by no means constituted a rejection of faith; his work is imbued with positive references to religion.

Indeed, he attributed the West's progress precisely to its religious heritage: "it is Christianity which has accomplished everything in Europe."[23] Europe's Christian identity guaranteed its further success and set it apart from places like ancient Greece and modern China, which succumbed, respectively, to decay and stagnation. Unlike other societies, Chaadaev claimed, "Christian nations must always go forward."[24] This forward path, this "indefinite progress," is a spiritual journey that will culminate in God's reign on earth.[25] Rejecting purely secular notions of progress, Chaadaev cautioned against "that imaginary perfectibility which philosophy dreams of and which is refuted by every page of history, a vain agitation of the soul which satisfies only the needs of our material being and which has ever raised a man to a height only to dash him into a still deeper abyss."[26]

We can readily spot rejections of Euro-imitation, promotion of communal bonds and opposition to excessive individualism, and support for religion as the key to progress in the works of the Slavophiles. Where the Slavophiles split with Chaadaev was in their forceful rejection of rationalistic philosophy and their embrace of Orthodoxy and traditional Russian modes of life.[27] A loose collection of gentry nobles led by Alexei Khomiakov (1804–1860) and Ivan Kireevsky (1806–1856), the Slavophiles had already familiarized themselves with Western philosophy and especially the works of Georg Hegel (1770–1831) and Friedrich von Schelling (1775–1854) before Chaadaev issued his indictment of Russia and his call for a new philosophy of history. Cognizant of the major intellectual movements of the West, the Slavophiles found more inspiring certain ideas that had long ago taken root in their native Russian soil.

A failing of Western thought, for Kireevsky and Khomiakov alike, is that it is too "one-sided." In an 1852 letter "On the Nature of European Culture and Its Relationship to Russian Culture," Kireevsky argues that Western philosophy dug its own grave by prizing rationalistic investigation and discounting all other modes of inquiry. Westerners "believed that, by using their own abstract mind, they could forthwith create a new, rational life for themselves and build a veritable paradise on the earth they had transformed."[28] But after having lost faith in all conclusions not stemming from reason, they lost their trust even in reason itself: rationalistic philosophy had developed as fully as was possible, and no new discoveries could be made on the basis of reason alone. As a result, Westerners faced a conundrum: they could learn to content themselves by focusing purely on material well-being, or, if they aspired to something higher, they could return to their spiritual heritage. The problem with the latter option, however, was that remembering and returning Europe to a time prior to the reign of reason was "well-nigh impossible."[29]

Even if Westerners had given religion its due and had not privileged rationalism at the expense of spiritualism, Khomiakov suggests, the particular traditions from which they had to draw were insufficient to sustain the West's forward development. Europe developed first under Roman Catholicism, which, stressing the unity of Christendom, failed to allow for freedom. Catholicism's emphasis on unity could be seen in Western Europe's use of Latin as the language of liturgy and diplomacy, in the evangelizing mission of the Crusades, in European legal principles, and in the hierarchical arrangement of feudal society. Having imposed an outward unity, Catholicism provoked a resistance that manifested itself in the Protestant Reformation. Protestantism, however, was "as one-sided as Roman Catholicism had been but leaning in the opposite direction—for Protestantism retained the idea of freedom and sacrificed to it the idea of unity." Casting aside the dogmas of the medieval Church of Rome, Protestantism sowed the seeds of its own demise: by advancing the idea that individuals were free to question the rules and rites of old, Protestantism unwittingly allowed individuals to become skeptics, too, of the various Protestant churches.[30]

Russian religious thought suffered none of the defects of Western thought; on this, Khomiakov and Kireevsky agreed. Whereas Catholicism had grown too oppressive in its quest to maintain unity and Protestantism had grown too lax by making religion purely a matter of individual conscience, the Orthodox Church represented "the coincidence of unity and freedom, manifested in the law of spiritual love."[31] And while Western thinkers, including religious thinkers,[32] had become overly enthralled by rationalistic inquiry, "the Eastern Church did not get distracted by the one-sidedness of syllogistic constructs, but retained the fullness and wholeness of speculation that comprise the distinctive feature of Christian philosophy."[33] "Because of the comprehensiveness and completeness of Russian principles," Russia had the duty and the right "to take the lead in universal enlightenment."[34] Developing these principles for itself was Russia's first task; its "mission" and "future destiny" was to "be their exponent before the whole world."[35]

Thus, when Chaadaev condemned Russian thought and argued that Russia had nothing to offer the world, the Slavophiles responded with a counterargument: the West might have contributed to world progress in the past, but it had grown stale; the time was now ripe for Russia to leave its imprint on the pages of history.[36] Glorifying as it did Russian thought and culture, Slavophilism would seem to have been more congenial to Nicholas I than was Chaadaev's rebuke of Russia. It was not. Frederick Copleston remarks that, in spite of all the things the tsar could have found praiseworthy in Slavophile thought—emphasis on Orthodoxy's virtues, lack of a revolutionary agenda, idealization of the Russian nation—he remained suspicious of its propagators.[37] Khomiakov, Kireevsky, and their collaborators were not to be praised for their celebration of Russia, but denounced for their implicit criticism of the autocracy. Khomiakov's heralding the "return of Russians to . . . Russian principles,"[38] for instance, suggested a deviation from the status quo. Likewise, his claim that "a better fate awaits future generations"[39] implied an unsatisfactory present that needed to be changed.

Nicholas I was right to be wary of the Slavophiles, to an extent. Kireevsky, Khomiakov, and their allies were certainly not enamored of their present. They supported Orthodoxy, but not theocracy. Patrick Michelson writes that "Khomiakov in particular found lifelong sustenance in the spirituality, ritualism, and piety of the Russian Church, even as he abhorred its reliance on civil authority to enforce canon law."[40] Likewise, while the Slavophiles granted that the sovereign had a monopoly on political power, they believed this power should be wielded infrequently, and that more issues could be settled among the Russian people themselves. Their praise of the Russian *people* and village commune[41] could be seen as implicit criticism of the centralized Russian *state*.[42]

Nevertheless, the Slavophiles were not nearly as subversive as Nicholas I feared them to be. Feeling that they had discerned "the mission of Russia in world history," they pondered how that destiny should be fulfilled.[43] Their answer was far from radical; indeed, they made pains to denounce revolutionary activity. Kireevsky contrasted Russia's history with that of the West, arguing that the former revealed a society that had "developed distinctively and naturally, under the influence of a single inner conviction that was nurtured by the Church and customary tradition."[44] In Europe, on the contrary, "revolution was the precondition of all progress, until it became not a means to an end, but in itself the distinctive end of popular aspirations."[45] Just as Russia had developed "naturally" and organically in the past, its future development was to be similarly natural and gradual.[46] The Slavophiles might have yearned for "further improvement of the law" on the basis of ancient customs,[47] but they did not advocate political upheaval to bring about that improvement.

If he feared political insurrection, the tsar had greater cause to be wary of proponents of the Petrine reforms than to distrust Peter I's critics. Whereas Slavophilism did not begin as a political movement, the Westernizers became resolutely political almost from the get-go. Emerging contemporaneously with Slavophilism, the Westernizing campaign aimed at many of the same things as the rival camp. But, as Susanna Rabow-Edling writes, "compared to the Slavophiles' solution to Russia's predicament, the version presented by the Westernizers' [sic] was somewhat more practical, action-oriented and explicitly related to the contemporary social and political situation."[48] And when (in 1849) the government disbanded the Petrashevsky Circle, a clandestine group that met to discuss proscribed Western socialist literature, the Westernizers turned resolutely against the autocracy.[49]

With their hearts hardened against the autocracy and their minds set on change, the Westernizers, led by critic Vissarion Belinsky (1811–1848) and activist Mikhail Bakunin (1814–1876), preached a complete overhaul of Russian society. Whereas the Slavophiles could tolerate the tsarist system, the Westernizers could not. "Halfheartedness," Bakunin decreed, "is the putrid source of all evil."[50] No stopgap measures would satisfy the Westernizers; compromise did nothing but stifle legitimate efforts at reform.[51] True reform could come only through revolution: "My God is negation!" Belinsky proclaimed, and "my heroes are the destroyers of the old—Luther, Voltaire, the Encyclopaedists, the Terrorists."[52] Bakunin concurred with Belinsky on the need to negate their Russian present, but he added that "the passion for destruction is a creative passion, too."[53] The Westernizers aimed not simply to undermine the status quo, but to usher in "an original, new life which has not yet existed in history."[54] That new life would be socialism.[55]

The Westernizers' appetite for destruction tied into their philosophy of history, which trusted in and demanded continual advancement. "History today which is alien to the idea of progress," Belinsky wrote, "will not be conceded the merits of history."[56] Analysis of concrete historical facts had revealed that moral and material progress alike were not merely possible, but could be discerned in the unfolding of time.[57] "The goal of the historical progress of man"[58] added Bakunin, "the real object of history," was freedom.[59] He conceived freedom as "the humanization and emancipation . . . the prosperity and happiness of each individual living in society."[60] On these points, the Slavophiles could agree, for they, too, sought the recognition of a freedom that would reconcile the rights of individuals and the societies in which they lived.

But the Slavophiles believed in traditional social obligations, too, and on this point the Westernizers offered a dissenting opinion. Belinsky, for instance, looked forward to the day "when there will be no senseless forms and rites, no contracts and stipulations on feeling, no duty and obligation, and we shall not yield to will but to love alone; when there will be no husbands and wives, but lovers and mistresses."[61] Such a vision of the future was unacceptable to the Slavophiles. But if, as Belinsky claimed, "there is no limit to human progress,"[62] and if progress and individual freedom are coterminous, as Bakunin claimed, then surely the trajectory of history pointed to the steady undoing of traditional restraints on individual liberty. Certain social norms and legal obligations, Belinsky granted, had played important roles in preparing the world for the "golden age," but these institutions had become "stupid and vulgar."[63] Rejecting these institutions, Bakunin admitted: "we are really Anarchists."[64] The Westernizers demanded nothing short of "a total transformation of [the] world."[65]

Believers in progress though they were, the Westernizers did not believe in inevitable progress. They could not count on fortune to usher in the new age: they could "concede no true power to chance in history."[66] Nor could they rely on the hand of God to turn the pages of mankind's story toward happily-ever-after; God and his representatives on earth were in fact impediments to the progress of liberty. From the moment that a people accepts the idea of an interventionist God, there comes forthwith a hierarchy amongst that people, with God's elect given the power to direct the affairs of the less inspired.[67] Christ had preached the ideals of equality and liberty, but his martyrdom remained humankind's salvation only until a church was built around this act. Both the Eastern and Western Churches were and remain champions of inegalitarianism.[68] Working hand-in-hand with states, the churches are "institutions of slavery,"[69] and God Himself the Supreme Slavemaster. "A master," Bakunin reasons, "whoever he may be and however liberal he may desire to show himself, remains none the less always a master. His existence necessarily implies the slavery of all that is beneath him. Therefore, if God existed, only in one way could he serve human liberty—by ceasing to exist."[70]

Determined foes of mysticism and superstition,[71] the Westernizers believed that rational man was responsible for bringing about his own progress. "History is made," Bakunin insists, "by acting, living and passing individuals."[72] Allowing that the mind of any individual man was finite, Belinsky argued that the common stock of reason allotted to humankind was infinite. And over the course of human history, the shared treasury of knowledge grows such that "all that is false and finite in the human being vanishes without leaving a trace, and all that is true and rational yields fruit a hundredfold."[73] With education comes the moral and even the physical improvement of humankind. But, again, such improvement could not be left to the grace of God or the whims of the Fates: "it is absurd to imagine that this could happen by itself, with the aid of time, without violent changes, without bloodshed."[74] Individuals needed to push back against barriers to change, such as church and state, if there was to be progress. And, to Bakunin and Belinsky alike, there *would* be progress.[75]

### Hesitation: The Qualified Optimism of Alexander Herzen and Fyodor Dostoevsky

To be sure, not every Westernizer accepted the idea of progress uncritically. (Nor as, will be shown, did every writer with Slavophile sympathies trust in progress reflexively.) Alexander Herzen, for instance, gives a fair reading to skeptics of the idea in *From the Other Shore*. In that work appears a dialogue between a proponent of the idea and a decided opponent. Herzen allows the enthusiast of the doctrine of progress to make his points, but the detractor fights back powerfully:

> If progress is the end, for whom are we working? Who is this
> Moloch who, as the toilers approach him, instead of rewarding
> them, only recedes, and as a consolation to the exhausted, doomed
> multitudes crying "morituri te salutant," can give back only the
> mocking answer that after their death all will be beautiful on earth.
> Do you truly wish to condemn all human beings alive to-day to the
> sad role of caryatids supporting a floor for others some day to
> dance on . . . or of wretched galley slaves, up to their knees in mud,
> dragging a barge filled with some mysterious treasure and with the
> humble words 'progress in the future' inscribed on its bows? Those
> who are exhausted fall in their tracks; others, with fresh forces
> take up the ropes; but there remains, as you said yourself, as much
> ahead as there was at the beginning, because progress is infinite.
> This alone should serve as a warning to people: an end that is
> infinitely remote is not an end, but, if you like, a trap; an end must

be nearer—it ought to be, at the very least, the labourer's wage, or pleasure in the work done. Each age, each generation, each life had and has its own fullness; en route, new demands arise, new experiences, new methods; some capacities improve at the expense of others.[76]

Strong critique though it is, the proponent of the idea of progress has a ready rejoinder, latching on to the notion that some capacities develop in man at the expense of others. Echoing the Slavophiles, he suggests that modern thought has become stultified or "one-sided," with an over-attachment to idealism leading to the decline of practical thought. The day will come, though, when people "will be cured of idealism as they have been of other historical diseases—chivalry, Catholicism, Protestantism."[77]

The dialogue seems to represent an internal debate for Herzen. And, at times, Herzen seems to have decided that the critic of the idea of progress has the stronger case. When the revolutions of 1848 brought forth in Europe and Russia not the bright sun of a better day but the dark clouds of reaction, Herzen could not help but feel his own spirit darken.[78] He noted that "after such convulsions the human being cannot remain what he was. Either his soul becomes more religious, clinging with desperate stubbornness to its convictions and finds comfort in the very absence of hope, and the man flowers again, singed by the lightning, carrying death in his breast; or else gathering up all his strength he bravely surrenders his last hopes, grows soberer still and does not try to retain the last feeble leaves which the rude, autumn wind carries away."[79] The first response, he claimed, led to "the bliss of lunacy," while the second brought about "the unhappiness of knowledge." Having come to a fork in the road, Herzen claimed to have chosen the second path to follow, and he pledged to "wander as a moral pauper through the world," tearing out along the way "childish hopes" and "youthful dreams."[80]

But Herzen never felt entirely at peace along the lonesome journey that he had embarked upon, and he always qualified his sober reflections. In his introduction to the second edition of *From the Other Shore*, published five years after the first, Herzen remarked: "I was accused of teaching despondency."[81] This was clearly far from his aim. Aileen Kelly points to letters exchanged in the 1860s between Herzen and the novelist Ivan Turgenev (1818–1883), revealing that the former could in no ways support a philosophy of resignation à la that of Schopenhauer.[82] But even in *From the Other Shore*, the reader can sense that Herzen had stopped far short of embracing pessimism. In another dialogue found in that work, a character remarks: "I am neither a pessimist nor an optimist; I watch, I examine, without any preconceived notion, without any prepared ideals, and I am in no hurry to reach a verdict."[83] Such a wait-and-see attitude seems to have been Herzen's own stance in the 1850s. We can see this cautious stance in the introduction to *From the Other Shore*, where Herzen reflects on his being in Europe, which he asserted was in its dying days but which he believed would be the place of history's next great act: "will I succeed in achieving something?" he asks rhetorically. "I do not know. I hope so."[84]

What Herzen hoped for, as did Belinsky and Bakunin, was the advent of socialism. In *From the Other Shore*, the author's hope was heavily qualified. But even there he insisted that "one or the other must fall; either monarchy or socialism," and that he had hedged his bets on the latter's success. Granting that some readers might find the victory of socialism difficult to imagine, he retorts that "well, it was hard to imagine that Christianity would triumph over Rome."[85]

Not normally one to give in to flights of fancy, Herzen sounds positively exuberant regarding the prospects of socialism and the future of his homeland in an "Open Letter to Jules Michelet." There he writes that "the great question, Russia's 'to be or not to be,' will soon be resolved," adding that "before battle, one has no right to despair of the outcome."[86] To his own mind, there was no justification for such defeatism. True, Nicholas I was trying "to stamp out all civilization,"[87] "smothering all progressive ideas,"[88] but Herzen and his countrymen "shall not despair."[89] There was just cause to believe in a "future of a truly remarkable vitality," not for Russia alone, but for all of Slavdom.[90] For evidence of past progress, Russians could look to their aristocrats, who demonstrated moral certitude during the Decembrist uprising of 1825.[91] For evidence of current success in "backward" Russia, one need look only to the literary movement flourishing even under adversity.[92] And when looking for signs of a bright future for Russia, one's attention should turn to the peasant (*muzhik*), whose simple, communal way of living paved the way for socialism.[93] Thus, contrary to some interpretations, Herzen's was not a pessimistic philosophy; he merely gave pessimism a fair hearing in his works.[94]

One reader who appreciated Herzen's giving both sides in the optimism-pessimism argument was none other than Fyodor Dostoevsky (1821–1881).[95] Dostoevsky would give a similar pro and contra in one of his own works, *The Brothers Karamazov*. In that novel, two of the titular characters, Ivan and Alyosha, address (among other things) the problem of evil and the goal of history,[96] with the former taking a pessimistic view and the latter holding to an optimistic vision of mankind's future. And, just as Herzen dutifully presented the pessimist's position in his work, so too did Dostoevsky.

Dostoevsky makes Ivan's pessimistic beliefs most manifest in the chapters "Rebellion" and "The Grand Inquisitor." In these chapters, Ivan gloomily describes all the misfortune he sees in the world. Although he could discuss at length "the suffering of mankind in general," he is particularly struck by the torments suffered by innocent children.[97] Recognition of this evil leads Ivan to reject the world. "It's not God that I do not accept," he tells his brother, Alyosha, "it is this world of God's, created by God, that I do not accept and cannot agree to accept."[98] The world that Ivan rejects is both evil and chaotic. "The world stands on absurdities," he tells Alyosha.[99] Life on earth is nothing more than an "offensive comedy of human contradictions."[100]

If the world is full of tremendous evil, people themselves are responsible for much of this suffering. Man is, Ivan claims, "a wild and wicked animal."[101] He reiterates that there is "a beast hidden in every man, a beast of rage."[102] Although he calls man an animal and a beast, Ivan searches for a better epithet. He must retract his claims that man is a beast, for "no animal could be so cruel as a man, so artfully, so artistically cruel."[103] As evidence of this cruelty, Ivan points to several stories of child abuse culled from newspaper articles or learned of otherwise. That innocent children should be the victims of such barbarous treatment, Ivan reasons, is sufficient grounds for his misanthropy.

The suffering imposed upon and inflicted by people stretches to all corners of the earth and to the earliest points in human history. Ivan reflects upon the "human tears that have soaked the whole earth through, from crust to core."[104] He recognizes that human suffering is not a recent phenomenon, but instead something that has been present throughout time. Nor is torture a localized phenomenon. Ivan's anecdotes of cruelty come not only from Russia, but from Bulgaria and Switzerland as well.[105] That suffering and torture exist across time and space belies the notion of progress.

Thus, Ivan can be seen as a pessimist. He regards the world in which he lives as fundamentally evil. He similarly judges mankind to be inherently flawed. And he gives no sense that the defects he finds in the world or in mankind can be dramatically altered. Ivan should not, however, be mistaken for a nihilist.[106] Despite his bleak assessment of the world and its inhabitants, Ivan recognizes that good exists. He confesses that, although "I do not believe in the order of things, still the sticky leaves that come out in the spring are dear to me, the blue sky is dear to me, some people are dear to me" and "some human deeds are dear to me."[107] It is not that Ivan has no values, but that what he values seems to be trampled on and debased.

Whether Ivan's views of man and history reflect Dostoevsky's own is a matter for debate. Joshua Foa Dienstag contends that Dostoevsky can be considered a pessimist, because for Dostoevsky "the universe is as apt to produce ugliness and depravity as beauty and virtue."[108] David Walsh does not affix the pessimist label to Dostoevsky, but suggests that Dostoevsky looked with dismay at "the chaos of the modern world." This disenchantment, Walsh claims, prompted the author to look to Christianity as a source of order.[109] Dostoevsky's contemporary, Konstantin Leontiev, accuses him of introducing into his works a "too rosy hue" of Christianity.[110] In *The Brothers Karamazov*, the character Zosima promulgates this "rosy" Christian vision, teaching that "life is paradise."[111] However, as Walsh notes, Zosima's outlook does "not necessarily coincide with Dostoevsky's own more somber assessment of history."[112]

We can see this "somber" view of history in Dostoevsky's nonfiction works. In a letter addressed "to a mother," he declares that "it is beyond doubt that every human being is born with evil tendencies."[113] This evil, contrary to the idea of historical progress, grows ever stronger. In an entry in his *Diary of a Writer*, Dostoevsky acknowledges "that in days past there has also been much evil," but laments that "at present it has unquestionably increased ten times."[114] Richard Pipes says of Dostoevsky that, "while he never ceased to condemn cruelty and hatred, he was morbidly fascinated by both."[115] *Diary of a Writer* bears testament to this dark side of Dostoevsky's character (for example, in his extended discussion of the Kronenberg child abuse case, which was infamous in Dostoevsky's day).

Still, there is cause to reject the conclusion that Dostoevsky accepted Ivan Karamazov's pessimism. *The Brothers Karamazov* ends, after all, with the triumph of Alyosha's point of view and Ivan's succumbing to paralysis from the weight of his ideas. And, though Dostoevsky did admit that horrors had existed throughout history and into his own day, he also projected a better future. He makes manifest his prophetic vision in the *Diary*:

> The Slavophile doctrine, in addition to that assimilation of the Slavs
> under the rule of Russia, signifies and comprises a spiritual union of
> all those who believe that our great Russia, at the head of the united
> Slavs, will utter to the world, to the whole of European mankind
> and to civilization, her new, sane, and as yet unheard-of word. That

word will be uttered for the good and genuine unification of mankind as a whole in a new, brotherly, universal union whose inception is derived from the Slavic genius, pre-eminently from the spirit of the great Russian people. . . . Now, I belong to this group of the convinced and the believing.[116]

This passage is emblematic of Dostoevsky's faith that the historical process would culminate in universal brotherhood. John D. Simons argues that, for Dostoevsky, imagination and the freedom to experiment with different types of social organization are necessary requisites for this harmonious Golden Age to prevail, whereas "systems which impose harmony on man from without deny the possibility of progress and negate what has already been accomplished."[117] Other readers of Dostoevsky, however, suggest that their subject parted company from the Slavophiles of old by adopting a more aggressive political stance: whereas the first generation of Slavophiles had aimed principally to defend Russian virtues against the infusion of nonnative ideals, the pan-Slavs (like Dostoevsky) who succeeded them sought to actively export Russian beliefs and practices, by force, if necessary.[118] On either reading of him, Dostoevsky emerges as a figure who was critical of his own time but confident that a brighter day would dawn.

### The Idea of Progress During the Reign of Nicholas I

Rabow-Edling observes that "change, enlightenment, and progress were the goals for both Slavophiles and Westernizers, although they interpreted them in somewhat different ways."[119] For the Slavophiles, progress would come through the embrace of spiritual rather than material values. Russia, with its unique Orthodox tradition, could act as a guide for the rest of the world by revealing how a religion could preserve social unity while still allowing individual freedom. So distinctive was Russia's place in the world to the later pan-Slavs that they professed a duty to spread Russian culture and values to other nations. The shift from the Slavophilism of the 1840s to the pan-Slavism of the latter half of the nineteenth century marked a change from romantic nationalism to national chauvinism. In the words of Hans Kohn, the generation following Khomiakov and Kireevsky "emptied the [Slavophile] doctrine of its theological and humanitarian content and discovered in it a crude appeal to the nationalist and xenophobe instincts of the masses."[120]

If Slavophilism underwent a transformation in the 1860s, so, too, did Westernism. Thornton Anderson observes that "from the beginning various personalities among the Westerners responded differently to the flow of ideas and events, at home and abroad, and gradually the reformers and the revolutionaries parted company, developing Western thought along the divergent lines of liberalism and socialism."[121] At odds with one another over how quickly and by whom changes should be introduced in their country, Russian liberals and radicals of the nineteenth century agreed on the need for major reform. They sought the destruction of the Orthodox Church, which they not incorrectly viewed as a pillar of the autocratic system, and they looked forward to the collapse of autocracy itself. "Progress" meant increasing individual and social freedom by shattering the twin shackles of church and state.

Nicholas I understood that talk of future progress implied dissatisfaction with the present. And as a fierce defender of the status quo, he sought to limit the free discussion of ideas—like "progress"—that he feared could undermine his authority. The challenge posed by the Westernizers, who demanded massive political reforms, is clear enough. Nicholas perhaps misjudged the threat posed to his regime by the Slavophiles, who became propagandists for the monarch's policies at home and abroad. But he could not have been certain of the path that Slavophilism would take.[122] In any case, he did not seek approbation: "'Neither praise nor blame,' Nicholas himself wrote, 'is compatible with the dignity of the government or with the order that fortunately exists among us; one should obey and keep one's reflections to one's self.'"[123]

Not privy to the tsar's memo, one writer who opted not to keep his reflections to himself was Leo Tolstoy, who, while indisputably a critic of Nicholas I, shared with the tsar a belief that the idea of progress was dangerous. Though the tsar's opposition to "progress" may have been reflexive, Tolstoy's was an integral part of a well thought-out philosophy of history, which is described below.

### The Lion Who Wished to Be a Lamb: Leo Tolstoy on History and Politics

Born into a well-to-do family and destined to become a prince, Siddhārtha Gautama lived a privileged life free from worry. His carefree existence came to a sudden end when, as a young adult, he ventured from his palace to meet his subjects. Shielded from tragedy as a child, Siddhārtha had not heretofore encountered the phenomena he witnessed on his voyage beyond palace walls: disease, death, and poverty. His experiences outside his royal home led him to a simple, yet fundamental conclusion: "life is suffering." Having attained this knowledge, the young prince sought a way to overcome the suffering of the world. Renouncing both his princely title and the world itself, Siddhārtha initially pursued a policy of extreme self-denial. Nearly dying as a result of his asceticism, the former prince modified his behavior, finding a "middle way" that led to enlightenment and charting a path for those who would follow him.

The well-known story of the Buddha has a near analogue in the life of Leo Tolstoy. The son of Nikolai Tolstoy and Maria Tolstoya (nee Volkonskaya), Lev Nikolayevich Tolstoy descended from nobility on both sides of his family. His Tolstoy grandfather had served as the governor of Kazan, while a more distant ancestor had acted as Peter I's ambassador to Constantinople and, later, as a member of Catherine II's Privy Council. The even more illustrious Volkonsky family could trace itself back to the days of Rurik, the fabled founder of Kieven Rus'. But Tolstoy would not take his rightful place at court, as so many of his relations had done. Instead, he opted in his later years to live an ascetic life modeled after the Russian peasantry. The austere lifestyle he adopted and his advocacy of the nonresistance to evil became the basis for a religious movement, Tolstoyism.[124]

Between his noble birth in 1828 and his death some eighty years later as an advocate for simple living and nonaggression, Tolstoy played a number of roles. He was the proud owner of Yasnaya Polyana, the estate on which he was born and which he inherited in 1847. He was a military man, serving in the Crimean War in 1854–1855. He was a husband, marrying Sophia "Sonya" Bers in 1862. He was a father to thirteen children, eight of whom survived into adulthood. He was an education reformer, having created and taught at a school for the peasant children of his estate. Each of these experiences, important in its own right, shaped the mature Tolstoy's outlook and influenced him in his best-known role, that of a writer.

Tolstoy, the man of letters, was also the product of his time. A. N. Wilson observes that Tolstoy's birth occurred three years after the abortive Decembrist uprising, while his death in 1910 came just seven years prior to the October Revolution.[125] This means that for his entire existence, Tolstoy lived under the highly repressive but relatively stable regimes of Nicholas I, Alexander II (1818–1881), Alexander III (1845–1894), and Nicholas II (1868–1918).

This chronology also points to the fact that Tolstoy's formative years took place during the dawn of Russian literature's golden age—Alexander Pushkin (1799–1837), Mikhail Lermontov (1814–1841), and Nikolai Gogol (1809–1852) published their most important works during the 1830s. The literary output of the 1830s and 1840s included, as well, works by figures engaged in the flowering Slavophile-Westernizer debate.

Growing up under an autocratic regime that discouraged political participation, the young Tolstoy was free to remain indifferent to politics. And indifferent he was and remained well into adulthood.[126] The romantic attitude of the Decembrists[127] had some superficial appeal to the young Tolstoy. And if he had been forced to pick a side in the Slavophile-Westernizer debate, he would have chosen the Westernizers, whose ideas of reform appealed to the youthful idealist. As Tolstoy would later recount in his *Confession*, upon his return to St. Petersburg after the Crimean War, he met up with a motley group of writers, and: "before I had time to look round I had adopted the views on life of the set of authors I had come among. . . . The view of life of these people, my comrades in authorship, consisted in this: that life in general goes on developing, and in this development we—men of thought—have the chief part; and among men of thought it is we–artists and poets—who have the greatest influence. Our vocation is to teach mankind."[128] Even prior to his meet-up with the St. Petersburg literary set, Tolstoy had tacitly endorsed the Westernizers: in 1852, he submitted for publication his first novel, *Childhood*, to their leading periodical, *The Contemporary*.[129] But he was hardly a zealot for change: as a soldier he acquiesced without complaint to the military's harsh rules of discipline and punishment; he defended serfdom as a "very benevolent evil" until the mid-1850s; and he openly deplored what he perceived as extreme radicalism in figures like Turgenev.[130]

In a letter to a cousin at court, Tolstoy identified the very moment he became politically minded. During the summer of 1862 he had left Yasnaya Polyana in search of relief for a nagging cough, putting his sister and aunt in charge of the estate. While he was away, the secret police raided the premises on the suspicion that he was printing seditious literature. The police uncovered nothing, but news of the raid hardened his heart against the government, as his letter to Countess Alexandra Tolstoya explained: "If you will recall my political attitude you will know that always . . . I have been entirely indifferent to the Government. . . . Now I can longer say this. I possess bitterness and revulsion, almost hatred for that dear Government."[131]

Although the search of his home turned Tolstoy irrevocably against the autocracy, it did not make him a card-carrying Westernizer. In the same letter in which he recounted the details of this incident, he decried "the present liberals whom I scorn with all my soul."[132] What should be made, then, of an ardent opponent of the government who paid no heed to the liberal and radical activists of his day? Henri Troyat suggests that Tolstoy was, "in his heart of hearts" a Slavophile.[133] Troyat's assertion merits consideration, but a more convincing argument comes from Wilson, who states that "at no stage, really, can one 'place' Tolstoy on any political spectrum, any more than you could fit him into any of the circles of literary movements of his day."[134] "From the beginning," Wilson says of Tolstoy, "he is alone."[135]

One of the ways in which Tolstoy stood apart from other thinkers of his time was in his rejection of the idea of progress. His dismissal of this idea is implicit in *War and Peace* and *Anna Karenina* and explicit in *A Confession.* His critique, and his philosophy of history more generally, in turn undergirded a unique political philosophy.

Reflecting on his years in St. Petersburg after the Crimean War, Tolstoy notes in *A Confession* that his then-acquaintances promulgated an idea of progress, without referring to it as such. Instead, they spoke of "development." Echoing Hegel, they argued that "'all that exists is reasonable.'" Their theory contained the additional premises that "'all that exists develops. And it all develops by means of Culture.'" From these premises, they reached the conclusion that writers had the special duty of contributing to historical development by producing great works of art. Having reached this conclusion, the writers—Tolstoy included—excused and justified their aggressive dealings with one another, their exploitation of the peasants, and all manner of deceit and debauchery so long as they continued to create worthy poetry or prose.[136]

Quitting St. Petersburg for one of his few trips abroad, Tolstoy spent the spring of 1857 in Paris. There he spent his time sightseeing and meeting with now-forgotten writers.[137] From these "leading and learned Europeans," Tolstoy learned the language of "progress." Not fully comfortable with the dissolute lifestyle he had led in St. Petersburg, he had started inquiring as to how he should live instead. The answer he received was "'Live in conformity with progress.'" What this meant, he did not know: "I was like a man in a boat who when carried along by wind and waves should reply to what for him is the chief and only question, 'whither to steer,' by saying, 'We are being carried somewhere.'" With no map to guide him, the young author resolved to let the current carry him where it may.[138]

Tolstoy found his trust in the idea of progress shaken by two events. The first event took place while he was still in Paris. A witness to a public execution, Tolstoy reacted viscerally to the spectacle before his eyes: "I understood, not with my mind but with my whole being, that no theory of the reasonableness of our present progress could justify this deed." If we take Tolstoy at his word, then the seed of his future pacifism appears to have taken root at this time. The second event that nearly capsized the *S.S. Progress* occurred in 1860 in the seaside town of Hyères in southeastern France. The fourth of five children, Tolstoy watched incredulously and inconsolably as his eldest brother, Nikolai, succumbed to tuberculosis far from their native Russia: "Wise, good, serious, he fell ill while still a young man, suffered for more than a year, and died painfully, not understanding why he had lived and still less why he had to die. No theories could give me, or him, any reply to these questions during his slow and painful dying." But these two events were exceptional—"rare instances of doubt"—and for the next couple of years, Tolstoy "continued to live professing a faith only in progress."[139]

To distract himself when the big life-and-death questions crept into his consciousness, Tolstoy devoted himself to his family—his wife gave birth to their first child within a year of their 1862 wedding—and to his writing. With his steadily growing brood—the Tolstoy nest grew again in 1864 and 1866—his home life offered plenty of diversions. But over time, the act of writing became not a respite from introspection, but an occasion to wax philosophical. In *War and Peace*, in particular, readers can perceive Tolstoy's use of the novel as a vehicle for philosophical speculation. More specifically, *War and Peace* offers Tolstoy's fullest statement on the nature and study of history: as Isaiah Berlin observes, "the problem of historical truth" is "the central issue round which the novel is built."[140]

Ostensibly an intricate story of love and loss, *War and Peace* brings to life some of fiction's most renowned characters, including the young and alluring Natasha Rostova and two of the men who compete for her affections, the military man Andrei Bolkonsky and the aimless, wealthy landowner Pierre Bezukhov. Not far beneath the surface, however, the reader finds that *War and Peace* is much more than an artistic rendering of the lives of Russian aristocrats during the Napoleonic Wars. Woven throughout the story are interjections from the narrator that draw the reader's attention to some of the themes that are treated at greater length in the two-part epilogue. Acknowledging that his work is no ordinary piece of fiction, Tolstoy declares to his audience that *War and Peace* "is not a novel, still less an epic poem, still less a historical chronicle. *War and Peace* is what the author wanted and was able to express, in the form in which it is expressed."[141]

Chief among the things Tolstoy wished and was able to convey in *War and Peace* was his rejection of the methods and assumptions of contemporary historians. "Modern history," he declares, "is like a deaf man, answering questions that no one has asked him." Historians give the when and where of events, and they name the prominent personae who lived during such and such a period. But they fail in their essential aim: "to describe the movements of mankind and of peoples." Or, rather, historians fail to identify the force responsible for the movement of humankind and the groups which comprise it.[142]

When they do seek to understand the historical trajectory of a nation or group, historians often focus on leaders, purporting to understand the psyches of generals or rulers and imputing to them motivations for their behaviors. The focus on leaders is misguided, however, for two reasons. First, the assumption that there is but one cause of any event—and that a leader could be that one cause—is erroneous. Neither Napoleon nor Alexander I alone, for instance, could claim responsibility for the war between France and Russia in the early 1800s: "billions of causes—coincided so as to bring about what happened."[143] Second, historians put too much stock into the notion of free will and neglect the role necessity plays in human affairs. Studies of the Napoleonic Wars focus on the whims of the wars' namesake, but "the actions of Napoleon . . . on whose word it seems to have depended whether the event took place or not, were as little willed as the action of each soldier who went into the campaign by lot or by conscription."[144]

As an alternative to what is now commonly referred to as the "Great Man" theory of history, Tolstoy offers his own vision. This is a vision that, Berlin points out, has failed to inspire much admiration from lay or scholarly readers.[145] The most common charge against Tolstoy's philosophy is that it is fatalistic. This critique is not unjust: the narrator of *War and Peace* frequently opines, as in the passage above, that marches and battles, like all events, take place independently of men's individual wills. That Tolstoy's opinion and that of his narrator are the same, there can be no doubt. In "A Few Words Apropos of the Book *War and Peace*," Tolstoy remarks that Napoleon, Alexander, and their retinues interested him only in that their activity illustrated "that law of predetermination which, in my conviction, governs history."[146]

A fatalistic philosophy of history is not necessarily antithetical to the idea of progress—one can believe that immutable laws govern human action and also believe that nature or God directs humankind toward a brighter future—but in Tolstoy's case, fatalism goes hand in hand with a rejection of "progress." Tolstoy's dismissal of progressive visions of history is less transparent than his critique of the notion of free will, but it comes to light if one considers a metaphor that runs throughout *War and Peace*: that of man as a bee. Tolstoy's narrator defines history as "the unconscious, swarmlike life of mankind."[147] Such a definition merely reformulates Tolstoy's fatalism: men, like social insects, blindly follow where providence directs them.[148] But the narrator extends the metaphor, asking the reader to answer the question of a bee's purpose. Some respondents might say that a bee's purpose is to sting people. Others might claim that a bee's purpose is to protect his queen. Another might insist that the bee exists to create honey. Still another might argue that the bee exists to pollinate flowers. Any of these answers sounds plausible, but none clearly reflect an ultimate end for the bee. And just as we are unable to discern a chief purpose for bees, the situation is "the same for the purposes of historical figures and peoples."[149]

Having raised questions about human destiny in *War and Peace*, Tolstoy turned to philosophy for answers. The best answers, he found in the summer of 1869, came from a German author then little known in Russia. That author was Schopenhauer, whose portrait would come to grace Tolstoy's study.[150] Writing to Afanasy Fet (1820–1892), the poet who introduced him to the great German pessimist, Tolstoy asked rhetorically "Do you know what my summer has been?" He answered: "One continuous roar of approval of Schopenhauer, a series of spiritual joys such as I have never known before. I wrote away for his complete works and I have read them and am reading them again. Certainly, no student ever learned as much in his entire course of study as I have in this one summer."[151]

The "spiritual joy" that Tolstoy felt when reading Schopenhauer was not the sense of relief a convert feels when finding religion, but the kind of self-contentedness a parishioner feels when sympathetic to a preacher's sermon. Schopenhauer did not so much teach Tolstoy something new as he did confirm conclusions that the author of *War and Peace* had reached independently. In his great work, Tolstoy concludes that "we can never imagine either total freedom or total necessity."[152] This nuanced statement echoes Schopenhauer's doctrine of the will to life: to paraphrase, a man is free to do as he wants, but his wants spring from a universal, ceaseless, striving force that is the source of all desires.[153] To Tolstoy and Schopenhauer alike, the laws that govern man give history a changeless quality. Tolstoy writes that, having studied the legends, letters, and diaries of figures associated with the Napoleonic Wars, he "did not find all the horrors of that brutality in a greater degree than . . . now or at any other time. In those times, too, people loved, envied, sought truth, virtue, were carried away by passions."[154] This is the position of Schopenhauer, who suggests that only a fool would expect something new to emerge in the history of human activity, given that "we yet always have before us only the same, identical, unchangeable essence."[155]

Tolstoy's rapture with Schopenhauer outlived the summer of 1869. Entering the new decade with a Schopenhauerian attitude toward the world in which he lived, Tolstoy chose as the epigram for his next major work, *Anna Karenina*, a biblical quotation he originally chanced upon in Schopenhauer's writings: "Vengeance is mine; I will repay."[156] But *Anna Karenina* shows Tolstoy's affinity with Schopenhauer in ways other than the cribbed epigram. The theme of freedom versus necessity, present in *War and Peace*, recurs in the later novel, which looks at the behavior not of nations or armies but rather of individuals. Focusing on the titular character and her inner circle, *Anna Karenina* reaffirms Tolstoy's position that fate, rather than free will, rules the day. As Sigrid McLaughlin demonstrates, Anna pursues an adulterous relationship less of her own volition and more because some preternatural force (what Schopenhauer terms the will) drives her to do so. This same force drives Anna to end her life by flinging herself into the path of an oncoming train.[157]

The train acts as an important symbol in *Anna Karenina*. As Elisabeth Stenbock-Fermor observes, the railway, "a sign of progress for so many," represented for Tolstoy an "evil" and "destructive" force.[158] In the mind of many a Westerner, the train stood for the spread of material wealth and European civilization, that is, progress. By making the train Anna's killer, rather than the bearer of good fortune, Tolstoy implicitly rejects this Western vision of progress. Schopenhauer had earlier remarked that steam engines could not "ever make anything that is essentially better."[159] But, again, this reveals only a similarity between Schopenhauer and Tolstoy, rather than the influence of the one on the other. For Tolstoy had connected trains and the idea of progress as early as 1862, well before he became aware of Schopenhauer. In "Progress and the Definition of Education," Tolstoy remarks that "those who believe in progress . . . say that the railways are an increase of the people's well-being." He contends, though, that railroads "increase the temptations; they destroy the forests; they take away labourers; they raise the price of bread."[160]

By highlighting certain negative aspects of material development, Tolstoy bears a resemblance to the author of the *Discourse on the Origin and Foundation of Inequality Among Mankind*, Jean-Jacques Rousseau. In the so-called *Second Discourse*, Rousseau suggests that "most of our ills are of our own making" and that "we might have avoided them all by adhering to the simple, uniform and solitary way of life prescribed to us by nature."[161] Tolstoy's article calls the reader's attention to some of the "ills" brought about by modern technology and industry, including not only trains, but steamboats, telegraphs, and even printing. It also gives praise to the "simple" life characteristic of the Russian peasantry, whom other observers erroneously characterize as mere "savages."[162] However, though the lion of Russian literature may have ventured down a trail first tread by Geneva's renowned solitary walker, Berlin goes too far when he claims that Tolstoy's "greatest affinity . . . is with Rousseau."[163] Tolstoy, despite issuing a verdict on modern civilization similar to Rousseau's, parts from his predecessor in important ways, particularly with respect to his political stances.[164]

Anticipating much of his later nonfiction work, Tolstoy's 1862 essay hints at the direction his critique of "progress" would take him. First, the essay highlights the Crimean War veteran's nascent pacifism. Tolstoy observes that, for promoters of the idea, "progress . . . is a common law of humanity . . . except for Asia, Africa, America, and Australia."[165] He finds this perspective curious: how can a law be said to govern humanity, if the majority of humankind are found to contravene that law? Maybe, he muses, "progress is a law discovered only by the European nations, but one that is so good that the whole of humanity ought to be subjected to it."[166] That is, perhaps progress truly is the common law of humanity, but, heretofore, large segments of the earth's population have flouted this law and must now, finally, be coerced into obeying it. Tolstoy entertains arguments in favor of this view, but ultimately he cannot endorse such a conclusion. To him, evangelists of the gospel of progress care little for the well-being of those they would convert; instead, these missionaries preach a faith from which they alone would benefit.[167] The zeal to "help" other parts of the world is simply a pretext for war, and so we see Europeans "go with cannon and guns to impress the idea of progress upon the Chinese" and other nations.[168]

European elites terrorized not only far-off populations, but exploited even their own countrymen in the name of progress—or so Tolstoy argues in his 1862 article. His critique of domestic policies in Europe points toward the second predominant feature of his mature political philosophy, his anarchism. Lumping government officials with the gentry and educated merchants, Tolstoy declares that these members of the leisure class derive benefits at the expense of the rest of society. The fruits of civilization are "the monopoly of a certain class" and "advantageous only for the people of that class, who by the word 'progress' understand their personal advantage, which thus is always contrary to the advantage of the masses."[169] Neither the expansion of railways nor the introduction of the telegraph nor the spread of printing, Tolstoy argues, have increased the average person's lot in life one iota. In fact, we can safely say that "progress has done more evil than good to the people, that is, to the majority."[170] Inasmuch as governments sponsor "progressive" reforms, one must conclude—and Tolstoy leaves it for his reader to make such an inference—that they are detrimental to the well-being of the common man and woman.

Still inchoate in 1862, Tolstoy's thoughts on pacifism and anarchism found full expression some thirty years later, this time as part of a religious appeal. In *The Kingdom of God Is Within You*, published in Germany in 1894 after having been banned in Russia, Tolstoy offers his final verdict on a number of questions that had racked his brain for years. The answer to many of the questions, such as why he should live, was faith. Religious devotion, so important to Tolstoy in his later years, counted for little during his adolescence and early middle age, and not without cause do some authors bifurcate Tolstoy's life into pre- and post-conversion periods. Rene Fueloep-Miller, for instance, argues that these two parts of Tolstoy's life "do not merely differ from each other, but seem almost incompatible with each other."[171] Indeed, Tolstoy the elderly preacher of celibacy stands in marked contrast to Tolstoy the youthful womanizer and later father of thirteen children. Tolstoy the cantankerous art critic bears little resemblance to Tolstoy the vibrant artist.[172]

In vital ways, however, Tolstoy's later thought is not incompatible with, but fully consonant with or even an elaboration of his earlier work. Commenting particularly on Tolstoy's philosophy of history, G. W. Spence argues that "the ideas [Tolstoy] held in his earlier period to some extent determined the nature of those put forward after the so-called 'conversion.'"[173] Not a focus of Spence's essay, one constant in Tolstoy's thought is the rejection of the idea of progress. Tolstoy's criticism of progressive theories of history is clear in "Progress and the Definition of Education," can be discerned in *War and*

*Peace* and *Anna Karenina*, and is explicit in the post-conversion *Confession*. In the first of these works, Tolstoy writes that "the law of progress, or per- fectibility, is written in the soul of each man, and is transferred to history only through error. As long as it remains personal, this law is fruitful."[174] In the last of them, he continues to object to the "superstitious belief in [his- torical] progress,"[175] and maintains his faith in the possibility of "moral per- fection" for the individual.[176]

Tolstoy's renewed interest in religion altered the presentation of his ar- guments, but not necessarily his conclusions. In his earlier years, Tolstoy ob- jected to a man's execution or a war against the Chinese on humanitarian grounds. In his later period, he railed against corporal punishment and military conflict from a Christian perspective. At every stage, however, he argues based on his understanding of what constitutes good conduct. As Alexandre Christoyannopoulos observes, "Tolstoy's idiosyncratic exegesis of the Bible . . . ignored established commentaries and understood Jesus' teach- ing in a very literal and rational manner. He stripped away all elements of supernatural mystery and was thus left only with an ethical system."[177]

At the heart of Tolstoy's religioethical system is his reading of the Sermon on the Mount, particularly Jesus' injunction not to repay evil with evil.[178] To readers who objected to his nonrecognition of certain rituals or his interpretation of certain parables, Tolstoy reiterated his contention that there is no way "to harmonize what was clearly expressed in the teacher's [Jesus'] words . . . about forgiveness, humility, renunciation, and love of all men, of our neighbours and of our enemies . . . with the demand of military violence exerted against the men of one's own nation or another nation."[179] Erasmus long before him had argued with Tolstoy that the idea of a "just" war is contrary to Christ's teaching.[180] But Tolstoy followed the admonition not to resist evil to a conclusion not reached by Erasmus or any other major writers. The state's defining characteristic, its raison d'être, in Max Weber's words, is the "monopoly of the legitimate use of physical force."[181] From Tol- stoy's perspective, however, Christ's example suggests that there can be no legitimate use of force, and thus the state's very existence is illegitimate and participation in its maintenance is unjust. Tolstoy concludes, then, that "Christianity in its true meaning destroys the state."[182]

In no way does Tolstoy's talk of the destruction of the state represent a call to arms against the institutions of government. As Copleston observes, if "all coercion and violence are wrong," then "political revolution is also wrong."[183] Janko Lavrin modifies this observation by noting that Tolstoy's theory "does not manifest any tendency to overcome the evils of our civilization through direct action" whatsoever, revolutionary or otherwise.[184] Instead, Tolstoy seeks after self-perfection, and he asks those in his audience to strive for the same. The individual's quest for moral improvement does not depend on the machinations of the state.[185] Nor do—or should—a good number of other things depend on politics: neither "the dethronement of King Otho" nor "the speeches made by Palmerston and by Napoleon III" affect the peasant's ability to work the field and sustain himself and his family.[186] The destruction of the state will come not at the hands of revolutionary terrorists, but from the collective indifference of those people who recognize that the state is not instrumental to their well-being. States, Tolstoy notes, can defend themselves against acts of terror. However, he asks rhetorically, "what are the governments to do against those men who point out the uselessness, superfluity, and harmfulness of all governments, and do not struggle with them, but only have no use for them, get along without them, and do not wish to take part in them?"[187]

## Conclusion

The official credo of Nicholas I's reign was "Orthodoxy, Autocracy, and Nationality." After a long search for answers to some of life's thorniest questions, Leo Tolstoy emerged as an apostate, anarchist, and individualist. But in a certain sense Nicholas I proved less objectionable than other monarchs to Tolstoy. Despite undeniably great differences in their ideas, Tsar Nicholas and Tolstoy could find common ground in at least one area: their judgment of "progress." "The most widely debated of all the 'cursed questions' during Nicholas' reign," James Billington observes, "was the meaning of history."[188] Writers of various stripes—Slavophile, liberal, and radical—looked to history and judged from their studies that the future entailed progress. Nicholas understood that the very term "progress" had political undertones. So did Tolstoy. And both men, contrary to so many other major figures of their day, rejected the idea.

Although Nicholas I could not earn any praise from Tolstoy, and, in fact, inspired in him a lasting enmity toward Russia's "dear government," the tsar actually caused less trauma to Russian and global society than did other monarchs. For an anarchist-pacifist, the two towering figures most associated in the West with enlightened rule in Russia, Peter I and Catherine II, share greater culpability. In the words of Marc Raeff, "the effect of Peter the Great's reign was to tear Russian society apart," the legacy of a pronounced effort to "build a well-ordered state in Russia."[189] This well-ordered police state, according to Anderson, "approached modern totalitarianism," with "even the sphere of personal habits" having been "invaded by the will of the tsar."[190] Evgenii Anisimov, too, affixes the "totalitarian" label to Peter,[191] singling him out as the instigator of a peculiarly Russian "doctrine of progress through violence."[192] With respect to domestic policy, "Catherine shared with Peter the Great the goal of creating in Russia a well-ordered police state," and in foreign affairs she "pursued an expansionist imperial policy based on military force."[193] It is small wonder then, that Tolstoy regarded Peter as "the greatest of evildoers"[194] and Catherine as a "stupid illiterate and lewd wench."[195]

For his part, Tolstoy, vociferous critic of the government though he was, posed less of a threat to the regimes of Nicholas I and his successors than did other writers. His writings on religion challenged the symbiotic relationship between church and state in Russia and won him excommunication from the Orthodox Church. But these writings also praised the Russian peasantry—that is, the bulk of the population—for their religious devotion. Tolstoy considered the state to be an instrument of oppression. But he held no higher hopes for democracy than he did for monarchy,[196] and he argued against revolutionary attacks on the system.[197] Thus, Tolstoy won begrudging acceptance from the tsars and their inner circles.[198] "Throughout the reign of three emperors," Wilson writes, those in the government "were to be wary of [Tolstoy] and frightened of his capacity to stir up discontent through his writings. But there was always admiration for his genius, and something more: a vein of indulgent tolerance such as, in a family, might be felt for a wayward uncle. Tolstoy was 'one of them.'"[199]

Tolstoy was, at the very least, more at one with the tsars than he would have been with the radicals who executed Nicholas II and instigated a reign of terror unlike any seen before. True, the tsars ruled with iron fists. But even the authoritarian Nicholas I, moved by his sincere spiritual convictions, sometimes relaxed his grip; as Nicholas Riasanovsky argues, there is "a sharp line between the system of Nicholas and those twentieth-century states which have known no religious or moral inhibitions."[200] Reflecting on her own experience under a regime that knew no limits, the Croat writer Slavenka Drakulić remarks that "the word 'progress' was always one of the key words in the political speeches of my youth."[201] For a measure of technological and industrial development, millions of people living under communist regimes paid dearly. A holder of views that won him scorn from Vladimir Lenin (1870–1924), Leo Tolstoy would have been appalled at the totalitarian system that emerged in Russia after his death.[202] With Tsar Nicholas and few others, Tolstoy would have been able to say that he had warned his countrymen and the world about the potential harm done in the name of progress.

### Addendum

Of nineteenth-century Russian critics of the idea of progress, Tolstoy is assuredly the most renowned. But another critic merits our attention today, not due to any particular notoriety in his own time, but due to the nature of his critique: Nikolai Danilevsky (1822–1885), a naturalist and opponent of Darwinism who dabbled in other fields, including history. The fruit of Danilevsky's historical investigations was *Russia and Europe*, which, as its title suggests, offers comparisons between the author's homeland and its neighbors to the west. The cross-cultural focus of his work marks Danilevsky as a late participant in the Slavophile-Westernizer debate. But Danilevsky's place in this debate is unusual. Anderson regards Danilevsky as a corrupter of Slavophilism,[203] while Robert MacMaster insists that Danilevsky reached conclusions closer to Herzen and Bakunin than to Kireevsky or Khomiakov.[204] In truth, Danilevsky's thought shows the influence of both Slavophiles and Westernizers. What strikes readers of *Russia and Europe* today, however, is not the ways in which Danilevsky develops or distorts earlier thought. What is most striking is Danilevsky's cyclical theory of civilizations and its broad similarities to the philosophy of history propounded by Oswald Spengler.

As Spengler would later do, Danilevsky made his key arguments through the use of analogy. For instance, to help explain the history of *international* relations, he invited his readers to consider *interstellar* phenomena. If we look to the pages of human history, we see certain groups appear seemingly from nowhere and then just as suddenly disappear; these are the comet-like Huns and Mongols of the world, peoples that shine brightly for a moment before fading away. Then there are the peoples of true world-historical significance like Egypt, Greece, India, and Rome; these civilizations fill the earth just as individual planets dot the skies, and are notable for both their magnitude and their duration.[205]

Modern astronomy teaches that even planets disappear, and history shows that the longest-lasting civilizations have eventually petered out. In Danilevsky's estimation, this latter fact should come as no surprise: civilizations obey the same laws as everything else in the natural world. "To all living things," plant and animal, individual, genus, and species, he writes, there "is given only a certain span of life, and when it is finished they must die." This rule applies no less to individual humans and particular groupings of people, which "are born, attain various degrees of development, grow old and decrepit, and die."[206]

Certain conclusions follow from the idea that the world ought to be viewed in terms of historically significant civilizations and lesser, ephemeral groupings of people; the theory that all groups follow patterns of growth and decline has other implications. To the first point: by taking civilizations or nations as our units of analysis, as Danilevsky asks us to do, we downgrade the importance of our shared humanity. Danilevsky rejects as nonsensical those schemas in which all human history is divided into ancient, medieval, and modern periods. Global histories gloss over the fact that each nation and civilization has its own ancient, medieval, and modern era; in any given year, some nations and civilizations are at higher levels of development than others.[207] Since each people has its own unique experience, we should not speak of *universal* progress; a late and fruitful period for one group might occur as another group experiences its fitful beginnings.[208] But the historical laws that Danilevsky lays out also preclude perpetual *national* or *civilizational* progress. A group's development from ancient origins to so-called modernity may parallel an individual's growth from infancy to adulthood. But, as noted above, we should not forget that development ultimately becomes decay and death, for the group and the individual alike.

The links between Danilevsky's philosophy of history and his political vision for Russia are hard to miss. Danilevsky argues that Russia is an entity separate from Europe, the dominant civilization of the day. Unlike its neighbor, Russia has not yet attained world-historical status, but it still might. Danilevsky offers his Russian readers an ultimatum: do nothing and remain nothing, or take the steps necessary to grow from awkward youth to vigorous adulthood.[209] He writes that "the very character of Russians and Slavs in general is a stranger to violence, filled with gentleness, deference, and respect,"[210] noting, too, the "moderation, equanimity, and prudence characterizing both the Russian people and Russian society."[211] The path that he would have his co-nationals follow would seem to require a break in character. For

Danilevsky argues that Russia can achieve importance only if it is unified with all the other Slavic peoples, from the Baltic coast to the Bosporus and the Balkan Peninsula.[212] The pursuit of this pan-Slav union would necessarily bring Russia into conflict with competing interests, which Danilevsky recognizes. He asserts: "the most important goal of Russian state policy, which it must never renounce, is the liberation of the Slavs from the Turkish yoke, and the destruction of Ottoman power and the Turkish state itself."[213] He recognized, too, that Slavs suffered not only as vassals of the Turkish suzerain, but also as subjects of the Austrian and other European monarchies. This being so, there would necessarily be "an ongoing recurrent struggle with Europe, without which Slavdom cannot fulfill its destiny."[214] (So much, then, for nonviolence and moderation!)

Danilevsky, thus, while sharing Tolstoy's rejection of the doctrine of progress, ends up with conclusions completely different from his more renowned countryman.[215] This is because, even while rejecting the idea of perpetual improvement, he admits the possibility of temporary national or civilizational advance. Danilevsky's philosophy gives people a goal: "originality in politics, culture, and industry constitutes the ideal to which all historic peoples must aspire."[216] And Danilevsky suggests that war is the primary means by which this end might be reached. As will be shown, his successors Spengler and Brooks Adams (1848–1927) would come to the conclusion that war could also be used by a civilization to stave off its inevitable decline. The latter's ideas are analyzed in the following chapter.

# CHAPTER 3

# "The Path to Hell": Henry (and Brooks) Adams on History and Politics

I apprehend for the next hundred years an ultimate, colossal, cosmic collapse; but not on any of our old lines. My belief is that science is to wreck us, and that we are like monkeys monkeying with a loaded shell; we don't in the least know or care where our practically infinite energies come from or will bring us to. . . .

This is, however, a line of ideas wholly new, and very repugnant to our contemporaries. You will regard it with mild contempt.

## Introduction

So wrote Henry Adams (1838–1918) in a letter to his younger brother, Brooks. Adams's candid self-appraisal was fitting in many respects. He aptly recognized that his gloomy prognosis for the future was out of sync with the rosy picture painted by his contemporaries. He also understood the novelty of his ideas: his thoughts challenged not only the ethos of his day, but a line of thinking that stretched back at least as far as the American founding. Americans had long trusted in mankind's continual progress and their country's role in bringing about that progress, ideas that Adams dared to suggest were mere fiction.

A diverse set of scholars have noted the prominent role played by the idea of progress in American thought. Commenting on representative selections from speeches or writings by the Founders, Rutherford Delmage convincingly shows that "the dominant note in American thought between 1750 and 1800 was that of progress."[1] Robert Nisbet concurs, suggesting that the Declaration of Independence can be viewed as "the product of minds . . . which were steeped in faith in human progress."[2] Even political adversaries of the Declaration's drafter, Thomas Jefferson, shared such faith: "the often dour, occasionally pessimistic John Adams was capable of the most eloquent appreciation of human progress."[3] The founding moment, Mariana Mathiopolous argues, was a manifestation of the Founders' historical optimism: the Founders regarded their country's birth as "a bold liberal experiment and model of an ideal democracy for universal, sociopolitical, ethical, economic, and scientific human progress."[4] For the Founders, the political dawn of their country forebode for that country and the world a bright future.[5]

Trust in progress outlived the Founding Fathers, and such faith extended beyond the political class to all rungs of society.[6] Dorothy Ross suggests that post-independence Protestant Americans regarded the founding of their republic as the start of the millennium, a hallmark that would lead to mankind's final salvation. Throughout the nineteenth century, Americans assumed that their bountiful lands and republican tradition would "insure [their country's] progress virtually in perpetuity."[7] The American intelligentsia lent credence to the popular belief in progress, which even the Civil War could not dispel. Warren Susman writes that "mid-nineteenth-century American intellectuals adopted an approach to the study of the past that led to a fundamentally utopian outlook." Through their historical writings, these intellectuals presented "a way of understanding what was happening [in their own day] through an almost mystical notion of the divine law of progress."[8] And Thomas Pangle, who denies that the Founders believed in progress, nevertheless concedes that by the late nineteenth century the idea "dominated" intellectual circles.[9]

Given the ubiquity of the idea of progress in America, Henry Adams must have cut a strange figure when he took his place in the intellectual scene. As Ernst Breisach writes: "the historians gathered for the 1894 annual meeting of the American Historical Association must have been perplexed not only that their president, Henry Adams, would send them his presidential address from faraway Guadalajara, but even more by the address itself. In it he raised questions of substance rather than of method when he expressed radical doubts about the optimistic premise held by most American historians on the modernization of history."[10] Indeed, while other historians wrote with the expectation that the great American eagle would soar ever higher, Adams dared to ask whether she might nosedive instead. For his raising the specter of his country's stagnation or decline—among other reasons—Adams stands out among American men of letters. Henry Adams, iconoclastic historian, is this chapter's subject. I focus here on the nexus between Adams's political ideas and his philosophy of history. I argue that Adams, a critic of postbellum American politics, developed a philosophy of history that served to justify his withdrawal from active political participation and, in so doing, unknowingly secured for himself a unique position in American intellectual history.

This chapter proceeds as follows. I first discuss the idea of progress in nineteenth-century American historiography, with particular reference to five major historians of the time: George Bancroft (1800–1891), John Lothrop Motley (1814–1877), John Fiske (1842–1901), Herbert Baxter Adams (1850–1901), and Frederick Jackson Turner (1861–1932). I then offer a brief biographical portrait of Henry Adams and situate him in his intellectual milieu. In turn, I provide a more in-depth account of Adams's rejection of the faith in progress manifest in his contemporaries' works, connecting his critique of democracy with his historical pessimism. Here, I draw from the analysis of Brooks Adams, and I assess the influence of the two Adams brothers on one another. The chapter concludes with a short discussion of the Adamses' influence and their importance at a time when the promise of "hope" and the meaning of "change" are being debated.

## The Idea of Progress in Nineteenth-Century American Histories

In November 1854, George Bancroft, the preeminent nineteenth-century American historian, delivered an oration to the New-York Historical Society on the occasion of that society's semicentennial. The topic of Bancroft's speech was "the necessity, the reality, and the promise of the progress of mankind."[11] Progress was inevitable, Bancroft declared to his audience, because God endowed mankind with the power to discover immutable truth.[12] Through its collective wisdom, the human race had already realized progress over time: "in surveying the short period since man was created, the proofs of progress are so abundant that we do not know with which of them to begin, or how they should be classified."[13] Great artistic works and creative endeavors, the slow but certain march toward equality for women, improved conditions for workers, and the purification of the Christian religion should be hailed as marks of progress.[14] But the real promise of progress, its "last triumph," is the organization of society "on the basis of equality and freedom."[15] By its example, the United States would entice other states into adopting freer political institutions and realizing this final aim.[16]

Fourteen years after Bancroft's address, John Lothrop Motley presented remarks of his own to the New-York Historical Society. In that 1868 speech, published the following year as "Historic Progress and American Democracy," Motley echoed many of his predecessor's sentiments. Like Bancroft, Motley insisted that there is meaning in history; he believed that it was "possible to discover a law out of all this apparently chaotic whirl and bustle; this tangled skein of human affairs as it spins itself through the centuries."[17] The law he ascribed to history was progress, which he suggested could easily be discerned: the leading lights of science, religious martyrs, artists, adventurers, and patriots all contributed to progress in their own ways.[18] But "the chief event thus far recorded in human progress" was the discovery of America.[19] Out of colonial origins the United States came into being, and the United States would come to serve as a model for the rest of the world: "progress and liberty are identical," and the United States represented the paradigmatic free society.[20]

Bancroft and Motley were part of America's autochthonous tradition of historians, a group that also included Francis Parkman (1823–1893). Amateurs, these writers were known more for their impressive narrative styles than for their attention to method. By the 1870s, however, authors of romantic histories found themselves challenged by another camp as professional historians inspired by German research techniques came to the fore.[21] These professional historians modeled themselves after Leopold von Ranke (1795–1886), whom they esteemed for his objectivity in presenting historical facts and for his use of seminars as a means of training future scholars.[22] Conceiving of their discipline as a science, historians in the last quarter of the nineteenth century borrowed terminology from other fields, notably biology, and employed it in their own works.[23]

We can perceive the shift in American historiography from the romanticism of Bancroft and Motley to a more scientific approach in the works of John Fiske. In "Manifest Destiny," Fiske proclaims that his remarks stem from "historical or philosophical rather than by patriotic interest," and that he aims "to characterize and group events as impartially as if" he had been born in Europe rather than the United States.[24] His commitment to objectivity is one mark of his scientific approach; his utilizing the language of evolution is another.[25] Fiske appropriates Darwinian notions to argue that mankind had developed from barbarism to civilization and that the civilized portions of the species were evolving still further, from militarism to industrialism.[26] What makes industry possible, along with "all the other kinds of improvement," is peace, and peace comes through the union of smaller polities into larger.[27] "The history of human progress politically" is "the history of the successive union of groups of men into larger and more complex aggregates."[28] If Bancroft and Motley stressed American democracy as a model for the world, Fiske promoted federalism as the key American attribute worthy of imitation.[29]

Like Fiske, Herbert Baxter Adams appropriates scientific methods and metaphors in his historical studies. In "The Germanic Origin of New England Towns," Adams attempts to trace the development of American institutions back to ancient Germanic traditions. "The science of Biology no longer favors the theory of spontaneous generation," he writes, and neither should historians, who ought instead to search for the causes of events.[30] Adams's thesis, known to posterity as the "germ theory," stresses historical continuity: American practices and norms are but modifications of English behaviors and beliefs, themselves outgrowths of Germanic customs. "Magna Carta and the Bill of Rights," Adams proclaims, "are only the development of those germs of liberty first planted in the communal customs of our Saxon forefathers."[31] For Adams, to progress means to allow unabated more of the same, namely, the flourishing of inherited liberal and democratic traditions.[32]

If Adams emphasized historical continuity, Frederick Jackson Turner, his former student, stressed change. "The peculiarity of American institutions," Turner writes, lies in "the fact that they have been compelled to adapt themselves to the changes of an expanding people—to the changes involved in crossing a continent, in winning a wilderness, and in developing at each area of this progress out of the primitive economic and political conditions of the frontier into the complexity of city life."[33] The pioneering spirit that led settlers west and the continual redefining of the country's outermost limits shaped American national character. Proponents of the germ theory, focused as they were on the commonalities between the United States and Europe, neglected "The Significance of the Frontier in American History," the topic of Turner's 1893 address to the American Historical Association.[34] But understanding the frontier, Turner insists, is the key to understanding the United States itself. For one thing, easy mobility led to the breaking down of *local* attachments, which in turn allowed for the emergence of American *na-tional* identity.[35] For another, readily available land and the freedom to settle or uproot oneself at one's pleasure fostered a sense of rugged individualism.[36] Such individualism and resistance to control from higher authorities in turn cultivated "the most important effect of the frontier," namely, "the promotion of democracy here and in Europe."[37]

Whatever his differences with them, Turner shared with earlier historians a similar belief in progress. As Lloyd Ambrosius argues, this trust in progress "represented an essential element of continuity" between the older generation of historians and the so-called progressive historians of the turn of the century.[38] Each historian articulated his idea of progress differently, to be sure, but all proponents of the idea stressed the link between progress and the American political system. Ralph Henry Gabriel and Robert Harris Walker write that "one of the most frequently repeated concepts in the rhetoric of the Middle Period was that of the uniqueness of the American democratic contribution to the world."[39] We certainly see this motif in Bancroft, who proclaims that "our country is bound to allure the world to freedom by the beauty of its example."[40] But such rhetoric was hardly limited to the Middle Period in American history: Richard Hofstadter writes of Turner that he promoted "a gentle and basically humane nationalism" centered on "the democracy of the common man."[41] Conservative nationalists like Motley and Baxter Adams and social Darwinists like Fiske dominated the period between Bancroft and Turner, and while they might not have shared the egalitarian values of their brother historians, they did share their trust in the idea of progress and their faith in American democratic practices.[42]

### Henry Adams and His Time

In exceedingly rare circumstances could Henry Adams find a man with ties to the pantheon of democrats stronger than his own. The descendants of Theseus or Athena could perhaps challenge him for bragging rights on that matter, but scarcely anyone on State Street or Constitution Avenue could claim a more illustrious lineage. Walking among demigods was so routine for the young Adams that he remained blissfully ignorant of his unique situation, unaware, he observes, that "it was unusual for boys to sit behind a President grandfather, and to read over his head the tablet in memory of a President great-grandfather, who had 'pledged his life, his fortune, and his sacred honor' to secure the independence of his country and so forth."[43] Democracy ran through Adams's blood, and being at the hub of American government was part of his life.

As the scion of an important political dynasty, Adams had every reason to believe that his own destiny lay in politics. If this was his expectation, however, then the fates left him sorely disappointed; the thread Clotho spun for him entailed that he would leave his mark not in higher office, but as a historian. Although posterity remembers him best for *The Education of Henry Adams*, the semi-autobiographical book for which he was posthumously awarded a Pulitzer Prize in 1919, Adams's literary output went far beyond *The Education*. He also authored the nine-volume *History of the United States During the Administrations of Thomas Jefferson and James Madison*, a series of essays on the profession of teaching history, and the novels *Democracy* and *Esther*. Through his writings, rather than through direct political involvement, Adams offered his greatest contributions to the national conversation about America's democratic experiment.

A Bostonian by birth, Henry Adams was familiar with other major commentators on American political development; Bancroft, Motley, Fiske, and Herbert Baxter Adams all had deep ties to Massachusetts.[44] Sharing a similar background with these leading lights of history, Adams also shared, for a time, some of their views. For instance, not only did he subscribe to the germ theory popularized by Herbert Baxter Adams, but his own work precipitated his namesake's: as Edward Chalfant suggests, the book that became a "bible" of sorts for Herbert Baxter Adams was none other than *Essays in Anglo-Saxon Law*, a compilation of pieces by Henry Adams and some of his Harvard graduate students.[45] However, Adams's intellectual affinities with his peers were shorter-lived and less keenly felt than his personal sympathies. He disassociated himself from his work on the Anglo-Saxons,[46] and his reviews of his intimates' work could be scathing.

A motive force in American historiography's shift to a more scientific approach, Adams found fault with his predecessors' romantic style. Michael Kraus and Davis Joyce explain the differences between Adams and the amateur writers of old: "The romantic historians stressed narrative, appealed to the emotions, selected colorful episodes. . . . Adams concentrated on the sources, appealed to the intellect, brought the past to the reader, and emphasized the evolution of societal institutions."[47] Adams broke with the past not only as a writer; he introduced novel methods as a teacher as well. Jurgen Herbst acknowledges Adams as among the first social scientists to make use

of the seminar method.[48] Not without cause do Gerald Grob and George Billias suggest that Adams stands with Turner as the best exemplification of
the shift from amateur to professional historiography.[49]

Adams's concern was as much with his forerunners' message as it was
with their methods. As Ernest Samuels notes, Adams, in his review of Bancroft's *History*, "spoke rather scornfully" of his elder's "naïve faith in the abstract virtues of democracy."[50] If unwavering trust in democracy was a fault
of Bancroft, it was one he shared with the younger generation of historians,
whom Adams also took to task. Well before Adams launched his professional
career, Gabriel and Walker argue, he had been increasingly convinced "that
democracy is the process of degradation."[51] Where his peers linked democracy with progress, Adams associated it with decline; his works challenged
the ideas proffered by his complacent contemporaries.[52]

If anyone had a bird's-eye view of American democracy, it was Adams,
who from his earliest life had been immersed in politics. By the time of
his birth, his ex-president grandfather, John Quincy Adams, had resumed
his place in the halls of Congress. At ten, he witnessed his own father,
Charles Francis Adams, campaign for the vice-presidency of the United
States as Martin Van Buren's running mate on the Free Soil Party ticket.
Having acquired in his boyhood a familiarity with Washington, he gained
an outsider's perspective on American politics as a young adult: when President Abraham Lincoln selected Charles Francis Adams for the post of minister to the United Kingdom, the younger Adams accompanied his father in
Britain and served as his personal secretary. When he returned to Washington after his long stay in London, Adams recalls in the *Education*, he was "a
young reformer of thirty."[53] His zeal for reform, though, was short-lived:
when Ulysses Grant announced the composition of his cabinet, Adams
recognized that his ambition to help clean up the nation's capital was "an
absurdity so laughable," a promise so far from possible, that he was ashamed
to have entertained the idea.[54]

### Democracy

Garry Wills notes that there is a tendency to read Henry Adams backward:
cognizant of Adams's pessimistic narrative in *The Education*, readers try to
find that same pessimism in his earlier works.[55] I wish to read Adams forward, as it were, beginning with an interpretation of his novel *Democracy*

before turning to two late pieces published posthumously by his brother Brooks in *The Degradation of the Democratic Dogma*. Though Wills suggests that the Adams who authored the *History* (1889–1891) was optimistic about the United States, I will show that the author of *Democracy* (1880) certainly seems to have had misgivings about his country's future; if Adams ever sounded a positive note in his projections for American political development, he was playing off-key in an otherwise melancholy requiem.

Published anonymously in 1880, Adams's first novel turns a critical eye to Reconstruction-era American government.[56] The novel tells the tale of a young and wealthy widow, Mrs. Lee, who travels to Washington, D.C., to get at "the heart of the great American mystery of democracy and government."[57] In Washington, Mrs. Lee becomes fully engaged in political life; her home becomes a salon of sorts. She meets senators and representatives, bureaucrats and diplomats, and even greets the president. Well-liked immediately, she finds as suitors the powerful Senator Ratcliffe and the earnest lawyer John Carrington. But the love triangle is merely a subplot; Mrs. Lee goes to Washington not because she has romantic ambitions, but because "she wanted to learn how the machinery of government worked" and "the quality of the men who controlled it."[58] Her aim is singular: she insists that "the one thing in life" that she must know is "whether America is right or wrong."[59] She spends her months in the capital learning how politicians operate and how government works behind the scenes. What she discovers horrifies her to such an extent that she decides to quit Washington and travel as far from the capital as she can. She departs for Egypt, declaring to a confidante that "democracy has shaken my nerves to pieces."[60]

In an essay on the uses of novels for political theorists, Catherine Zuckert suggests that "we cannot identify the novelist with any one of his characters."[61] Elisha Greifer issues a similar warning—"one should not too hastily identify an author with his leading character"—but he argues that in the case of Adams and *Democracy*, the novelist clearly represents himself in his novel's heroine.[62] Several other commentators likewise see the disenchanted Mrs. Lee as a stand-in for Adams himself. Michael Colacurcio, for instance, suggests that Adams's response to the corrupting influence of Washington was the same as Mrs. Lee's: flight from the city.[63] Ernest Samuels sees Mrs. Lee not as a mirror of Adams alone, but as a composite of the author and his wife Marian,[64] a view B. H. Gilley shares.[65] Whether her character is based on Adams alone or is a composite, she clearly speaks Adams's point of view.[66]

But Adams inserts himself into *Democracy* in other ways. The narrator, for instance, echoes much of what Mrs. Lee thinks or says, and thus is a voice for Adams as well. Ernest and Jayne Samuels write that the noble Mr. Carrington represents Senator Lucius Lamar, a friend of Adams.[67] In that Carrington is one of the protagonists of the novel, he too might be taken as a mouthpiece for Adams. Indeed, any of Mrs. Lee's friends, inasmuch as they guide her and shape her views of government, might be regarded as Adamslike. Such friends also include Nathan Gore, an earnest reformer whom Vernon Parrington asserts is "quite evidently Henry Adams himself."[68]

The reader can easily sense Adams's disappointment with democracy, voiced alternatively through Mrs. Lee, her acquaintances, and the narrator. In his novel, Adams critiques both politicians and the public they are supposed to represent. One of his criticisms is that congressmen spend too much of their time politicking and too little time governing. Mrs. Lee's sister regards Congress as "a place where people went to recite speeches." The narrator adds that many congressmen hold this same view of Congress.[69] They make "noisy demonstrations," but the narrator maintains that they would be put to better use "doing nothing."[70]

Some congressmen do busy themselves with a lot of nothing when not speechifying. Senator Ratcliffe can be seen "signing papers without reading them, answering remarks without hearing them . . . and appearing immersed in labor." But not all his colleagues share his work ethic; they do not even *pretend* to be busy. Rather, they spend their time "lounging about . . . reading newspapers, or beguiling their time in tobacco in various forms."[71] Their chief sport, after all, is chasing after offices.[72] Once actually in office, there is not much for them to do.

The little real work politicians do gets achieved in an overly partisan environment. Asked by Mrs. Lee whether he has ever refused to align himself with his party, a shocked Senator Ratcliffe declares "Never!" When pressed further, the senator admits that national allegiance is more important than party affiliation.[73] However, Ratcliffe's actions suggest that concern for his party does trump concern for his country. Throughout his career, "he had done his best for his party," and had willingly "sold himself to the devil" to see that party succeed.[74] Although denied his party's nomination for the presidency, Ratcliffe wields considerable influence in Washington. After having schemed his way into the president's cabinet, he sees to it that civil servants are replaced with friends of his own.[75] Loyalty in Washington means favoritism.

If politicians were guilty only of making bombastic proclamations on the floors of Congress, idling their time, or being too closely guided by partisan considerations, they would hardly be worth the worry. But one of the major themes of *Democracy* is corruption. Adams presents a world in which congressmen use their offices to enrich themselves, not to serve the public interest. Senators live by the maxim that "democracy, rightly understood, is the government of the people, by the people, for the benefit of Senators."[76] Washington is a place where "wealth, office, power are at auction."[77] Votes, too, can be bought; the denouement of the story comes when Senator Ratcliffe admits to Mrs. Lee that he has taken $100,000 in bribes.[78] Having gone to Washington to see how the government works, Mrs. Lee finds that she and her compatriots are "at the mercy of thieves and ruffians."[79]

While politicians are corrupt, they are merely representatives of a depraved citizenry. Having had a chance to wed Ratcliffe (and declined the opportunity), a disgusted Mrs. Lee laments to Carrington that "nine out of ten of our countrymen would say I had made a mistake."[80] That is, most Americans would unhesitatingly have turned a blind eye to Ratcliffe's corruption. Sharing Mrs. Lee's low opinion of the masses, the narrator asks if there is not "some mistake about a doctrine which makes the wicked, when a majority, the mouthpiece of God against the virtuous."[81]

Being moved by material interests is not the only way in which politicians represent the society from which they come. Politicians and their constituents also share a need for approval. Congressmen seek office not solely to enrich themselves, but because of vanity. "One general characteristic of all Senators," Mrs. Lee learns, is that all possess "a boundless and guileless thirst for flattery."[82] But senators' need to be flattered is coupled with an inclination to heap praise upon their constituents. Mrs. Lee tells Ratcliffe that if monkeys were voters, he "would be very enthusiastic about their intelligence and virtue."[83]

In some respect, Ratcliffe, his colleagues in government, and the American public are no better than monkeys. They are certainly little smarter than primates. Senator Ratcliffe cannot engage with foreign diplomats, who try to speak with him on a range of topics of which he is ignorant. He attempts to steer such conversations to safer topics, but when he cannot, his replies reveal plain "ignorance of common literature, art, and history."[84] And the senator is not alone in his ignorance: the president and his wife stand "stripped of every sign of intelligence." But these "automata" are merely "representatives of the society which streamed past them."[85]

Washington society does not hide its collective stupidity. The city "swarms with simple-minded exhibitions of human nature," men and women "whom it would be cruel to ridicule and ridiculous to weep over."[86] Politicians sometimes seem even to flaunt their intellectual shortcomings. Or, if not proud of their lack of intellectual aptitude, they are at least unashamed. To the Bulgarian diplomat Baron Jacobi, American politicians combine "the narrowest education and the meanest personal experience" with "the utmost pragmatical self-assurance" that he has witnessed in any government.[87] Through foreign eyes, Americans seem base.

American democracy, thus, is a system that allows the ill-educated and self-interested masses to elect from their ranks men who will remain uninformed and self-interested once in positions of power. By the end of her time in Washington, Mrs. Lee has "got to the bottom of this business of democratic government," and she has determined that it is "nothing more than government of any other kind."[88] Corruption runs unchecked, party interests trump public interest, and the best that can be hoped of politicians is that they fritter away their time rather than doing any lasting harm.

Adams clearly shared his heroine's concerns about American politics, misgivings that were hardly novel. Others before him, as far back as Plato, had voiced similar fears about democracy; he himself acknowledged Alexis de Tocqueville and John Stuart Mill as his early models. In *Democracy*, Adams depicts the political elite as men hardly worth esteeming; in *Democracy in America*, Tocqueville denies that the most meritorious individuals necessarily rise through the political ranks in the United States, noting that while universal suffrage may have its benefits, ensuring that worthy men direct public affairs cannot be counted among those advantages.[89] Adams's novel shows the masses to be woefully ignorant; in *On Liberty*, Mill suggests that the public constitutes "a few wise and many foolish individuals."[90] Other parallels between Adams and the men he once claimed as his "high priests"[91] might readily be found.[92]

But Adams departs from Tocqueville and Mill in at least one important way. *Democracy* raises the question whether the American political system's deficiencies are ameliorable, a question to which the two Europeans would have answered in the affirmative. As Alan Kahan says of Tocqueville: "In *Democracy in America*, he is, on the whole, an optimist."[93] And Mill, despite his concerns about the effects of public opinion on individual liberty, could still look favorably upon "the stage of progress into which the more civilized portions of the species have now entered," could still speak of "man as a progressive being," and could recognize "improvement which has taken place either in the human mind or in institutions."[94] He also believed that "left without a government, every body of Americans is able to improvise one, and to carry on that or any public business with a sufficient amount of intelligence, order and decision."[95] Adams did not share his predecessors' optimism.

Adams's heroine, Mrs. Lee, notes that "half of our wise men declare that the world is going straight to perdition; the other half that it is fast becoming perfect. Both cannot be right."[96] She ultimately concludes that American government and society are devolving and that chaos will ensue. Witnessing the spectacle of a state function, she sees the president and his wife shaking hands with well-wishers, and feels a sense of dread. The narrator notes of Mrs. Lee that "She felt a sudden conviction that this was to be the end of American society; its realisation and dream at once. She groaned in spirit. 'Yes! At last I have reached the end! We shall grow to be wax images, and our talk will be like the squeaking of toy dolls. We shall all wander round and round the earth and shake hands. No one will have any object in this world, and there will be no order."[97] Sharing his protagonist's sense of impending doom sets Adams apart from European predecessors such as Tocqueville and Mill and from his contemporaries in the United States. In addition to his caustic fictionalized portrayal of postbellum America, his numerous nonfiction works and letters to his intimates manifest a preoccupation with finding order amid chaos and trying to remain moored when historical laws pointed to decline.

## The Law of Entropy

The heroine of *Democracy* concludes that "I could do nothing sillier than to suppose myself competent to reform anything."[98] Adams had concluded the same for himself years before he wrote his novel. He had returned to the United States from Europe in July 1868 upon his father's resignation as minister to the United Kingdom, hoping to carry on the family tradition of public service. The political post he had imagined for himself did not materialize, however, and he swiftly became a fierce critic of the very administration he had initially sought to join. As a freelance journalist, writing for such outlets as the *Nation* and *North American Review*, Adams lambasted Grant's presidency for its various shortcomings.[99] In a certain sense, however, his concern was less about Grant per se and more about the general tenor and trend of American politics: the executive branch had become too weak, the legislative branch too strong, and the spoils system too deeply entrenched.[100] His (perhaps) pedestrian objections to the practice of democratic politics disregarded by others, Adams turned to the study of history to find a reason for his country's decline.

To this day, professional historians regard Adams's *History of the United States* as an impressive piece of scholarship.[101] But what sets Adams apart from other historians (of his day or ours) is the unique philosophy of history he elaborated in his later works.[102] While he had taken from Tocqueville and Mill certain insights about liberty and democracy, he looked to a different pair of European thinkers when developing his philosophy of history: in *The Education*, he claimed that he "drew life from Hegel and Schopenhauer rightly understood."[103] Such a statement might seem on first glance to be paradoxical, but it is not. Adams shared with Hegel the desire to achieve a scientific understanding of history; with Schopenhauer, he reached the conclusion that historical changes have not resulted in progress. In "The Rule of Phase Applied to History" (1909) and "A Letter to American Teachers of History" (1910), he used insights from the natural sciences to create a theory of social development.

In his role as a professional historian, Adams had surveyed an immense array of literature dealing with human social and political change. What he found was that most published histories stressed the continued improvement of humankind. "The historian of human society," he writes, "has hitherto . . . preferred to write or to lecture on a tacit assumption that humanity showed upward progress, even when it emphatically showed the contrary."[104] Society, historians assumed, must be moving toward a superior state of being: surely scientific, technological, and educational improvements were improving society as a whole, even if not leading to some ultimate telos.

As noted earlier, many nineteenth-century historians justified their faith in progress by appropriating lessons from science to the social sphere. The theories of evolution that Charles Lyell and Charles Darwin developed in midcentury, for instance, seemed to validate the progressive view of history. Although used to explain biological development, these theories could be used to explain social change as well. When applied in such a way, the theories seemed promising for mankind, and for a full "fifty years, society flattered itself that science stood solidly behind it, lifting it up from lower powers to higher."[105] There were even times, Adams suggested, when turn-of-the-century Americans proclaimed their belief in continual progress with more dogmatic certainty than had generations prior.[106]

But for all the inspiration they had drawn from biology, historians were unwilling to consider lessons from physics. To Adams, this was a serious oversight. In his view, everything—human interactions not excepted—must be susceptible to the laws of physics.[107] And because nothing can defy physical laws, Adams contended that historians ought to turn away from biology for their models and look instead to physics. With no sense of irony, Adams maintained that "the future of Thought, and therefore of History, lies in the hands of the physicists," and therefore "the future historian must seek his education in the world of mathematical physics."[108] As William Jordy argues, whether Adams properly understood or presented the laws of physics is immaterial: what matters is the lesson he took from physics and the metaphors he employed to argue against his contemporaries.[109] Adams argued that if the historian should become acquainted with advances in physics, he would understand the cardinal teaching of that discipline: "all grow old and die."[110]

In his studies of physics, Adams was particularly drawn to Lord Kelvin's Second Law of Thermodynamics, a law that (on his reading, anyway) asserts "the constant dissipation of energy."[111] Energy moves through phases: solids turn to liquids, liquids to vapor, and vapor to ether. The end result of this transformation of energy from one phase to another is a matter of philosophical speculation.[112] Adams, however, saw that Kelvin's Law points one way: to "catastrophe."[113] Adams understood the laws of physics to mean that "everything, animate or inanimate, spiritual or material, exists in Phase" and that "all is equilibrium more or less unstable."[114] Since physical laws apply to all spheres of being, even society exists in phase and its peace could be shattered at any moment.

Kelvin's Law forced biologists to reconsider the doctrine of evolution: even scientists who were committed in principle to Darwin's theory had altered their terminologies by the late nineteenth century, no longer speaking of positive "evolution," but instead using the more neutral word "transformation."[115] But while scientists adapted their theories to new evidence, Adams's fellow historians clung to a progressive view of history, paying little heed to the lessons of physics. They treated "the Degradationist," as Adams called the alternative theorist, as persona non grata, an enemy and an outlaw.[116] Adams had gleaned from his lessons in physics that "man is a bottomless sink of waste unparalleled in the cosmos," a being who "can already see the end of the immense economies which his mother Nature stored for his support."[117] His colleagues peddled the idea that man had no limits; this was the safe view, one supported by artists, politicians, and other groups.[118]

Adams believed that if his peers in the humanistic sciences would confront the law of entropy, they would find in America's short history evidence of social and political decline. He writes in his *Education* that "evolution, from President Washington to President Grant, was alone evidence enough to upset Darwin."[119] This might sound like a proclamation made in jest, but, in light of his trenchant critique of Gilded Age politics in *Democracy*, we should not treat it as such. Letters exchanged with his intimates also reveal that American decline was no joke to Adams. In an 1895 letter to his youngest brother, for instance, he laments that he tends to "look on our society as a balloon, liable to momentary collapse."[120]

The kind of pessimism that we might attribute to Adams, Francis Wilson notes, "is not common in America." Where others, for example Henry George (1839–1897), may have been what Wilson terms "contingent" or "conditional" pessimists who foresaw decline if their political prescriptions or social reforms were not adopted, Adams stands alone for his total rejection of the idea of progress.[121]

### Degradation and Democracy

Roger Shumate notes a paradox in Adams's thinking: on the one hand, he freely castigates American government and society for their decrepitude, while on the other hand his own philosophy professes the inevitability of such decay.[122] If society necessarily sinks into a great morass, how can people be blamed for being uneducated, uncultured, self-serving, or materialistic? Moreover, if all societies are subject to physical laws and are bound to deteriorate, then what difference does it make whether the people rule, a monarch reigns, or a military junta exercises control? Adams does not make explicit the connection between democracy and social collapse.

There are two plausible responses to the dilemma posed by Shumate. The first is to argue that Shumate's objection is beside the point: Adams's contention is not that democracy is *worse* than alternative political systems, but that it is simply *no better*. Such a reading of Adams can be defended; his was the pen, after all, that inked a novel in which the heroine concludes that democracy is "nothing more than government of any other kind."

A second rejoinder to Shumate's paradox is this: though Adams may not have connected all the dots for his audience, nothing precludes readers from drawing inferences themselves. One very attentive reader, in fact, engaged in just such a project of connection-making: in his contribution to *The Degradation of the Democratic Dogma*, Brooks Adams, a noteworthy economist and historian in his own right, links his brother's political thought and his philosophy of history. His reading of Henry merits consideration, because the two brothers were not merely kin, but kindred spirits as well. Daniel Aaron writes of the affinities between the two: "Henry's heavy correspondence with Brooks, earnest for the most part and without the veneer of flippancy that characterized most of his other correspondence, is merely one indication of their close intellectual relationship. 'We are too much alike, and agree too well in our ideas,' Henry remarked to a friend. 'We have nothing to give each other.'"[123]

Brooks's best-known work, *The Law of Civilization and Decay* (1895), played a special role in the development of Henry's ideas.[124] Acting as his brother's chief sounding board, Henry carefully read drafts of the manuscript. Letters exchanged between the two brothers reveal an earnest give and take of ideas. And the end result was a book of which not only Brooks, but Henry, as well, was proud. In a letter to his close confidante, Elizabeth Sherman Cameron, Henry writes of Brooks and the fruit of his labors:

> In my private opinion—not to be lisped abroad for fear of total
> ruin to it and mankind at large—I think it is astonishing. Indeed it
> is the first time that serious history has ever been written. He has
> done for it what only the greatest men do; he has created a startling
> generalisation which reduces all history to a scientific formula, and
> which is yet so simple and obvious that one cannot believe it to be
> new. My admiration for it is much too great to be told. I have
> sought all my life those truths which this mighty infant, this seer
> unblest, has struck with the agony and bloody sweat of genius. I
> stand in awe of him. He is in History what Schopenhauer is in
> Metaphysics.[125]

Henry's praise of Brooks would be revealed to the public in due time. In *The Education*, Henry writes that Brooks was "a strong writer and a vigorous thinker." The two brothers were "absorbed in the same perplexities," and as they formulated their ideas, they became "used to audiences of one."[126]

The philosophies of Henry and Brooks Adams are not identical, and I do not purport them to be. I reject claims, though, which suggest that Brooks's contribution to *The Degradation of the Democratic Dogma* was somehow at odds with Henry's philosophy.[127] I would contest that the Adams brothers shared fundamental agreement in their diagnoses of society's ailments, but parted ways when it came to acting on their findings. Brooks became an apologist for American imperialism, arguing that the United States could stave off its ultimate collapse so long as it kept expanding its territory to incorporate new energies. Henry, however, approached politics with resignation, finding his country's faults irreparable. While the two Adamses disagreed on what (if anything) could be done, they shared similar concerns about capitalism, industrialism, and the modern family.

For both Adams brothers, capitalism plays a vital role in hastening America's decline. In their view, the more capitalism develops, the more energy is wasted. The more resources are put in private hands, the fewer can be developed for the public good. "Of all forms of society or government," Henry confesses, capitalism "was the one he liked least."[128] But the capitalist impulse cannot be separated from democratic governance. Brooks claims that "the whole theory of modern democracy" falsely proclaims "that it is possible by education to stimulate the selfish instinct of competition . . . so as to coincide with the moral principle that all should labor for the common good."[129] Excessive competition does not raise society to a higher moral plane, it promotes only disunity. "Social war," Brooks predicts, "would seem to be the natural ending of the democratic philosophy."[130]

For Brooks, Henry's philosophical essays prove the inevitability of such a social war. He claims that these essays attest to certain "facts" that point to nothing less than society's total dissolution; democracy must "ultimately end in chaos."[131] Technological innovation and industrialization, intimately connected with modern democracy, push society towards that bitter end.[132] As Benjamin Barber notes, the pace of change in the twentieth century was staggering, but Henry had already keenly observed that in the previous century, "measured by any standard known to science—by horsepower, calories, volts, mass in any shape—the tension and vibration and volume and so-called progression of society were fully a thousand times greater."[133] This rapid change, which Henry famously symbolized in the dynamo, would contribute to the great undoing of society. No longer did the Church, represented by the cult of the Virgin, emit the centripetal pull that unified medieval society, and though the dynamo could and did supplant the Virgin as a force in the

world, it could not help replicate the unity of a bygone age.[134] The result of
the unceasing technological changes ushered in by democracy, Brooks
argued, will be catastrophic. In the end, he suggests, industrial society
"becomes resolved into what is, in substance, a vapor, which loses collective
energy in proportion to the perfection of its expansion."[135]

If not in outright war, society will dissolve itself by other means. In a
speech before the American Academy of Arts and Letters, Brooks describes
the undoing of America's social fabric by excessive individualism. This great
undoing starts in the family. When women reject their duties as wives and
mothers—when they cease to be the "cement" that holds families together—
they hasten society's decline. Brooks goes so far as to say that women shirk-
ing their traditional duties constitutes "the ultimate form of selfishness" and
tends toward "the final resolution of society into atoms."[136] Henry laments,
too, in the *Education* that "the American woman was a failure."[137] The modern American "woman had been set free," but women "were not content."[138]
Unable to find her footing in the new age, the modern woman could not
succeed in any of her old roles: "she had failed even to hold the family together."[139] This was not, Henry argued, entirely the fault of women, for he
regarded the female sex as superior. Modern democratic life had simply
de-sexed American society.[140]

The philosophies of history elaborated by Henry and Brooks are thus
deeply pessimistic. A common thread running through these theories is that
the human race is governed to a great extent by laws beyond its control. These
forces push civilization toward a cataclysmic end, and the only influence
people have is on how quickly or slowly that end will be reached. Self-
interestedness, whether in the form of materialism or manifested by the
rejection of traditional obligations, will hasten a decline that is already visi-
ble in American government and society. In this sense, we might argue that
democracy *is* worse than its alternatives.


### Staving Off the Decline

William A. Williams writes that "both Brooks and Henry Adams considered
The Law [the law of civilization and decay] to be the central problem of their
life."[141] The gist of that law is that human societies experience "oscillations
between barbarism and civilization," or the "movement from a condition of
physical dispersion to one of concentration." In its early stages, society is

motivated by fear, which "creates a belief in an invisible world, and ultimately develops a priesthood." Later, greed supplants fear as the dominant motivating force. In the course of civilization, "the imagination fades, and the emotional, the martial, and the artistic types of manhood decay," while "the economic, and, perhaps, the scientific intellect is propagated." At the peak of civilization or centralization, when "unrestricted economic competition prevails," there is a marked "loss of energy . . . manifested by a gradual dissipation of capital, which, at last, ends in disintegration."[142] The United States and Europe, as they appeared to the Adams brothers, had reached a high point of civilization; all that lay ahead was collapse and displacement as the center of global capital.

Neither Adams brother liked the conclusion of *The Law of Civilization and Decay*, and Brooks went to work almost immediately to find a way for the United States to defy historical precedent.[143] The result of his effort was *America's Economic Supremacy* (1900). Much of the later work echoes its predecessor: there is the same discussion of centralization, energy, and capital. But Adams qualifies his pessimism in the later work. He observes that "for upward of a thousand years the social centre of civilization has advanced steadily westward,"[144] from Constantinople, to Venice, to Antwerp and Amsterdam.[145] If the center of civilization should continue along the same trajectory, "it will presently cross the Atlantic and aggrandize America." But, "if, on the contrary, it should recede, America may have reached her prime."[146] The future of the United States is thus up in the air: it might have reached the end, but it might yet live to fight another day.

In *The Law of Civilization and Decay*, Adams treats a civilization's eventual end as an inevitability. "When a highly centralized society disintegrates," he writes, "it is because the energy of the race has been exhausted" by economic competition. "Consequently, the survivors of such a race lack the power necessary for renewed concentration, and must probably remain inert, until supplied with fresh energetic material by the infusion of barbarian blood."[147] In *America's Economic Supremacy*, Adams posits a way for the United States to avoid this bitter end. The United States risks losing its status in the world by having nowhere to offload its surplus production. The key, then, is to penetrate a market that has not yet been saturated—East Asia. "Whether we like it or not," Adams writes, "we are forced to compete for the seat of international exchanges."[148]

"Competition" is a gentler term for what Adams really had in mind—the creation of an American Empire. To wrest the seat of global trade will be no easy feat: "competition, in its acutest form, is war."[149] And once won, it will be difficult to sustain: "to maintain such an empire presupposes an organization perfect in proportion to the weight it must support and the friction it must endure." Consequently, "it is the perfecting of this organization, both military and civil, which must be the task of the next fifty years."[150] If the United States should take up its dangerous challenge, the odds would be in its favor: "Anglo-Saxons have little to fear in a trial of strength," since "they have been the most successful of adventurers."[151]

Thus, the gloomy Brooks Adams modified his law of decay. Noting that "the civilization which does not advance declines,"[152] he supported the one thing that looked like a possible way for his country to advance. In an 1896 letter to Theodore Roosevelt, Adams wrote that "the whole world . . . seems to me to be rotting." At the same time, he spoke of "hope for us." That hope was for "war, war which shall bring down the British empire." He told Roosevelt that "you are an adventurer and you have but one thing to sell—your sword."[153] War would come two years later, with Spain. And shortly thereafter, a man of the martial type would occupy the White House, showing that American energy had not yet dissipated.

## Conservative Christian Anarchism

In contrast with his brother, Henry Adams could not find an "out" from the disarray in which the United States found itself.[154] Had he more consistently applied his theory of phase, he may have arrived at a cyclical theory similar to his brother's or to the Roman republicans. Instead, he became transfixed by the idea of decline, and he could not countenance the idea of regeneration. As a consequence of his preoccupation, Adams was able to paint a vivid portrait of a society in its final throes, while failing to provide a complementary vision of revivification. His failure in this regard, however, was only partial: he may have been unable to offer the American public solutions to the problems of social and political decline, but he successfully absolved himself of the duty to formulate any such solutions. In elaborating a philosophy of history that posited inevitable decay, Adams had freed himself from the need to be a reformer or to take direct political action—in terms of his philosophy, political activity would be mostly futile. Schopenhauer had observed that "constructive histories, guided by a shallow optimism, always ultimately end in a comfortable, substantial, fat State."[155] Adams, having proposed a philosophy of history shorn of any optimism, reconciled himself to being the equivalent of an anti-statist; he was a self-styled "anarchist."

Disillusioned with the world in which he lived, Adams opted to withdraw. The most extreme form of withdrawal short of suicide is total separation of self from society and renunciation of the world. At times Adams seems to have embraced this kind of resignation. He writes to his brother, Brooks, that "the process of turning a machine like ours round a corner will be dangerous in proportion to its sharpness," continuing on to lament that "neither its dangers, nor its successes, nor its failures seem to me now to be worth living to see." He reiterates his disenchantment with the world: "Nothing can come of it that is worth living for; nothing so interesting as we have already seen."[156] Henry's world-weariness even seeps into his fiction. Mrs. Lee, the semi-autobiographical protagonist of *Democracy*, declares that "I do not cling very closely to life, and do not value my own very highly."[157]

A less drastic option than complete resignation, and the one Adams chose, was to separate himself not from the entire world, but simply from the part of the world that so disgusted him, Washington, D.C. Though he maintained a home on Lafayette Square until the end of his life, he made frequent sojourns outside the United States and looked askance at American political happenings. Hofstadter observes of Adams that he stands alone for "the unparalleled mixture of his detachment and involvement."[158] Seeing politics as a corrupt endeavor, and holding no hope of its becoming less corrupt, washing his hands of the mess may have been the only logical solution for him. In a letter to his brother Charles, Henry writes: "I will never make a speech, never run for an office, never belong to a party."[159] Brooks insists that, even if it had been offered him, Henry would not have accepted political office.[160]

By the end of his life, Adams had become, in his own estimation, a "conservative Christian anarchist."[161] He was conservative in the sense of dreading his society's further erosion and clinging, in the nineteenth and twentieth centuries, to "eighteenth-century principles."[162] He was Christian in wish only; although he found much to admire about faith-centered societies, he confessed that, for himself, "the religious instinct had vanished and could not be revived."[163] And he was an anarchist in ways already alluded to: he resisted centralization,[164] and, given his idiosyncratic views, he could not stand behind any political party. In a letter to Brooks, he refers to the latter's book as "the Bible of Anarchy" and remarks that "God knows what side in our politics it would help, for it cuts all equally."[165] Sharing much with his brother's, Henry's philosophy was one that likewise cut all equally.[166]

## Conclusion

To Henry Adams, Marcus Aurelius represented the pinnacle of human achievement, worthy of emulation.[167] But Adams himself was no emperor; lineage might have secured him a position of power in another place or time, but it could not in postbellum America. Nor can we situate Adams lower on the chain of command; he was not, as Russell Hanson and Richard Merriam deem him, a "watchful sentinel" warning his countrymen of imminent peril.[168] Marcus Aurelius crossed the River Gran to do battle with the Germanic Quadi; a sentinel not only stands guard, he is ready to take up arms against encroaching dangers. But Henry Adams engaged in no serious conflict with the barbarians of the Potomac. Rather, he chose flight over fight, quitting the dirty business of politics and seeking refuge where he could find it—in Tahiti, in his studies of medieval Chartres, and in cultivating relationships with people he deemed worthy of his affections.

Henry Adams is an important figure in American political thought not because of his influence on political actors or as the founder of an intellectual movement. Rather, he stands out as a unique thinker who raised questions about the promise of progress in a democratic society. At a time of widespread discontent with Washington and growing uncertainty about the future of the United States, these questions are worth our revisiting.

# CHAPTER 4

# Critics of the Idea of Progress in an Age of Extremes: Three Twentieth-Century Voices

Thus far, this book has shown most critics of the idea of progress to be leery of substantial political endeavors. To Arthur Schopenhauer, history revealed neither advancement nor decline, and new problems would simply replace any that could be fixed in the political arena—whack one mole, and up pops another. For Leo Tolstoy, "progress" was a cipher, an empty slogan with no agreed-upon meaning that the powerful could bandy about to justify their pet projects and policies. And in the eyes of Henry Adams, immutable laws degraded every sphere of human existence, the political realm not excepted.

However, not all critics of "progress" are critics of politics. As has been shown, Nikolai Danilevsky and Brooks Adams took a real interest in international affairs, advocating their countries' robust and even bellicose engagement with other parts of the world. Following in their footsteps was Oswald Spengler, a former *gymnasium* teacher who became twentieth-century Germany's most renowned philosopher of history. Hailed by some readers and maligned by others, Spengler's controversial masterwork, *The Decline of the West*, provoked a spirited discussion when its first volume appeared in 1918.

As Danilevsky had done in *Russia and Europe* and Adams had done in *The Law of Civilization and Decay*, Spengler provides in *The Decline of the West* a sweeping look at global history. He takes as his units of analysis not particular *epochs*, but identifiable *cultures*. As the title to his magnum opus implies, Spengler focuses primarily on those cultures most familiar to a European and North American readership. These include the Classical culture of the early Greeks and Romans, the Magian culture in which the Abrahamic religions arose, and a separate Western culture that took root in medieval Europe. Not entirely escaping Spengler's purview are ancient Babylon, China, Egypt, India, and Mesoamerica and the Russian culture still nascent in the twentieth century.

Also like Danilevsky and Adams, Spengler reveals a special interest in world politics. In the second volume of *The Decline of the West*, he declares that "domestic politics exist simply in order that foreign politics may be possible."[1] But foreign politics rarely means politics in the sense of give and take, negotiation and renegotiation between equal parties. "War is the primary politics of *everything* that lives," Spengler observes.[2] Granted, there are placid moments now and again. But "even world-peace, in every case where it has existed, has been nothing but the slavery of an entire humanity under the regimen imposed by a few strong natures determined to rule."[3] If domestic politics is simply a coda for the *real* performance of politics, politics on the global stage, and if international *politics* is merely international *warfare*, then one must conclude that politics requires a particular type of martial ruler. To Spengler, "the decisive problems" are not questions of morality or constitutional design, but questions of how best to secure "the steadiness, sureness, and superiority of political leadership."[4]

For Spengler no less than for Danilevsky, Adams, or any of the authors so far examined, there is a connection between historiosophy and political theory. At the heart of Spengler's philosophy of history is the idea of *culture* as distinct from *civilization*. To Spengler, each culture is an organic being that experiences the same life processes as all other living beings—birth, maturity, senescence, and death. A culture's early phases—its "spring" and "summer"—involve the birth of religion and artistic flourishing. As economic, technological, military, and political concerns and prowess supplant philosophical and aesthetic endeavors, a culture can be said to have entered its "winter" or civilization phase.

Spengler's use of analogy is deliberate: he states forthrightly that "the means whereby to understand living forms is Analogy."[5] Spengler wishes to show that not only are entire cultures analogous to individuals, their experiences are analogous to one another's. The claim is thus not merely that all cultures are born, grow, and die just as all organisms must, but that all cultures are born, grow, and die according to particular and discernible patterns. For Spengler, this means that Western man ("Faustian" man) may learn from the example of other cultures. The culture most relatable to the Western mind, and the one from which Spengler draws most of his inferences, is the Classical ("Apollonian").

There are several distinct phases in the Classical experience, but nothing so striking as the period marking the decline of Greece and the ascendancy of Rome (though Rome, of course, would suffer a decline of its own). As Spengler puts it, "in a word, Greek *soul*—Roman *intellect*," Greece a culture, Rome a civilization.[6] Plato, in the *Republic*, characterizes Athenian democracy as colorful and vibrant.[7] And this is how Spengler and many other contemporary readers regard ancient Athens, the heart of the Hellenistic world—as a place in which artists and artisans bedazzled onlookers with their works and wares. Rome, by contrast, Spengler regards as "uninspired," "disciplined," and "practical."[8] Casting aside the tone of a detached and impartial observer, Spengler makes manifest to the reader that "I prefer one Roman aqueduct to all Roman temples and statues."[9] Its artistic achievements are merely derivative and its religious rites pale in comparison to earlier practices; Roman civilization reveals its privileging of function over form.

Athens, that "coat of many colours,"[10] certainly has its appeal. But a present-day Athens is no more than a daydream—neither its spiritual and artistic flourishing nor its democratic practices are to be expected. The West has experienced its spring, summer, and fall, which correspond roughly to the Medieval period, the Renaissance, and the Enlightenment. And although "we [Westerners] cannot help it if we are born as men of the early winter of full Civilization," the West's inhabitants must confront what Spengler considers to be a fact of the current age.[11] If the West is looking for a model, he insists, "the parallel is to be found not in Pericles's Athens but in Caesar's Rome."[12] Based on the experience of its Classical analogue, the West can expect from its future only a further diminution of creative activity and a marked increase in irreligion, already apparent in staid works and apish behavior at the dawn of the nineteenth century.

Moving from description to prescription, Spengler confesses his "hope that men of the new generation may be moved . . . to devote themselves to technics instead of lyrics, the sea instead of the paint-brush, and politics instead of epistemology."[13] Technics—scientific investigation not with the aim of pure knowledge, but in the assistance of some end. Naval exploration—not for the sake of discovery, but in pursuit of new lands to conquer and new resources to exploit. Politics—not the impassioned speeches of rhetors in democratic Athens, but the tactical maneuverings of strong leaders in imperial Rome. This is what Spengler wants and expects of the West in its final phase.

*Time* magazine declared in 1934 that "when Oswald Spengler speaks, many a Western Worldling stops to listen."[14] *The Decline of the West*, according to Georg Iggers, "became a Bible, and a source of inspiration for tens of thousands of educated middle-class Germans during a period of bewilderment."[15] But the work was also translated into French, Italian, and Spanish, and sales of its English edition in the United States reached between twenty and thirty thousand by 1940.[16] What piqued the interest of Spengler's contemporaries, and what makes his work provocative nearly a century later, is not his sometimes plodding discussion of bygone times; expositions on Diocletian, Heraclitus, and Trajan can hardly be considered morsels for public consumption. Rather, what won Spengler lasting fame are his prognostications for the future, which he often expressed aphoristically.

One of Spengler's more famous prophecies, expressed in a short 1921 essay meant to clarify *The Decline of the West*'s main themes, is that "we Germans will never again produce a Goethe, but indeed a Caesar."[17] In light of what transpired in Europe during the 1930s and 1940s, Spengler's claim, just years after Germany had suffered a tremendous military defeat in World War I, seems prescient. According to the *Time* article mentioned above, Adolf Hitler fit to a "T" Spengler's ideal of a leader. The philosopher, the article claims, held out "a small hope, no bigger than Hitler's hand, for the salvation of Western civilization."[18] Even in the thick of World War II, when the Führer had made his depraved ambitions apparent to all, the popular press was lumping Spengler with the Nazi leader. Writing for *Foreign Affairs*, Hans Weigert noted "the close relationship between Spenglerism and Hitlerism."[19]

Yet Spengler repeatedly snubbed Hitler, and he saw his last book—*The Hour of Decision*—proscribed by the Nazi regime. In a 1924 speech before a student group, he warned Germany's youth not to be seduced by marches and parades, since, after all, "trumpeters are hardly generals."[20] Eight years later, as Hitler was on the ascendant, he reiterated this stance, proclaiming Germany's need for "a hero" rather than "a heroic tenor."[21] When asked by Joseph Goebbels to pen an endorsement of Hitler's party ahead of the November 1933 parliamentary election, Spengler replied that "I have never taken part until now in electoral propaganda and I will also not do it in the future."[22] Nazi race theory—an integral part of the German fascists' platform—he dismissed in his private papers as a "danger" and "idiotic."[23] After the Nazis had come to power, he declined university positions that would force him to compromise his beliefs and toe the party line.[24] And when the regime claimed Friedrich Nietzsche as one of its own, he resigned from the Nietzsche Archive's board of directors.[25]

For his intransigence and many slights against the ruling party, Spengler won not only the censorship of his final book, but the enmity of top Nazi officials. The propagandist Johann von Leers warned the German public that Spengler betrayed an "ice-cold contempt for the people,"[26] and Alfred Rosenberg touted a "salvation from the abyss . . . in exactly the opposite direction than, for example, Spengler sees."[27] Hitler himself opposed Spengler for speaking the language not of resurrection, but decline.[28] By the mid-1930s, Spengler's position in German society was so precarious that his death in 1936 may have spared him from imprisonment or exile.[29]

The conflation of Spenglerism with Hitlerism is understandable, however, as even readers sympathetic to the former readily admit. Northrop Frye opines of *The Decline of the West*'s author that "he was often his own worst enemy, and a stupid and confused Spengler is continually getting in the way of the genuine prophet and visionary."[30] H. Stuart Hughes goes a step further, claiming that "Spengler had played with fire" and "had tossed off wild phrases about a 'hard' philosophy of life, about blood and destruction, that could not fail to be misunderstood."[31] In the same vein, John Farrenkopf writes that Spengler launched a "corrosive assault on the political legitimacy of the Weimar regime" and popularized a "politics of cultural despair" that "helped to generate an intellectual climate receptive to Nazism's ideology and radical goals and thereby inadvertently helped Hitler."[32]

Although Spengler explicitly rejected Hitler and the Nazis, his relationship to non-German variants of fascism was murkier. He praised "the traditions of an old monarchy, of an old aristocracy, of an old polite society."[33] In Germany, the monarchy had not survived World War I, and Hitler, given his lower-class background, hardly reflected the interests of "polite" society. In Italy, by contrast, Benito Mussolini, though also of a less than illustrious lineage, sought the backing of King Victor Immanuel III. To Spengler, Mussolini displayed leadership qualities that Hitler did not. "The born statesman is above all a valuer," Spengler writes, "a valuer of men, situations, and things."[34] The statesman can assess the global arena, recognizing potential adversaries and allies who might jeopardize or augment his chances for political (read military) success. At the same time, a true leader demonstrates a mastery of domestic policy. "The great statesman is the gardener of the people," Spengler declares, who cultivates the masses and turns them into something other than they were.[35] Hitler, Spengler judged, exhibited none of the qualities of a true leader. "Mussolini," however, he wrote in *The Hour of Decision*, "is first and foremost a statesman, ice-cold and skeptical, realist, diplomat."[36]

Spengler's praise for Mussolini is difficult to overlook, though Farrenkopf obfuscates the matter by claiming that Mussolini "was admired by many foreigners in the twenties"[37] and that esteem for him was particularly "widespread among right-wing intellectuals in Germany."[38] What Spengler supported, Farrenkopf writes, was not fascism, but the creation of a more benign-sounding "Prussian, conservative, semi-authoritarian polity capable of executing a very successful foreign policy."[39] Hughes concurs about the conservative character of Spengler's political theory, writing that Spengler sought "the preservation of Germany's traditional ruling classes." But he is more direct than Farrenkopf regarding what a "successful foreign policy" would entail: victory would mean nothing less than "the attainment of world hegemony through war."[40]

In many ways, Spengler resembles his predecessors Schopenhauer, Burckhardt, and Nietzsche. "Optimism is cowardice," he thunders in *Man and Technics*.[41] History for him is "a drama noble in its aimlessness, noble and aimless as the course of the stars, the rotation of the earth, and alternance of land and sea, of ice and virgin forest upon its face."[42] And the business of written histories, particularly those focused on politics, "is not to show how 'humanity' advances to the conquest of its eternal rights, to freedom and equality, to the evolving of a super-wise and super-just State, but to describe the political units that really exist in the fact-world, how they grow and flourish and fade."[43] Pessimism, the plain rejection of an ideal polity, and conservatism are all aspects of his thought that Spengler shared with his above-named precursors.

Yet Spengler's departure from Schopenhauer, Burckhardt, and Nietzsche is as important as his debts to them. Spengler agreed with his predecessors that art and culture were in decline. But unlike any of these other authors, he simply renounced aesthetics in favor of more practical endeavors.[44] His turning his back on the arts in favor of politics would have been sufficient to earn him the evil eye from his forerunners. His turn to nationalism would have won their outright scorn. Spengler writes in the first volume of *The Decline of the West* that his approach "admits no sort of privileged position to the Classical or the Western Culture as against the Cultures of India, Babylon, China, Egypt, the Arabs, Mexico."[45] But he certainly seems to admit a "privileged position" *within* Western culture. He writes in the second volume of *Decline* that "the way from Alexander to Caesar is unambiguous and unavoidable, and the strongest nation of any and every Culture, consciously or unconsciously, willing or unwilling, has had to tread it."[46] In his later works, Spengler made clear his hope that Germany would be the nation to lead the West into its twilight (or even forestall it).

Spengler's short-term hopes[47] for Germany are most readily apparent in *Prussianism and Socialism*, which appeared between the publication of the first and second volumes of *Decline*. Here Spengler predicts a struggle in the West over two competing ideologies, British liberalism and Prussian socialism. "Up to now," he writes, Western civilization "has been largely British civilization."[48] But the dominance of British ideas and practices is lamentable: "England has succeeded in poisoning all countries to which it has offered the 'medicine' of its own form of government."[49] In England, the "every man for himself" ethos rules the day.[50] Liberalism means selfishness, competition, and the individual's pursuit of wealth for wealth's sake.[51] Germany offers an alternative: "every man for every other man."[52] Socialism means "suprapersonal community spirit,"[53] cooperation and the pursuit of a shared goal,[54] and the state's administering of goods for the well-being of the totality.[55] Either the British or the Prussian way will win out,[56] but these two modes of life cannot coexist: "neither can accept a restriction of its will, and neither can be satisfied until the whole of the world has succumbed to its particular idea. This being the case, war will be waged until one side gains final victory."[57]

The war of which Spengler spoke was not metaphorical, something to be contested in the realm of thought. He writes that "the Viking spirit [British] and the spirit of the knights [Prussian] will fight it out to the finish, even though the world may emerge weary and broken from the bloodbath of this century." "Ideas," he adds, "when they press for decisions, assume the form of political units: countries, peoples or parties. They must be fought over not with words but with weapons." England, the embodiment of the liberal idea, must compete with Germany, the representation of the socialist impulse, in much the same way that Athens and Sparta symbolized the classical conflict between democracy and oligarchy.[58] And, just as Sparta bested Athens and gained control of the Peloponnesus, Germany will win supremacy in the modern West.[59] The West itself may be in decline, but Germany is on the ascendant within that dying civilization: "the year 1919 is the nadir of German dignity," which leaves nowhere for the Germans to go but up.

Spengler declared forthrightly that "Weimar is doomed," and he insisted that it was only a matter of time before Germany's post–World War I government was replaced by a regime more suited to the German national character.[60] "Parliamentarism as a political scheme is worn out," he writes, and it already showed signs of decrepitude in foreign places before a few ill-advised Germans imported the system for their countrymen. The parliamentarism of old could persist under the aegis of the British aristocracy. But "the new parliamentarism will present the struggle for existence with barely civilized manners and with much poorer success. The relationship between party leaders and party, between party and masses, will be tougher, more transparent, and more brazen." This further breakdown of parliamentarism, he declares, "is the beginning of Caesarism."[61] Should the British maintain their privileged position in the hierarchy of Western states, then Caesarism will entail the rule of billionaires, as an already limping parliamentary democracy is finally put to death by plutocrats. But if the Germans should come out on top, then the global empire will be led by able generals, administrators, and civil servants.[62] Spengler presents these two alternatives not so as to offer his readers a choice—"in politics as in other ways, there is no choice"[63]—but so as "realistically" to assess the current political climate and to draw implications for the future.

What Theodor Adorno writes of Spengler is apt: he "seemed to have inherited all the historical force" of German ideas.[64] Spengler effectively synthesized two strands of thought, uniting the pessimism of Schopenhauer and his heirs with the nationalism and statism of Fichte and Hegel. In no uncertain terms, Spengler rejected the idea of progress. Even so, history was in his eyes dynamic: multinational cultures grew and decayed according to a pattern of identifiable stages. Such a philosophy of history allowed Spengler to do something his gloomier predecessors could not: imagine a proud role for Germany in the future of the West.[65] In the end, Spengler's philosophy was less a philosophy of pessimism, but what he was "proud to call," in the preface to the revised edition of The Decline of the West, "a German philosophy."[66]

*   *   *

Spengler found Russia comparatively more difficult to assess than the West; it was, he claimed, an example of "pseudomorphosis," a young culture that cannot grow while in the shadow of some older culture. Echoing the Slavophiles of old, Spengler said that Russia had gone off track with Peter the Great's reforms; Russia was emphatically not the West, and Peter did not represent the Russian people.[67] Peter's Westernization campaign ultimately

culminated in the October Revolution, but Lenin and his cadre spoke for the masses no more than Peter had. "The real Russian is a disciple of Dostoyevski," Spengler claimed. Fortunately for those "real" Russians, the two-hundred-year period from Peter to Lenin was an aberration. Spengler predicted for Russia that "to Dostoyevski's Christianity the next thousand years will belong."[68]

Born the year that Volume 1 of *The Decline of the West* appeared, Aleksandr Solzhenitsyn (1918–2008) would have welcomed the coming to pass of Spengler's prophecy for Russia. In a 1983 address, the Soviet dissident writer himself insisted that "no matter how formidably Communism bristles with tanks and rockets, no matter what successes it attains in seizing the planet, it is doomed never to vanquish Christianity."[69] As for the form this Christianity should take in his native land, Solzhenitsyn had three years earlier confessed in an interview that "the spiritual values of Dostoyevsky are closer to me than Tolstoy's."[70]

If Spengler and Solzhenitsyn shared certain visions of Russia's future, they likewise held in common a particular view of the West. The West, Spengler declared, had entered a time of irreligion; in a culture-turned-civilization, spirituality played less of a role than did politics, economics, and technology. Solzhenitsyn shared this diagnosis of the West. But what was for Spengler a matter-of-fact observation was for Solzhenitsyn a cause for alarm. And whereas Spengler sat comfortably within the walls of his German study to make comparisons of a fledgling Russia and a dying West, the exiled Solzhenitsyn had firsthand experience of both worlds. A Tocqueville for the twentieth century, Solzhenitsyn used a long sojourn in the United States (1976–1994) to draw lessons for his homeland. His most famous commentary on the West vis-à-vis Russia is his 1978 commencement address at Harvard, "A World Split Apart."

The Harvard address, although not of the same magnitude as Spengler's two-volume tome, is illustrative of the themes that Solzhenitsyn took up in his nonfiction work. Moreover, it generated the same volume of discussion that *The Decline of the West* had done a half-century earlier. As an implacable critic of communism, Solzhenitsyn knew all too well the defects of the Soviet system. When authorities intercepted a letter of his that mocked Stalin's leadership, they arrested him and sent him to the infamous gulag-run labor camps. Rehabilitated during the Khrushchev era, he won recognition in both the West and Russia for his realistic depiction of camp life in *One Day in the Life of Ivan Denisovich*, which censors allowed to be published in

1962. But Communist Party leaders could tolerate only so much: they pro-hibited publication of *The Gulag Archipelago*, which was printed in the West in 1973, and they exiled Solzhenitsyn to the Federal Republic of Germany in 1974. Westerners welcomed the arrival of the brave dissident, whose moral authority and condemnations of totalitarianism helped win him the Nobel Prize for literature in 1970. What many anticipated, however, differed from what they got: the fierce detractor of the Soviet Union was also a harsh critic of the West. In his address to Harvard's graduates, Solzhenitsyn admitted that "should I be asked . . . whether I would propose the West, such as it is today, as a model to my country, I would frankly have to answer negatively. No, I could not recommend your society as an ideal for the transformation of ours."[71]

Solzhenitsyn found many deficiencies with the Western way of life, but none troubled him as much as the debasement of religion. In Central and Eastern Europe, ordinary individuals could not breathe the vital spiritual air with the boots of the militantly atheistic apparatchiks on their necks. In the West, the masses have the freedom to worship, but people are intoxicated by crass consumerism that leads them astray.[72] Westerners are blind to a fact that members of other cultures recognize: "the human soul longs for things higher, warmer, and purer than those offered by today's mass living habits, introduced as by a calling card by the revolting invasion of commercial advertising, by TV stupor, and by intolerable music."[73] The problem, as Solzhenitsyn saw it, was less that Westerners had abandoned religious *rites*, and more that they had ceased to embrace traditional *values*. There are few exemplars of courage, self-restraint, generosity, and other virtues in the West, and many instances of cowardice, licentiousness, and avarice.[74] Ask-ing rhetorically how the West reached "its present debility," Solzhenitsyn argues that the main currents of thought since the Renaissance have been anthropocentric and have left God out of the picture; vice and irreverence for the Almighty go hand-in-hand.[75]

Solzhenitsyn continued his critique of modernity when he accepted the Templeton Prize in 1983. To his audience in London, he declared that "the combined vision of all the thinkers of the Enlightenment amounts to noth-ing."[76] He took particular issue with the Enlightenment idea of progress, de-claring in a later address: "we all have lived through the twentieth century, a century of terror, the chilling culmination of that Progress about which so many dreamed in the eighteenth century."[77] Turgot and then other thinkers contended that economic advancement would lead to improvements in other spheres and to the general melioration of the human condition. In truth, while "progress is indeed marching on . . . it is doing so only in the field of technological civilization (with especial success in creature comforts and military innovations)"[78]—neither morality, nor culture, nor the arts have kept pace.[79] The relentless pursuit of novelty and of material well-being has drawn mankind's attention away from higher pursuits.[80]

The West was not alone in its belief in progress; Solzhenitsyn suggested that Russian Marxism had its roots in the same Enlightenment tradition.[81] And years before he issued his "warning to the West," Solzhenitsyn had cautioned his countrymen about their pursuit of progress, asking them to mind the ecological costs of technical-industrial advancement. In his 1973 "Letter to the Soviet Leaders," he maintained that "the earth is a finite object" and "its expanses and resources are finite also." The "infinite progress dinned into our heads by the dreamers of the Enlightenment cannot be accomplished on" a finite earth, just as "a dozen worms can't go on and on gnawing the same apple forever." The idea of perpetual progress is a "nonsensical myth" that lured humanity into a dark alley.[82] "Unless mankind renounces the notion of economic progress," unless industrial societies reverse course, "the biosphere will become unfit for life even during our lifetime."[83]

The Soviet Union did not abandon its pursuit of technological innovation and improved industry; Solzhenitsyn was a modern-day Cassandra, a prophet whose warnings no one believed.[84] And in the West, that part of the world to which Solzhenitsyn had made unflattering comparisons with his homeland—the USSR's modeling itself on Western societies, he said, would mean "improvement in certain aspects, but also a change for the worse on some particularly significant points"[85]—the response was largely the same. Some commentators reacted to Solzhenitsyn's Harvard address with smug self-congratulation. Writing in the New York Times, James Reston claimed that the ideas expressed in "A World Split Apart" were no more than "the wanderings of a mind split apart," and that, although Solzhenitsyn may not have appreciated it, "at least he was allowed to say all these things," to make his criticisms of the West.[86] Along the same lines, the Washington Post editorial board accused Solzhenitsyn of having used "the tolerance and diversity that are the splendors of the West to attack tolerance and diversity."[87] Other writers offered not a kneejerk defense of Western values, but the argument that a non-Westerner really had no business critiquing the West in the first place and thus could be safely ignored. In a Washington Star column, for instance, Mary McGrory mused that "maybe we would be better off if we stopped grappling with the politics and even the morality of what Solzhenitsyn said at Harvard and look at it in a different way—as the personal statement of a conservative, religious, and terribly home-sick Russian."[88]

To be fair, not everyone dismissed Solzhenitsyn's ideas out of hand. A member of Harvard's graduating class of 1978, Charles Kessler, argued that Solzhenitsyn's critics "miss his whole point,"[89] reminded those critics that Solzhenitsyn had plainly said in his speech that he spoke as a friend, and characterized the address as "part warning, part prophecy, but also part en-couragement" to do better.[90] Columnist George Will argued that Solzhenit-syn was a proud member of an illustrious intellectual tradition that included Cicero, Augustine, and Edmund Burke, that he shared misgivings about the United States with such respected figures as Tocqueville and Henry Adams, and that his views were "not exclusively Russian."[91] On this last point, Will was rebuffed by other writers who, even if not entirely sympathetic toward Solzhenitsyn, at least tried to make sense of him. Arthur Schlesinger, Jr., maintained of Solzhenitsyn that he was "a fervent Russian nationalist"[92] whose "ideal is a Christian authoritarianism governed by God-fearing despots without benefit of politics, parties, undue intellectual freedom or undue concern for popular happiness."[93] Or, in the words of Jack Fruchtman, Jr., "Solzhenitsyn sounds very much like a 19th-Century Slavophile."[94]

Solzhenitsyn's relationship with his literary forebears is complicated, and to label him a twentieth-century Slavophile, still less a pan-Slav, is to over-simplify if not grossly distort his views. To his critics, Solzhenitsyn was an advocate for "Orthodoxy, Autocracy, and Nationality" born a century too late. In fact, he endorsed no part of the tripartite slogan the Russian tsars used to rally loyalists in the 1800s. True, he had a deep personal attachment to the Orthodox Church. And he did claim that Dostoevsky's spiritual values were close to his. However, Solzhenitsyn shared few of the Slavo-philes' misgivings about the Christian denominations that took root in the West, and still less did he reveal the outright hostility to Catholicism that Dostoevsky had. As Daniel Mahoney writes, "Solzhenitsyn had a remark-ably ecumenical understanding of religious truth" and recognized the validity of ideas preached outside Orthodoxy.[95] Solzhenitsyn himself recounted to his biographer, Joseph Pearce, the excitement with which he anticipated a 1993 meeting with Pope John Paul II in Rome, an encounter that left the Russian writer convinced the Polish pontiff was "very bright, full of light."[96]

With respect to the suggestion that autocracy represented for Solzhenitsyn an ideal form of government, the reality again differs from the charge. In truth, Solzhenitsyn denied that an ideal form of political organization existed. Citing Spengler, he argued that "the very concept of the state is differently understood in different cultures," adding that "there is no definitive 'best' form of government which needs to be borrowed from one great culture for use in another."[97] Moreover, as James Pontuso observes, while Solzhenitsyn appreciated the stability tsarism had provided Russia for centuries, he also recognized that autocratic systems have their drawbacks. With authoritarian regimes there exist, in Solzhenitsyn's words, "the danger of dishonest authorities, upheld by violence, the danger of arbitrary decisions and the difficulty of correcting them, the danger of sliding into tyranny."[98] Such dangers existed to a much lesser extent in the West, with "its historically unique stability of civic life under the rule of law—a hard-won stability which grants independence and space to every private citizen."[99] Far from something to be rejected wholesale, the Western model had much to offer the post-communist world. On the eve of the Soviet Union's dissolution, Solzhenitsyn told his countrymen that his "critical comments about contemporary democracy . . . are not meant to suggest that the future Russian Union will have no need for democracy. *It will need it very much.*" But democracy was something to be introduced gradually, from the bottom to the top, rather than to be imposed from the top down.[100] Russian leaders from Peter I to Lenin had already shocked Russia by forcing Western ideas on it; to let a new strongman do the same would be folly.

Nor did Solzhenitsyn, for all his alleged national chauvinism,[101] wish for Russia to force Russian ideas and institutions on other groups. He says forthrightly to his co-nationals that "*we don't have the strength* for sustaining an empire," and he adds that "it is just as well."[102] To Solzhenitsyn, real patriotism is not a matter of supporting political expansionism or clamoring for an increased role for one's country in world affairs. Nor does real patriotism demand an uncritical allegiance to one's homeland without consideration of whether it is right or wrong. Instead, true patriots offer both an "unwavering love for the nation" *and* a "frank assessment of its vices and sins."[103] In his accounting, Solzhenitsyn ranks among his nation's gravest sins its treatment of other nations that were part of the Soviet Union, including groups that had their own titular republics and indigenous peoples in Russia proper. And he called on Russians to atone for their transgressions not only by recognizing the rights of linguistic minorities but, in the case of the most endangered communities, by "offering our help in restoring them to life and vigor."[104] Even in the case of Ukraine and Belarus, which he considered to be connected with Russia as part of the same organism, Solzhenitsyn argued for linguistic and cultural rights and supported political self-determination.[105]

If scholars tend to exaggerate Solzhenitsyn's affinities with the Slavophiles and pan-Slavs of the nineteenth century, they likewise distort the relationship between Solzhenitsyn and Tolstoy. Edward Ericson and Alexis Klimoff write that Solzhenitsyn's *The Red Wheel* "can be understood as, in large part, a running argument against Tolstoy's philosophy of history."[106] Citing the same work, Andrew Wachtel concurs that "Solzhenitsyn radically disagrees with Tolstoy's concept of history."[107] But a more accurate statement would be that Solzhenitsyn disagrees with *part* of Tolstoy's philosophy of history. Where Tolstoy had argued that impersonal forces drive human history, Solzhenitsyn suggests instead that individual people can and do shape events. Rejecting the fatalism of his predecessor, Solzhenitsyn writes that "we might look for consolation to Tolstoy's belief that armies are not led by generals, ships are not steered by captains, states and parties are not run by presidents and politicians—but the twentieth century has shown us only too often that they are."[108] The catastrophes of the twentieth century were not predetermined; they occurred as a result of choices made by particular individuals, and they could have been averted.

Granted, Solzhenitsyn departs from Tolstoy with respect to the matter of fate versus free will in history. But neither his nor Tolstoy's philosophy of history touches solely on the question of individual agency in world-historical events. A critical component of both authors' views is their rejection of the Western pursuit of material progress and their dismissal of the idea of historical progress more generally. Tolstoy scoffs at the notion that "progress is a law discovered only by the European nations, but one that is so good that the whole of humanity ought to be subjected to it."[109] Solzhenitsyn, too, mocks the "naïve fable of the happy arrival at the 'end of history,'"[110] countering that "the Western way of life is less and less likely to become the leading model" for the rest of the world.[111] But, whereas Tolstoy and Solzhenitsyn challenge the dominant belief in historical advancement, they both believe in the possibility of individual self-improvement. Tolstoy writes that "the law of progress, or perfectibility, is written in the soul of each man, and is transferred to history only through error. As long as it remains personal, this law is fruitful."[112] Solzhenitsyn echoes this sentiment, claiming that "there can be only one true Progress: the sum total of the spiritual pro-gresses of individuals; the degree of self-perfection in the course of their lives."[113]

Solzhenitsyn's belief in personal redemption and skepticism of the possibility of universal progress led him to reach a conclusion similar to Tolstoy's regarding the importance of politics. Tolstoy writes of "the useless-ness, superfluity, and harmfulness of all governments."[114] Solzhenitsyn does not endorse the anarchist extreme; indeed, he claims that "anarchy is the ultimate peril," citing the October Revolution as a tragic example of what happens when there is a power vacuum.[115] As noted above, he appreciates the stability and peace that come with the rule of law. Nevertheless, he avers that "we have placed too much hope in politics and social reforms."[116] Like Tolstoy, he urges each individual to tend to her or his spiritual life, a matter that is separate from, but not independent of political engagement. Solzhenitsyn argues that there is an inverse relationship for political partici-pation and spiritual development: "the more energetic the political activity in a country, the greater is the loss to spiritual life."[117] As Pontuso puts it, "Solzhenitsyn wishes to diminish what people expect of politics, while raising their expectations of themselves."[118]

* * *

Ericson and Mahoney write of Solzhenitsyn that "the final note in his work is . . . one of hope."[119] Such a proclamation might seem indefensible, in light of Solzhenitsyn's well-documented and, in the eyes of many, exaggerated forebodings about a future global catastrophe. But "hope" is indeed a ban-ner under which Solzhenitsyn marched. This is evident even from the speech that caused such a backlash in the United States and cemented his reputa-tion as a crank, his commencement address at Harvard. Solzhenitsyn, after having identified serious problems with Western society and his own, con-cludes his address by insisting that "no one on earth has any other way left but—upward."[120] He may have meant this as an injunction to look upward toward God. If so, he clarifies that trusting in the Almighty does not pre-clude people from taking the future into their own hands. Each individual is responsible for his or her own fate: "man's hope, salvation and punishment lie in this, that we are capable of change, and that we ourselves, not our birth or environment, are responsible for our souls!"[121] The futures of entire com-munities and the world at large are likewise matters not left to chance;

whether the future holds something good or evil in store depends on the choices people make. And Solzhenitsyn expresses a cautious confidence that humanity is capable of leaning from history: "surely, we have not experienced the trials of the twentieth century in vain. Let us hope."[122] What Solzhenitsyn offers his readers, then, is a frank denial of the idea of progress but also an imperative to hope for a better future.

Solzhenitsyn was not alone in occupying this precarious position between hope and expectation. Christopher Lasch (1932–1994), an American historian and cultural critic and a contemporary of Solzhenitsyn's, made pains to distinguish between hope on the one hand and optimism on the other. In *The True and Only Heaven*, the last of his books published while he was alive, Lasch offers a defense of hope and a critique of the optimistic belief in progress. Reflecting on the traumas of the twentieth century, he writes that "the same developments that make it impossible for those who believe in progress to speak with confidence and moral authority compel us to give a more attentive hearing to those who rejected it all along."[123] But, while siding with critics of the idea of progress, Lasch adds that "we need to recover a more vigorous form of hope."[124] The difference between optimists and the merely hopeful is that the former believe that a brighter future is inevitable, while the latter desire such a future while still recognizing that better days ahead are not guaranteed. Optimists are fatalists, but Lasch's heroes, like Solzhenitsyn's, know that the future is what people make of it.[125]

Lasch finds common cause with Solzhenitsyn, too, by arguing that progress-mongers have sold a faulty definition of their ware: what typically passes for "progress" should not be considered such. Tracing the idea of progress back to the Scottish Enlightenment, he argues that figures like Adam Smith did more to elucidate this idea than did "second-rate thinkers" like Condorcet.[126] Smith and others offered a wholly new philosophy of history, not merely an updated and secularized version of Christian millenarianism.[127] The "original appeal" of this philosophy, Lasch claims, rested in its thesis that "insatiable appetites, formerly condemned as a source of social instability and personal unhappiness, could drive the economic machine—just as man's insatiable curiosity drove the scientific project—and thus ensure a never-ending expansion of productive forces." Thus, the critical part of Smith's philosophy of the future is not some abstract new conception of time, but the more specific contention that pursuing one's desires leads to personal and social improvement.[128] Not only Smith and his devotees, but also large swaths of Lasch's contemporaries on all sides of the political spectrum, shared in the "noble dream of progress," that is, the dream of "luxury for all" brought about by the pursuit of wants.[129] The visionaries of progress, however, will one day wake up to reality, as all dreamers must. The eye-opening moment will be "the belated discovery that the earth's ecology will no longer sustain an indefinite expansion of productive forces." This discovery, Lasch claims, "deals the final blow to the belief in progress."[130]

According to Lasch, the idea of progress could survive the traumas of the twentieth century only in a stripped-down form that linked desire with development. This vision of progress proffered by political economists always had more cachet than the "vague utopianism of the French Enlightenment."[131] From its origins to the present day, Lasch claims, "the idea of progress never rested mainly on the promise of an ideal society."[132] Alternative visions of progress existed, to be sure. But the "more extravagant versions of the progressive faith, premised on the perfectibility of human nature—on the unrealized power of reason or love—collapsed a long time ago."[133] Two World Wars, Nazi genocide, and Soviet totalitarianism were sufficient to shake the flimsy foundations on which more ambitious schemes for social improvement were built.

Lasch bid good riddance to the visions of progress that petered out. But he wished to drive a stake through the one version—progress as material advancement—that refused to die. "The modern conception of progress," he writes, "depends on a positive assessment of the proliferation of wants."[134] Related to this is the notion that men and women should face no restraints in pursuit of their desires.[135] But Smith's "moral rehabilitation of desire,"[136] whatever its worth as a theory, bore bitter fruit in reality. Unchecked desire is voraciousness, and unchecked liberty is licentiousness. And, contrary to Smith's expectations, the extreme has become the rule rather than the exception. Sounding like Cotton Mather before a flock of wayward Salemites, Lasch writes:

> To see the modern world from the point of view of a parent is to see
> it in the worst possible light. This perspective unmistakably reveals
> the unwholesomeness, not to put it more strongly, of our way of
> life: our obsession with sex, violence, and the pornography of
> "making it"; our addictive dependence on drugs, "entertainment,"
> and the evening news; our impatience with anything that limits
> our sovereign freedom of choice, especially with the constraints
> of marital and familial ties; our preference for "nonbinding

commitments"; our third-rate educational system; our third-rate
morality; our refusal to draw a distinction between right and
wrong, lest we "impose" our morality on others and thus invite
others to "impose" their morality on us; our reluctance to judge or
be judged; our indifference to the needs of future generations, as
evidenced by our willingness to saddle them with a huge national
debt, an overgrown arsenal of destruction, and a deteriorating
environment; our inhospitable attitude to the newcomers born in
our midst; our unstated assumption, which underlies so much of
the propaganda for unlimited abortion, that only those children
born for success ought to be allowed to be born at all.[137]

The positive connotation of desire, novel in the eighteenth century, led to the
excesses of the proceeding centuries. The pursuit of material progress led not
to the improvement of the Western world, but to its debasement.

Lamentation about Western decadence was a common characteristic of
Lasch's works. More than a decade prior to the publication of *The True and
Only Heaven* came *The Culture of Narcissism*, a book that introduced many
of the ideas for which Lasch gained notoriety as a critic. In that 1978 book,
Lasch bemoans the "atmosphere of violence, danger, drugs, sexual promiscu-
ity, moral and psychic chaos" pervading the contemporary United States.[138]
But *The True and Only Heaven* is not simply a retread of Lasch's earlier work.
He opens *The True and Only Heaven* by asking "how does it happen that serious people continue to believe in progress, in the face of massive evidence that
might have been expected to refute the idea of progress once and for all?"[139]
Contrarily, *The Culture of Narcissism* begins with the observation that "the
question of whether the world will end in fire or in ice, with a bang or a whim-
per, no longer interests artists alone. Impending disaster has become an everyday concern."[140] Lasch's reading of the pulse of American society changed
during the 1980s, which surely led him to change the emphasis of his argument. A decade of social and political transformation, however, did not force
him to abandon his core ideas. *The True and Only Heaven* provided a ballast to
unbridled optimism, while *The Culture of Narcissism* provided a corrective
to unbridled pessimism. Running through both works is the contention that
Americans are unwilling or unprepared to deal with the future.[141]

His untimid reflections on American society won Lasch a meeting with
a sitting president of the United States. In his able biography of Lasch, Eric

Miller carefully reconstructs the circumstances of this meeting. *The Culture of Narcissism* had deemed the 1970s "an age of diminishing expectations," a characterization that rang true to President Jimmy Carter, who claimed to have speed-read the book. In May 1979, Carter adviser Jody Powell invited Lasch to dinner at the White House; the select few other notables present included Harvard sociologist Daniel Bell, civil rights activist Jesse Jackson, and journalists Haynes Johnson and Bill Moyers. The invitees had been brought to discuss the "malaise," as Lasch termed it, then afflicting the United States. Bell would recall that Lasch was reticent throughout the evening, a fact confirmed by Lasch himself. But Lasch attempted to continue the discussion after the night had ended, writing a letter to members of Carter's inner circle in which he clarified his diagnosis of society's ills and his proposed remedy.[142]

Further correspondence between Lasch and the Carter team continued after July 15, the night the president delivered his televised "Crisis of Confidence" speech before the American public. Writing to a friend weeks after the address, Lasch acknowledged that, although he "recognized certain phrases" of his in President Carter's speech, he felt his ideas had been rudely "torn out of context."[143] The echoes of Lasch in Carter's speech are clear enough. Carter's remark that "too many of us now tend to worship self-indulgence and consumption" could easily pass as a Laschism, as could the accompanying statement that "human identity is no longer defined by what one does, but by what one owns."[144] The problem with the president's address, Lasch complained to Carter pollster Pat Caddell, is that it painted all Americans with the same broad brush; where Carter had castigated the entire country, Lasch had meant only to draw negative attention to the country's elites and managerial class.[145]

Ronald Beiner writes that the impact of Lasch's ideas on President Carter "vastly exceeds the sort of influence that the average theorist or intellectual can hope to exert." At the same time, Beiner concedes, the fallout from Carter's address was not what Lasch—or, presumably, Carter—had wanted.[146] In his address, Carter told the American public that "we are at a turning point in our history."[147] The public agreed, and what Lasch would later quip about American historians turned out to be true of American voters—for them, "history has to have a happy ending."[148] American voters by and large agreed with Lasch's assessment of Carter's speech, finding the president too dour and scolding. They turned to Ronald Reagan, a man who promised them their happy ending, who told them it was morning in America. But Lasch himself was not impressed with the former California governor: uncertain whether to support Carter or a third-party candidate more to his style, Lasch opted for the former, writing to his parents that he "couldn't live with the thought of helping to elect Reagan" in a close election.[149]

Lasch writes that "resistance to the ideology of progress . . . did not always take a conservative direction."[150] And if not all critics of the idea of progress were conservative, nor were all self-declared conservatives critics of the idea of progress. Reagan gave lip service to cultural conservatism, addressing Lasch's concerns about abortion and family structure. But he was an outspoken advocate for the progress of capitalism, the very system responsible for so much of the upheaval in society. In *The True and Only Heaven*, Lasch attempted to provide an alternative to both Reaganism and what he called "liberal paternalism." His search for such a solution involved looking to the past. What he found worthwhile in the history of American ideas, and what he defended to his audience, was populism. Populism, to Lasch, meant localism, as opposed to centralization. And populists preached the two things Lasch claimed were the core of his argument: hope and a "sense of limits."[151]

The historical figures whom Lasch held in high regard were not his brother historians. He had nothing to say about the founding giant of American historiography, George Bancroft. Nor did he remark even in passing on social Darwinist John Fiske. Other optimistic historians—Herbert Baxter Adams, John Lothrop Motley, and Frederick Jackson Turner—were likewise pushed aside. Henry and Brooks Adams, who shared both Lasch's pessimism and his concerns about capitalism, received the briefest of mentions, rather than the sustained treatment their ideas would seem to merit.[152] Instead, Lasch held in high esteem Orestes Brownson, an impossible-to-pin-down oddball in the American intellectual tradition. But the appeal of Brownson to Lasch is not difficult to comprehend. Lasch describes the winding road Brownson traveled as he searched for answers to life's thorniest questions: "An Owenite socialist in his twenties, he later embraced the cause of working-class radicalism, briefly called himself a Jacksonian Democrat, soured on democracy after the log-cabin, hard-cider campaign of 1840, allied himself for a time with John C. Calhoun, and finally settled down as a Catholic conservative in the last twenty-five years of his life." Although the parallel is inexact, Lasch traversed a path similar to Brownson's. As Miller writes of

Lasch, "as he moved, he moved in the spirit of reckoning, freely casting judgment on all—left, right, and everyone in between."[153]

*   *   *

Nineteenth-century critics of the idea of progress berated various aspects of their own day and age—bellicose nationalism, statism, ochlocracy, capitalist corruption, and spiritual mediocrity. The twentieth century would have horrified these critics (as it did many of those who lived through the worst of the century). The nationalism of the nineteenth century was mild by comparison with that of the twentieth. The authoritarian regimes of the nineteenth century appear free when contrasted with the totalitarian regimes of the century following. Capitalism in the twentieth century, though shorn of many of its early defects (for example, child labor and poor work conditions), fostered a consumerist culture and corporate greed. Many critics of the idea of progress in the nineteenth century perceptively realized where their societies were headed, when the majority of their compatriots had failed to read the trend lines. These critics of the idea of progress, despite their prescience, were ultimately unable to alter the course of history.

And what of critics of the idea of progress in the twentieth century? We see in the case of Spengler how a pessimistic philosophy helped rationalize fascism, one of the most destructive ideologies of all time. Spengler, while rejecting *universal* progress, while positing *Western* decline, concocted a narrative of *national* greatness-through-politics. But in the cases of Solzhenitsyn and Lasch, we see two individuals doing what several earlier critics of the idea of progress had done before, arguing against totalizing political endeavors. Both Solzhenitsyn and Lasch looked to nonpolitical solutions to life's problems; when they did turn to politics, neither defended either of the dominant systems of their day (Soviet-style communism or American-style democratic capitalism) as the triumph of history or models for perpetuity.

In 1991 Christopher Lasch published *The True and Only Heaven*, his plea for readers and the Washington, DC, elite to dispense with the idea of limitless progress. Lasch had just suffered through Ronald Reagan's second presidential term, and he had had enough with optimism. It was precisely that optimism, however, that would earn Reagan the admiration of one of his successors, Barack Obama. One might be tempted to attribute the unrelenting faith in the future shared by the Illinois native Reagan and the Chicago transplant Obama to something in the Prairie State ground. But if there is something in the Illinois soil, then that something has spread to the other forty-nine United States, for Reagan and Obama are hardly alone in their outlooks. Reagan could earn a second term by promising that it was "morning in America," because members of the electorate were susceptible to the idea that their country's best days lay ahead and would only get brighter. Obama could secure another four years for himself by pledging to take the United States "forward," because that is where the American people wanted to be. What Louis Hartz controversially said of liberalism could incontrovertibly be said of optimism: there is no alternative tradition in America.[1]

There are signs, however, that optimism has its limits, even in the United States. By the end of his first term, the president who campaigned on a message of "hope" and "change" found himself on the defensive, declaring before a skeptical audience in his 2012 State of the Union address that "anyone who tells you that America is in decline or that our influence has waned, doesn't know what they're talking about."[2] In spite of President Obama's proclamations that the country remains as vibrant as ever, the American public was and remains uncertain. Citizens have voiced their unease in a number of ways, most obviously through polling. The Gallup Organization's "right track, wrong track" question revealed that a mere 18 percent of the public was satisfied with the state of the union at the time the president delivered his address.[3] The following year, Gallup found that Americans' satisfaction with their government had reached its lowest point in the poll's history.[4] Faith in American political institutions is at a nadir, with trust in both the Supreme Court and Congress lower than ever.[5] On top of this, Pew found in 2013 that, for the first time in forty years of polling, a majority (53 percent) of Americans believed their country's influence in world affairs was waning.[6] The general mood of discontent is captured in a September 2015 Bloomberg poll, which finds that "72 percent of Americans think their country isn't as great as it once was."[7]

For a country founded at the height of the Enlightenment and imbued with a faith in progress, this is a striking state of affairs. All governments have their critics and see their policies questioned by the public. What American citizens have not typically questioned, however, are their country's greatness and its prospects for continued flourishing. A few years' worth of public opinion is insufficient to portend a long-term trend, and ordinary Americans' vocalization of discontent with the present is not an indication of their having abandoned prospects for a better future. Nevertheless, given the recent uptick of pessimistic or even declinist rhetoric in public discourse, we have reason to ask what we can learn from critics of the idea of progress.

Figures like Henry and Brooks Adams, deeply skeptical of visions of future bliss, are rare in the history of American ideas; indeed, they are minorities in the history of thought more generally, which, at least in the modern age, has witnessed the dominance of progressive visions of history. But the Adams brothers and their intellectual kin, while assuredly iconoclasts, are not so far removed from their more optimistic adversaries that they cannot communicate with them. This book has shown the ways in which critics of the idea of progress respond to theories contrary to their own.

In the preceding chapters, I put critics of the idea of progress into conversation with other thinkers from the same national tradition.[8] One of my aims was to determine whether political and national context shapes critics' proposals for action or whether these critics advocate stances that can be adopted irrespective of time or place. My findings reveal a split among these thinkers that is based not on nationality, but on whether the authors in question view history as a bumpy but straight road to nowhere (or worse, to hell), or whether they discern in the passing of time a pattern of recurring hills and dales. Writers of the first sort tend to be critics of politics, while cyclical theorists are receptive to grand political projects, especially in the international arena. Whether a thinker rejects or adheres to a cyclical view of history is a more important determinant of whether or not he prioritizes politics than such things as whether he believes in fate or free will or whether he believes that God, nature, or man shapes history.

We may assign to the first typology Arthur Schopenhauer, Jacob Burckhardt, Friedrich Nietzsche, Leo Tolstoy, Henry Adams, Aleksandr Solzhenitsyn, and Christopher Lasch. To unite these figures by labeling them "critics of politics" is not to deny that each of these thinkers held strong political preferences, nor is this grouping meant to obscure the important differences between members of this motley crew. There is, for instance, a wide chasm between Schopenhauer, who defended despotism, and Tolstoy, who sought to undermine the Russian autocracy. Nevertheless, we must recognize that a bridge connects the monarchist Schopenhauer and the anarchist Tolstoy, with Burckhardt, Nietzsche, et al. standing on the planks in between, advocating neither absolute authority for the government nor absolute liberty for subjects or citizens. Schopenhauer writes that "the State and the Kingdom of God, or the Moral Law, are so entirely different in their character that the former is a parody of the latter, a bitter mockery at the absence of it. Compared with the Moral Law the State is a crutch instead of a limb, an automaton instead of a man."[9] On this point, the author of *The Kingdom of God Is Within You* assuredly agrees. Indeed, this is the unifying position of thinkers who find no rhyme or reason in history, antipolitical thinkers who seek refuge in art, religion, or intellectual pursuits. Thinkers of this sort recommend that individuals work out their own salvation rather than trust in the state to bring about national or universal progress.

Cyclical theorists, on the other hand, often justify political projects to their compatriots by drawing lessons from the past. To these thinkers, history reveals patterns of both progress and decline. Pointing to historical analogues, cyclical theorists argue that their own nations are fated to play important roles in global affairs, either in bringing about temporary civilizational advance or in managing inexorable decay. Oswald Spengler, Brooks Adams, and Nikolai Danilevsky alike felt that the West was nearing its natural end. In his vision of the future, Spengler portended a fateful day that would call upon the talents of a new Caesar to lead the West in its final years. Where Spengler cast Germany as the lead in the story of the West's twilight, Adams gave the starring role to the United States, which could forestall its ultimate collapse through expansionism and bringing new energy to the empire. For Danilevsky, it was immaterial whether Germany or the United States took center stage in the dramatic tale of the West's decline; drawing the curtains on that performance meant that a new show was about to begin, with Russia entering from stage right.

The set of thinkers I have examined in this book is relatively small, but a cursory look at thinkers outside my purview suggests that, even when we widen the scope of the investigation, the distinction between cyclical theorists and other critics of the idea of progress remains important. To the list of cyclical theorists we could add the father of the philosophy of history, Giambattista Vico (1668–1744).[10] Vico outlined his theory of *corsi e ricorsi* in *The New Science*, and, though he may not have shared the bellicose nationalism of Spengler, Danilevsky, or Brooks Adams, he, too had a sincere interest in international affairs, as evidenced by the Italian jurist's monumental work on *Universal Right*. To the subset of critics of "progress" who see no patterns in history, we could add the contemporary British philosopher Roger Scruton.[11]

Painting critics of the idea of progress with one broad brush, then, proves impossible, with important differences apparent between and among cyclical theorists and thinkers for whom history does not reveal patterns. Frequently critics of "progress" are conservative, though we should not equate historical pessimism with conservatism. As Joshua Foa Dienstag argues, pessimism has the ability "to unsettle, rather than confirm, existing political arrangements."[12] Tolstoy stands as testament to that fact. And contemporary American politics belies the notion that all self-proclaimed conservatives identify as critics of the idea of progress.[13] At the National Tea Party Convention in 2010, the 2008 vice-presidential nominee for the Republican Party, Sarah Palin, famously mocked Barack Obama's campaign motto, asking of Obama's supporters "How's That Hopey, Changey Thing Working Out for Ya?"[14] Two years later, though, the Republican Party's standard bearer, Mitt Romney, was far less dismissive of ideas of hope and change: accepting his party's nomination for the presidency, Romney approvingly claimed of the American people that they have always lived their lives "optimistic and positive and confident in the future."[15] The archetypal American conservative trusts in at least one form of progress, namely economic; as Christopher Lasch has convincingly shown, the capitalist impulse that is part and parcel to contemporary conservatism rests on the notion that material comfort can and should improve for perpetuity.[16]

If critics of the idea of progress are not uniformly conservative, still less are they, as a group, reactionary. Mark Lilla writes that "where others see the river of time flowing as it always has, the reactionary sees the debris of paradise drifting past his eyes."[17] Schopenhauer plainly rejects the reactionary's sense of a "lost Eden"—past societies had defects just as surely as do current societies and will future ones. Schopenhauer's heir, Burckhardt, may have abandoned himself in his studies of Renaissance Italy, and Henry Adams might have made mental pilgrimages to medieval Chartres, but neither man was moved by "the militancy of nostalgia" that Lilla attributes to reactionaries.[18] Militancy does characterize the thought of Spengler, Danilevsky, and Brooks Adams. But for these cyclical theorists there is no question of returning to some idealized past; Spengler, for instance, does not suggest that twentieth-century Westerners try to recover former glories, but that they (and the Germans, in particular) make the most of life "in the early winter of full Civilization."[19] Reactionaries, then, differ in important ways from the figures discussed in the present work. The reactionary may reject the idea of progress; just as likely, he simply defines "progress" differently from his contemporaries.

What the current aura of disenchantment means for the future of American and world politics is uncertain. Will members of the public turn their backs on politics and turn to aesthetic appreciation, enjoying the comforts of religion, or building Shangri-las in their own minds?[20] The post–World War II record-low voter turnout in the 2014 midterm elections might be one indication that Americans are washing their hands of even the most basic expressions of political engagement. But there are other indications that the legions of discontented do not reject the idea of progress *as such* and will not retreat from politics; instead what we are seeing is a rejection of *liberal universalist* visions of progress and the political programs associated with them. In a 2013 address before the Federal Assembly, Russian president Vladimir Putin declared that "attempts to push supposedly more progressive development models onto other nations actually resulted in regression, barbarity and extensive bloodshed."[21] Putin's military incursions in Russia's near (and not-so-near) abroad aside, increasing numbers of Westerners seem to agree with the sentiment of his remarks, punishing establishment politicians as "globalists" and rewarding inward-looking populists. From Brexiteers bucking the European Union to America-firsters looking to make their country "great again," from supporters of the National Front in France to loyalists of the Party for Freedom in the Netherlands or the Freedom Party of Austria, nationalists are on the ascent, seeking progress for themselves and their compatriots on their own terms.[22]

*   *   *

Leo Strauss observes that "political thought is as old as the human race."[23] This may be true, but as an academic field, political theory cannot be regarded as anything other than a contemporary and dynamic endeavor.[24] With this book, I have a made a modest offering to Aeternitas and Vertumnus alike: in deference to tradition, I have engaged with the history of ideas; with an eye to recent trends in the discipline of political theory, I have adopted a comparative approach.[25] My hope is that not only the gods of eternity and change, but also the mortals in academe who call themselves political theorists, will find something of worth in my project. The attributes of this book to which I would like to call attention are two: (1) the analysis of a contested concept; and (2) the bringing to light of important thinkers who have traditionally been marginalized by political theorists. By means of conclusion, I will briefly comment in turn on these two facets of my work.

Discourse is impossible without a shared understanding of some basic terms. But, as Voltaire learned from the outcry that followed the publication of his *Philosophical Dictionary*, certain words fail to find a consensus of meaning, a fact as true in our own day as it was in the eighteenth century.[26] More recent forays into developing a philosophical lexicon are Raymond Williams's *Keywords*[27] and Robert Nisbet's *Prejudices*.[28] In these works, readers will find a number of words that either are expressly political or have political connotations, including "liberty," "equality," and "democracy." Whether these concepts are "essentially contested,"[29] or are merely frequently disputed, they are at the heart of most political conversations, both mundane and profound. They are words that are difficult to define and that can cause even the most erudite to throw up their hands and say, as Justice Potter Stewart did with respect to "obscenity," "I know it when I see it."

Political theorists have good reason to study essentially contested or potentially contestable concepts. Words have the power to evoke a spectrum of responses from their readers or hearers—anger, pity, fear, longing, regret, and innumerable others. Political concepts, in particular, have the ability to inspire collective action. In late eighteenth-century France, calls for *liberté*, *égalité*, and *fraternité* were followed by a revolution to achieve these things. Two hundred years later, Polish workers demonstrated *solidarność* in opposition to an intransigent bureaucracy, setting the stage for a revolution of their own. As William Connolly writes, political concepts are part of political life itself—"they help constitute it, to make it what it is. It follows," Connolly adds, "that changes in those concepts, once accepted by a significant number of participants, contribute to changes in political life itself."[30]

In this book, I have focused on the changing and contested meanings of "progress." I have not sought to define this protean term myself;[31] instead, I have shown how prior writers have defined it, and what actions they hoped or feared the word would inspire. Though I have tried to zero in on a single idea, this book demonstrates the truth of James Farr's observation that "concepts are never held or used in isolation, but in constellations which make up entire schemes or belief systems."[32] The proponents of the idea of progress discussed in this work linked that idea with such concepts as "nation," "civilization," "democracy," and "equality." Most critics of "progress," in turn, objected not only to that idea, but to the nationalist movements, civilizing missions, democratic despotism, and radical egalitarianism that their opponents associated with that term.

Herein, I have suggested that we can learn from and appreciate critics of the idea of progress, who deserve a fairer hearing than they have received. Far too frequently, historical pessimism is conflated with the view that man is fallen or with skepticism. Our views on liberty and authority are determined in part by whether we hold Lockean or Hobbesian views of human nature. Our trust in or skepticism of rationally designed political institutions depends on how much we trust in reason more generally. And, I have argued, whether we view politics as an engine for positive and lasting social transformation or as something incapable of doing much to meliorate the human condition depends on whether we accept and how we define the notion of "progress." Each of these is a separate issue, however, and we err by assuming any necessary connections between our own or anyone else's views of human nature, epistemology, and the nature and trajectory of history.

The most famous historical optimists had deep interests in politics; critics opposed both their historiosophies and their political theories. One lesson that these critics teach us is that an individual may reflect thoughtfully about politics without being consumed by it. This is no small lesson for political theorists, who by nature are wont to emphasize (or overemphasize) the importance of politics. The figures who are front and center of this book were neither ignorant nor lazy; they were well-versed in the debates of their day but simply decided not to prioritize politics. Political observers today who bemoan nonparticipation—and this may well be lamentable—would be wise to consider that some of this disengagement might be principled, rather than due to citizens being uninformed or lethargic.

Another lesson from critics of the idea of progress is that one may dispense with optimism without succumbing to nihilism.[33] Schopenhauer, Burckhardt, Henry Adams, and Solzhenitsyn elaborated pessimistic visions of history without completely giving up on life. Schopenhauer, who taught that life was a curse, nevertheless had values, as evidenced by his moral and aesthetic philosophies. Burckhardt and Adams likewise had interests in the arts, and they shared with one another an interest in historical study. On top of these interests, Burckhardt found value in teaching, and Adams cherished his personal relationships. For his part, Solzhenitsyn turned to religious devotion. Their pessimistic visions of history led these authors to resist seductive calls for permanent and universal *political* solutions to the perennial problems of humankind, but critics of the idea of progress did not give up the search for *personal* mindsets and behaviors that would guide them through life.

Of course, criticism of the idea of progress does not come without its dangers; though the critics discussed in this work did not become completely socially disengaged[34] or fall prey to nihilism, these are potential pitfalls of losing one's faith in the future or in the ability of politics to meliorate intractable social problems. Schopenhauer, Burckhardt, and others, even while quitting direct political involvement, advocated or demonstrated altruism. But political scientists have found links between political disengagement and disengagement of other sorts (for example, refraining from volunteering or joining community groups).[35] And while Schopenhauer, Burckhardt, and company successfully navigated between the sirens on the rock singing "progress" and the whirlpool of crippling despair, not everyone reaches safe port in their intellectual voyages. The English philosopher John Gray, who challenges the idea of progress in such works as *Straw Dogs* and *The Silence of Animals*, declares in the former that "for the men and women of today, an irrational faith in progress may be the only antidote to nihilism. Without the hope that the future will be better than the past, they could not go on."[36] But to some reviewers of his work, Gray himself exemplifies a pessimist gone a few shades too dark, in need of a tonic of sorts. Calling *Straw Dogs* "crankish" and "unbalanced," Terry Eagleton in the *Guardian* labels Gray "a full-blooded apocalyptic nihilist."[37] And Danny Postel in the *Nation* claims that the effect of reading *Straw Dogs* in tandem with Gray's later *Al Qaeda and What It Means to be Modern* is a "moral numbness," suggesting that the reader is left asking "what difference does it make whether the human species avoids its collision course with doom?"[38]

Even if not guilty of antisocial behavior or the nihilistic rejection of all values, the critics mentioned in the present study are not faultless, and one may object to them for any number of reasons. One may not like the conclusions that these critics reached. (Are inequalities in wealth or status justified because they add to the world's variety, and thus make existence more pleasing from an aesthetic point of view, as Burckhardt's philosophy seems to suggest?) One may find these critics just as utopian as those whom they would correct. (What good does Tolstoyan pacifism serve in the face of evil?) One may even fault critics of the idea of progress as more culpable than their adversaries for the tragedies that their philosophies aimed to avert. (Who was more responsible for World War II, the glorifiers of nation and state, or the proponents of the idea that one should not muddy one's hands in politics, who thereby allowed the most ruthless of all to come to power?) One might regard the thinkers described in the foregoing as inconsistent. (If life is such a curse, and if there is no hope for its getting better, then why would Schopenhauer so oppose suicide, a perfectly acceptable end for the stoics of old?) One may find these figures simply futilitarian. (If decline is inevitable, then why heap scorn on the masses simply for obeying the laws of history, as Henry Adams did?) These are difficult challenges for the historical pessimist, any of whose works might have as their epigram these words from Herzen: "Do not look for solutions in this book—there are none." But, these authors would hasten to add, with Herzen: "in general modern man has no solutions."[39]

Critics of the idea of progress do not have the answers to all life's problems, but their works remind us that neither does anyone else. Nationalism, which appeals to its adherents as a panacea for present discontents, has been tried before. So too has relinquishing power to demagogues or vanguard political parties. Democratic capitalism is a relatively new phenomenon. But if, as Aristotle claims, politics is the means by which humans might attain a happiness that "renders life desirable and lacking in nothing,"[40] then this system, too, which (as per Lasch) encourages the "proliferation of wants" and continuous striving,[41] has also failed to hit the mark. Critics of the idea of progress do not ask us to stop caring about the ills that plague the world or our own little corner of it; rather, they ask us to temper our expectations of the good that politics can bring and to be on guard against the damage that can come from political excess. If only to force us to reconsider certain long-standing assumptions about historical change, politics, and the working of the world, these critics merit our attention.

# NOTES

## Introduction

1. James Wilson, "Oration Delivered on the 4th of July, 1788, at the Procession Formed at Philadelphia to Celebrate the Adoption of the Constitution of the United States (1787)," in *Collected Works of James Wilson,* vol. 1, ed. Kermit L. Hall and Mark David Hall (Indianapolis: Liberty Fund, 2007), 292.

2. For pertinent polls, see this book's concluding chapter.

3. "Gwen Ifill Interviews President Obama on Trump, Economic Recovery," PBS NewsHour, June 1, 2016.

4. "Shields and Brooks on Obama's NewsHour Interview, Presidential Legacy," PBS NewsHour, June 1, 2016.

5. Barack Obama, "Remarks by the President at Hillary for America Rally in Ann Arbor, Michigan," White House, Office of the Press Secretary (speech, University of Michigan, Ann Arbor, November 7, 2016).

6. Katie Glueck, "Clinton Decries Trump's 'Midnight in America,'" *POLITICO,* July 28, 2016.

7. Donald J. Trump, "Inaugural Address," White House, January 20, 2017. A majority of respondents in a POLITICO/Morning Consult poll found Trump's speech "optimistic"; see Jake Sherman, "Poll: Voters Liked Trump's 'America First' Address," *POLITICO,* January 25, 2017.

8. Gideon Skinner, "EU Citizens Think Things Across the Union Heading in the Wrong Direction—But Committed to Membership," *Ipsos in North America* August 31, 2015.

9. Simon Atkinson and Bobby Duffy, "What Worries the World—October 2016," *Ipsos,* November 15, 2016.

10. Marquis de Condorcet, *The Progress of the Human Mind,* in *The Idea of Progress Since the Renaissance,* ed. Warren W. Wagar (New York: Wiley, 1969), 81.

11. J. B. Bury, *The Idea of Progress: An Inquiry into Its Origin and Growth* (New York: Dover, 1955), v.

12. Robert A. Nisbet, *History of the Idea of Progress* (New Brunswick, NJ: Transaction, 1994), 8.

13. Friedrich Nietzsche, "Schopenhauer as Educator," in *Unfashionable Observations*, trans. Richard T. Gray (Stanford, CA: Stanford University Press, 1995), 171–255.

14. Cited in Erich Heller, "Burckhardt and Nietzsche," in *The Importance of Nietzsche* (Chicago: University of Chicago Press, 1988), 45.

15. Cited in Andrzej Walicki, *A History of Russian Thought: From the Enlightenment to Marxism* (Oxford: Clarendon, 1988), 329.

16. Henry Adams, *The Education of Henry Adams*, in *Novels; Mont Saint Michel; The Education*, comp. Ernest Samuels and Jayne N. Samuels (New York: Library of America, 1983), 1090.

## Chapter 1. "The Same, But Otherwise"

Note to epigraph: Schopenhauer writes in the second volume of *The World as Will and Representation* that "the motto of history in general should run: *Eadem, sed aliter*," which E. F. J. Payne translates as "the same, but otherwise" (Arthur Schopenhauer, *The World as Will and Representation*, vol. 2, trans. E. F. J. Payne [New York: Dover, 1969], 444). Hereafter cited as *WWR:II*.

1. David Cartwright, *Schopenhauer: A Biography* (Cambridge: Cambridge University Press, 2010), 513.

2. Bryan Magee, *The Philosophy of Schopenhauer* (Oxford: Clarendon, 1983), 202.

3. Ibid., 205.

4. Patrick Gardiner offers a four-page discussion of Schopenhauer's views of the state (Gardiner, *Schopenhauer* [Baltimore: Penguin, 1963], 267–70). Dale Jacquette writes that Schopenhauer's portrayal of the world as will "has startling ramifications for ethics, politics, aesthetics, and religious salvation" (Jacquette, *The Philosophy of Schopenhauer* [Chesham, UK: Acumen, 2005], 79). However, he does not expound upon what these ramifications are for politics. In his helpful primer on Schopenhauer's philosophy, Julian Young provides a single fleeting reference to Schopenhauer's conception of the state (Young, *Schopenhauer* [London: Routledge, 2005], 175). The terms "government," "politics," and "the state" are absent from the index to Christopher Janaway's work; the terms "i ching," "maya," and "dreams" make the cut (Janaway, *Self and World in Schopenhauer's Philosophy* [Oxford: Clarendon, 1989]).

5. Joshua Foa Dienstag, "'The Evils of the World Honestly Admitted': Metaphysical Pessimism in Schopenhauer and Freud," in *Pessimism: Philosophy, Ethic, Spirit* (Princeton, NJ: Princeton University Press, 2006), 84–117.

6. Yannis Constantinidès, "Two Great Enemies of the Enlightenment: Joseph de Maistre and Schopenhauer," in *Joseph de Maistre and the Legacy of the Enlightenment*, ed. Carolina Armenteros and Richard Lebrun (Oxford: Voltaire Foundation, 2011), 105–122.

7. See, for instance, Tracy Strong, *Friedrich Nietzsche and the Politics of Transfiguration* (Berkeley: University of California Press, 1975); Ruth Abbey, *Nietzsche's Middle*

*Period* (Oxford: Oxford University Press, 2000); Tamsin Shaw, *Nietzsche's Political Skepticism* (Princeton, NJ: Princeton University Press, 2007).

8. Raymond Marcin, *In Search of Schopenhauer's Cat: Arthur Schopenhauer's Quantum-Mystical Theory of Justice* (Washington, DC: Catholic University of America Press, 2006), 174.

9. Neil Jordan, "Schopenhauer's Politics: Ethics, Jurisprudence, and the State," in *Better Consciousness: Schopenhauer's Philosophy of Value*, ed. Alex Neill and Christopher Janaway (Chichester, UK: Wiley-Blackwell, 2009), 171–88.

10. Robin Winkler, "Schopenhauer's Critique of Moralistic Theories of the State," *History of Political Thought* 34, no. 2 (2013): 299.

11. John Gray, *Straw Dogs: Thoughts on Humans and Other Animals* (London: Granta, 2002), 39. Arthur Hübscher similarly labels Schopenhauer a "thinker against the tide" (Hübscher, *The Philosophy of Schopenhauer in Its Intellectual Context: Thinker Against the Tide*, trans. Joachim T. Baer and David E. Cartwright [Lewiston, NY: Edwin Mellen, 1989]).

12. Schopenhauer says forthrightly about the world that "its non-existence would be preferable to its existence." For him, the happy moments that may exist in the life of an individual do not compensate for that individual's having to experience misery at times. Moreover, even if a thousand people were able to live in an extended state of bliss, and only one person in the world were to experience evil, then the world's non-existence would still be preferable to its existence (*WWR:II*, 576).

13. Arthur Schopenhauer, *The World as Will and Representation*, vol. 1, trans. E. F. J. Payne (New York: Dover, 1969), xv. Hereafter cited as *WWR:I*. In this same section of the preface, Schopenhauer adds that if the reader "has also already received and assimilated the divine inspiration of ancient Indian wisdom, then he is best of all prepared to hear what I have to say to him." Schopenhauer has in mind the *Vedas* and the *Upanishads*. A later section of the present chapter notes his depiction of the Indian saint as a model—the archetypal individual who overcomes his attachment to the world.

14. Quoted in Rudiger Safranski, *Schopenhauer and the Wild Years of Philosophy*, trans. Ewald Osers (Cambridge, MA: Harvard University Press, 1990), 141.

15. Schopenhauer, *WWR:II*, 84.

16. Ibid., 590.

17. Ibid., 70.

18. Ibid., 40.

19. Ibid., 192–193.

20. Schopenhauer, *WWR:I*, 429.

21. Arthur Schopenhauer, *On the Basis of Morality*, trans. E. F. J. Payne (Indianapolis: Bobbs-Merrill, 1965), 15–16.

22. Ibid., 14.

23. Schopenhauer, *WWR:I*, xxiv.

24. Schopenhauer, *On the Basis of Morality*, 14.

25. Bryan Magee explains that a review of Schopenhauer's work, published in English in an 1853 issue of the *Westminster Review* and later translated into German, brought about an increase in awareness of—and appreciation for—Schopenhauer (Magee, *Philosophy of Schopenhauer*, 26).

26. Paul Gottfried suggests that Schopenhauer's invectives against Hegel should not be dismissed lightly. He argues instead that Schopenhauer came to criticize historical study *because* Hegel endorsed it. That is, Schopenhauer came to hate philosophies of history precisely because he hated Hegel the man and consequently hated anything Hegel supported (Gottfried, "Arthur Schopenhauer as a Critic of History," *Journal of the History of Ideas* 36, no. 2 [1975]: 335). For a critique of Gottfried's contention, see Harry Ausmus, "Schopenhauer's View of History: A Note," *History and Theory* 15, no. 2 (1976): 141–145.

27. For two different accounts of the idea of progress as it developed in German philosophy, see Georg Iggers, *The German Conception of History: The National Tradition of Historical Thought from Herder to the Present* (Middletown, CT: Wesleyan University Press, 1968) and Robert Nisbet, *A History of the Idea of Progress* (New Brunswick, NJ: Transaction, 1994), 220–224, 258–286.

28. Johann Gottfried von Herder, *This Too a Philosophy of History for the Formation of Humanity*, in *Johann Gottfried von Herder: Philosophical Writings*, ed. Michael N. Forster (Cambridge: Cambridge University Press, 2002), 334.

29. Ibid., 288.

30. Johann Gottfried von Herder, *Reflections on the Philosophy of the History of Mankind*, ed. Frank E. Manuel (Chicago: University of Chicago Press, 1968), 109.

31. Ibid., 112.

32. Ibid., 116.

33. Allen Wood, "Herder and Kant on History: Their Enlightenment Faith," in *Metaphysics and the Good: Themes from the Philosophy of Robert Merrihew Adams*, ed. Samuel Newlands and Larry M. Jorgensen (Oxford: Oxford University Press, 2009), 330.

34. Michael N. Forster, "Introduction," in Forster, ed., *Johann Gottfried von Herder*, xxxiii.

35. Immanuel Kant, "On the Common Saying: That May Be Correct in Theory, But It Is of No Use in Practice," in *Practical Philosophy*, ed. Mary J. Gregor (New York: Cambridge University Press, 1996), 309.

36. Ibid., 307.

37. Immanuel Kant, "An Old Question Raised Again: Is the Human Race Constantly Progressing," in *Religion and Rational Theology*, ed. Allen W. Wood and George di Giovanni, trans. Mary J. Gregor and Robert Anchor (New York: Cambridge University Press, 1996), 302.

38. Immanuel Kant, "Toward Perpetual Peace," in Gregor, *Practical Philosophy*, 324.

39. Kant, "Old Question," 308.

40. Kant, "Toward Perpetual Peace," 336.

41. Kant, "Old Question," 304.

42. Immanuel Kant, "Idea for a Universal History with a Cosmopolitan Aim," in *Anthropology, History, and Education*, ed. Günter Zöller and Robert B. Louden, trans. Allen Wood (Cambridge: Cambridge University Press, 2007), 119.

43. Others of his day may have wished to see the rest of the world become Europe writ large, but Herder laments Europe's acting as a "happiness-dispensing deity" that forces other parts of the world "to be happy in her way" (Herder, *Reflections*, 78).

44. As Forster notes: "Unlike Fichte for example, Herder never claimed or sought Germany's *superiority*, instead emphatically rejecting all such ideas of a 'Favoritvolk'" (Forster, "Introduction," xxxii).

45. Johann Fichte, *The Characteristics of the Present Age*, trans. William E. Smith (London: John Chapman, 1847), 64–65.

46. Ibid., 33.

47. Ibid., 15.

48. Fichte writes: "Rain, dew, abundant and hard years—these are all made by forces that we do not know and that are beyond our control; but the quite special life and times of man, human relations, these are made by men themselves, and not by any kind of power beyond their control" (Johann Fichte, *Addresses to the German Nation*, trans. Isaac Nakhimovsky, Béla Kapossy, and Keith Tribe [Indianapolis: Hackett, 2013], 179).

49. Ibid., 39–40.

50. Ibid., 187.

51. Ibid., 134. Fichte suggests that chief among the state's aims must be the enacting of a compulsory, universal education program from which the pupil will emerge "as a fixed and immutable work of art" (32) who is selfless and patriotic.

52. Karl Popper, *The Open Society and Its Enemies* (London: Routledge and Kegan Paul, 1962), 64.

53. Ibid., 56.

54. Shlomo Avineri, "Hegel and Nationalism," *Review of Politics* 24, no. 4 (1962): 464.

55. Friedrich Nietzsche, "The Utility and Liability of History," in *Unfashionable Observations*, trans. Richard T. Gray (Stanford, CA: Stanford University Press, 1995), 143.

56. Charles Taylor argues that there is "no particular chauvinism" in Hegel's discussion of history and that Hegel is wrongly associated with German nationalism (Taylor, *Hegel* [Cambridge: Cambridge University Press, 1975], 398, 457). Robert Nisbet takes the opposing view (Nisbet, *History of the Idea of Progress*, esp. 276–286). Yael Tamir characterizes Hegel as an illiberal nationalist (Tamir, *Liberal Nationalism* [Princeton, NJ: Princeton University Press, 1995], 63). Alan Patten downplays associations of Hegel with Prussian or German nationalism (Patten, *Hegel's Idea of Freedom* [New York: Oxford University Press, 1999]).

57. Georg Wilhelm Friedrich Hegel, *Lectures on the Philosophy of World History*, trans. H. B. Nisbet (New York: Cambridge University Press, 1975), 54, 93–97.

58. Ibid., 93.

59. Ibid., 93–97.

60. Herder, *Reflections*, 76.

61. I refer to Kant's categorical imperative. Kant writes in his *Groundwork of the Metaphysics of Morals*: "There is, therefore, only a single categorical imperative and it is this: *act only in accordance with that maxim through which you can at the same time will that it become a universal law*" (Kant, *Groundwork of the Metaphysics of Morals*, in Gregor, *Immanuel Kant*, 73).

62. Schopenhauer, *WWR:II*, 442–443.

63. Iggers, *German Conception*, 4.

64. Schopenhauer, *WWR:II*, 444.

65. Schopenhauer, *WWR:I*, 165.

66. Ibid., 312.

67. Ibid., 309.

68. Ibid., 326.

69. Schopenhauer, *WWR:II*, 583.

70. Ibid., 443.

71. Schopenhauer, *On the Basis of Morality*, 153.

72. Schopenhauer, *WWR:I*, 350.

73. Schopenhauer, *On the Basis of Morality*, 129.

74. Edmund Burke, "Thoughts and Details on Scarcity," in *The Writings and Speeches of Edmund Burke*, ed. Paul Langford and William B. Todd (Oxford: Clarendon, 1981), 120.

75. Arthur Schopenhauer, "On Jurisprudence and Politics," in *Parerga and Paralipomena*, vol. 2, trans. E. F. J. Payne (Oxford: Oxford University Press, 2000), 258–259.

76. Schopenhauer, *WWR:I*, 315.

77. Schopenhauer, "On Jurisprudence," 246–247.

78. Schopenhauer, *WWR:I*, 350. Throughout his scholarly career, Schopenhauer remained more interested in timeless problems than he did in the problems of the moment. In 1819 he wrote to the zoologist Martin Hinrich Carl Lichtenstein that "I would hold it as an abasement of myself, if I were to direct my intellectual powers to a sphere that appears to me so small and narrow as the present conditions of any particular time or country" (cited in Cartwright, *Schopenhauer*, 361). In the manuscript for *Spicilegia*, a work begun in 1837, Schopenhauer reiterates this point: "In my works one will look in vain for any consideration of the needs of the State and of any political tendency; the *private affairs of my times* do not concern me" (Schopenhauer, *Spicilegia*, in *Arthur Schopenhauer: Manuscript Remains in Four Volumes*, vol. 4, ed. Arthur Hübscher, trans. E. F. J. Payne, [New York: St. Martin's, 1990], 325).

79. Schopenhauer, *WWR:II*, 443. As a matter of pure "political prudence," however, the state should take measures to provide for the masses. If the state wishes to

avoid outright chaos, then "the people need panem et circenses" (Schopenhauer, *WWR:I*, 313).

80. Schopenhauer, *On the Basis of Morality*, 153.

81. Schopenhauer, *WWR:I*, 345.

82. See ibid., 114, 236, 294; and *WWR:II*, 442–443.

83. Schopenhauer, *WWR:I*, 369.

84. Ibid., 368.

85. Schopenhauer, *On the Basis of Morality*, 153.

86. Ibid.

87. Thomas Nipperdey, *Germany from Napoleon to Bismarck 1800–1866* (Dublin: Gill and Macmillan, 1996), 398.

88. James J. Sheehan, *German History, 1770–1866* (Oxford: Clarendon, 1989), 514–515.

89. See, e.g., Hans Kohn, *The Idea of Nationalism: A Study in Its Origins and Background* (New Brunswick, NJ: Transaction, 2005).

90. Arthur Schopenhauer, "What a Man Represents," in *Parerga and Paralipomena*, vol. 1, trans. E. F. J. Payne (Oxford: Oxford University Press, 2000), 360.

91. Magee, *The Philosophy of Schopenhauer*, 3–4.

92. Cartwright, *Schopenhauer*, 18.

93. Schopenhauer, *WWR:II*, 126.

94. Schopenhauer, "On Jurisprudence," 240.

95. Schopenhauer, *WWR:I*, 429.

96. Herder, *This Too a Philosophy of History*, 298.

97. Schopenhauer, "What a Man Represents," 361.

98. Benedict Anderson, *Imagined Communities: Reflections on the Origin and Spread of Nationalism* (London: Verso, 1991).

99. Schopenhauer, *WWR:II*, 442.

100. Schopenhauer, *WWR:I*, 244, 247.

101. Ibid., 247.

102. Ibid., 380–382.

103. Voltaire, *Candide*, trans. Lowell Bair (New York: Bantam, 1981), 120.

104. Schopenhauer, *WWR:I*, 385–386.

105. Ibid., Book IV, passim. Schopenhauer highlights the similarities between Christian mystics and Indian religious teachers with respect to their responses to the perceived evils of the world (cf. 389). Elsewhere, he draws favorable comparisons between "genuine Christianity" and Indian religions, insisting that on the fundamental issue of whether they are optimistic or pessimistic, both systems promote a pessimistic view of the world (Schopenhauer, *WWR:II*, 170).

106. Schopenhauer, *WWR:I*, 185–186, 196–197.

107. Voltaire, *Candide*, 119.

108. Ibid.

109. Jordan, "Schopenhauer's Politics," 173.

110. Schopenhauer, *Spicilegia*, 340.

111. Schopenhauer, "On Jurisprudence," 253.

112. Ibid., 257–258.

113. Ibid., 251.

114. George H. Sabine, *A History of Political Theory*, ed. Thomas Landon Thorson (Hinsdale, IL: Dryden, 1973), 816, 810.

115. György Lukács, *The Destruction of Reason* (London: Merlin, 1981), 197.

116. Schopenhauer writes: "A state constitution that embodied abstract right would be an excellent thing for natures other than human" ("On Jurisprudence," 252).

117. Ibid., 242.

118. Schopenhauer, "What a Man Represents," 360.

119. Hajo Holborn, "Origins and Political Character of Nazi Ideology," *Political Science Quarterly* 79, no. 4 (1964): 551.

120. Max Horkheimer, "Schopenhauer and Society (1955)," trans. Todd Cronan, *Qui Parle* 15, no. 1 (2004): 90.

121. Popper, *Open Society*, 306.

122. Schopenhauer, "On Jurisprudence," 257.

123. Safranski, *Schopenhauer*, 324. Schopenhauer qualified some of his more authoritarian sentiments. Although he opposed trial by jury and the like for German states, he claimed that such institutions were "natural and appropriate to the English people" (Schopenhauer, "On Jurisprudence," 256).

124. Popper, *Open Society*, 79.

125. Burckhardt writes: "The rivalry between history and poetry has been finally settled by Schopenhauer. Poetry achieves more for knowledge of human nature" (Jacob Burckhardt, *Force and Freedom: Reflections on History*, ed. James H. Nichols [New York: Pantheon, 1943], 153).

126. Burckhardt taught at Basel from 1843 to 1893, except for a brief stint in Zurich (1855–1858).

127. "Burckhardt refers to a number of specified passages from Schopenhauer's *World as Will and Representation*; they contain almost all that is needed for an understanding of Burckhardt's philosophy" (Erich Heller, "Burckhardt and Nietzsche," in *The Importance of Nietzsche* [Chicago: University of Chicago Press, 1988], 44).

128. Richard Sigurdson, *Jacob Burckhardt's Social and Political Thought* (Toronto: University of Toronto Press, 2004), 103.

129. Ibid., 157.

130. Sigurdson convincingly shows that "pessimism was evident in Burckhardt long before he read Schopenhauer's *The World as Will and Idea* in 1870. Thus reading this book did not occasion any radical change of mind or redirection of his life's plans" (107). This would suggest that, when speaking of the relationship between Schopenhauer and Burckhardt, one may speak of *affinities* between the two authors, if not a direct *influence* of the former on the latter.

131. Jacob Burckhardt, *Judgments on History and Historians*, trans. Harry Zohn (Boston: Beacon, 1958), 3.

132. Ibid., 231. Burckhardt remarks upon Darwin's theories of "survival of the fittest" as evidence of a permanent struggle in the world. Other historians of his day used Darwin's theory of evolution to support the idea of social and political progress. I say more about this in Chapter 3.

133. Ibid., 75.

134. Ibid., 230.

135. Ibid., 74.

136. Ibid., 113.

137. Burckhardt, *Reflections*, 184.

138. Burckhardt, *Judgments*, 171.

139. Ibid.

140. Ibid., 219.

141. Ibid., 233.

142. John R. Hinde writes of Burckhardt that his "political consciousness derived first and foremost from being a Basler. His deep-rooted psychological bonds with Basel defined his existence and his understanding of the world" (Hinde, "The Development of Jacob Burckhardt's Early Political Thought," *Journal of the History of Ideas* 53, no. 3 [1992]: 427).

143. There is some scholarly debate as to whether Burckhardt belongs in the liberal camp. Alan Kahan, for instance, deems him an "aristocratic liberal" (Alan S. Kahan, *Aristocratic Liberalism: The Social and Political Thought of Jacob Burckhardt, John Stuart Mill, and Alexis de Tocqueville* [New York: Oxford University Press, 1992]). Sigurdson suggests that he might be thought of either as a "liberal conservative" or a "conservative liberal" (Sigurdson, *Jacob Burckhardt's*, 165). Hinde calls him a conservative (Hinde, "Development," 427).

144. Burckhardt, *Judgments*, 218. The parenthetical remark about Hegel is Burckhardt's.

145. Ibid., 163.

146. Cited in Sigurdson, *Jacob Burckhardt's*, 113.

147. Burckhardt also writes of "war as a work of art."

148. Jacob Burckhardt, *The Civilization of the Renaissance in Italy: An Essay*, trans. S. G. C. Middlemore (New York: Phaidon, 1951), 2.

149. Ibid., 48.

150. Ibid., 55. In his lectures, Burckhardt proclaims that "there is a partial or momentary greatness in which an individual forgets himself and his own existence for the sake of a general aim. Such a man at such a moment seems sublime" (Burckhardt, *Reflections*, 306).

151. Sigurdson writes that, "for Burckhardt, historical contemplation substitutes for what 'The Philosopher' [i.e., Schopenhauer] describes as pure aesthetic experience—it is an escape, an interlude of peace; it is a transition from vain striving to pure

seeing, from desire to self-knowledge" (Sigurdson, *Jacob Burckhardt's*, 109). Historical contemplation would, of course, include investigations into political matters, though politics is for Burckhardt but one branch of the human story that needs to be told. For more on Burckhardt's aesthetic look at politics, see Nikola Regent, "A 'Wondrous Echo': Burckhardt, Renaissance and Nietzsche's Political Thought," in *Nietzsche, Power and Politics: Rethinking Nietzsche's Legacy for Political Thought*, ed. Herman W. Siemens and Vasti Roodt (New York: De Gruyter, 2008), 629–665.

152. Burckhardt, *Judgments*, 157–158. Burckhardt adds that "it is an illusion to expect lasting contentment with any victory, something for which man lacks the organ anyway."

153. Ibid., 160.

154. Cited in Heller, *Importance*, 49.

155. Kahan, *Aristocratic Liberalism*, 130. Sigurdson also notes this facet of Burckhardt's thought and life; Sigurdson, *Jacob Burckhardt's*, 43, 58.

156. Burckhardt, *Judgments*, 160. In the passage from which I quote, Burckhardt writes specifically about the need for "great individuals" to preserve Europe's political variety. But Sigurdson notes that, for Burckhardt, "in a world of declining standards and increased barbarization, outstanding achievements by striking personality types can stimulate new creation and spontaneity" (Sigurdson, *Jacob Burckhardt's*, 159).

157. Cited in Heller, *Importance*, 45.

158. In "Schopenhauer as Educator," Nietzsche writes that "I am among those readers of Schopenhauer who after having read the first page know with certainty that they will read every page and pay attention to every word he ever uttered" (Friedrich Nietzsche, "Schopenhauer as Educator," in *Unfashionable Observations*, trans. Richard T. Gray [Stanford, CA: Stanford University Press, 1995], 179).

159. Cited in Regent, "Wondrous Echo," 630.

160. Sigurdson, *Jacob Burckhardt's*, 203.

161. Nietzsche writes in the 1889 letter to Burckhardt: "Now you are—thou art—our greatest teacher" (cited in Regent, "Wondrous Echo," 629).

162. Heller, *Importance*, 50. Heller rightly states that Nietzsche maintained this personal affection and admiration even after he broke from his predecessors intellectually.

163. Nietzsche, "Schopenhauer," 237.

164. Friedrich Nietzsche, "The Utility and Liability of History," in *Unfashionable Observations*, trans. Gray), 143.

165. Nietzsche also writes that "we are experiencing the consequences of that dogma that has of late been preached from all the rooftops, a dogma that asserts that the state is the highest aim of humanity and that a man can have no higher duty than the service to the state. In this dogma I see a relapse not so much into paganism as into stupidity" (Nietzsche, "Schopenhauer," 197). For the same reasons that he felt politics to be a fruitless endeavor, Nietzsche thought nationalism could provide no fix to the

problems of the world. "Nationalism" was but another of his century's false slogans (237).

166. Shaw, *Nietzsche's Political*, 19. Shaw identifies Burckhardt as an ally of Nietzsche in the fight against politics.

167. For more on this topic, see Thomas Heilke, *Nietzsche's Tragic Regime: Culture, Aesthetics, and Political Education* (Dekalb: Northern Illinois University Press, 1998).

168. Regent, "Wondrous Echo," 642.

169. Nietzsche, "Schopenhauer," 176. Consider also: "everything stands in service of approaching barbarism, contemporary art and science included" (198).

170. Ibid., 230–231.

171. Burckhardt, *Reflections*, 224.

172. Ibid., 344.

173. Shaw, *Nietzsche's Political*, 13.

174. Kahan, *Aristocratic Liberalism*, 130.

175. Friedrich Nietzsche, *The Birth of Tragedy*, trans. Shaun Whiteside (New York: Penguin Books 1993), 32.

176. Nietzsche, "Schopenhauer," 173.

177. "That pessimism need not lead to resignation, that it properly leads to spirited activity, is Nietzsche's main contention in his long campaign to rid pessimism of the deformations with which it was saddled by earlier exponents" (Dienstag, *Pessimism*, 166). At the same time, Dienstag writes that "Nietzsche's pessimism advises each of us individually to cobble together a meaning for life out of lesser goals" (182). This hardly sounds any more daring than the courses of action proposed by Schopenhauer and Burckhardt.

178. Sigurdson, *Jacob Burckhardt's*, 38.

179. Nietzsche, "Schopenhauer," 200.

180. "Humanity should work ceaselessly at producing great individuals" (ibid., 215).

181. Ibid., 216.

182. Bruce Detwiler notes that "the Renaissance personality Nietzsche praises most and indeed associates with the superhuman is Cesare Borgia" (Detwiler, *Nietzsche and the Politics of Aristocratic Radicalism* [Chicago: University of Chicago Press, 1990], 133). Detwiler also spots a tension in the thought of the "anti-political" Nietzsche: "the difference between the worship of the superman and the worship of the state becomes a subtle one indeed as soon as the goal of the state becomes (as I think Nietzsche implies it should become) the promotion of a master race of supermen" (113).

183. Burckhardt commented on Nietzsche's "disposition towards possible tyranny," cited in Regent, "Wondrous," 660. Regent suggests, though, that Burckhardt's remark should not be considered scolding. Sigurdson disagrees (Sigurdson, *Jacob Burckhardt's*, 259).

## Chapter 2. The Autocrat and the Anarchist

Notes to epigraphs: So wrote the tsar on a ministerial report that contained the term (cited in Thomas Garrigue Masaryk, *The Spirit of Russia*, vol. 1, trans. Eden Paul and Cedar Paul [New York: Macmillan, 1955], 113); and Lev N. Tolstóy, "Progress and the Definition of Education," in *Pedagogical Articles; Linen-Measurer*, vol. 4 of *The Complete Works of Count Tolstóy*, trans. Leo Wiener (Boston: Colonial 1904), 167–168.

1. James Edie, James Scanlan, and Mary-Barbara Zeldin, "Preface," in *The Beginnings of Russian Philosophy; The Slavophiles; The Westernizers*, vol. 1 of *Russian Philosophy*, ed. James Edie, James Scanlan, and Mary-Barbara Zeldin (Knoxville: University of Tennessee Press, 1976), ix.

2. This was the case especially when Nicholas I closed philosophy departments upon his taking the throne!

3. Hugh Ragsdale, *The Russian Tragedy: The Burden of History* (Armonk, NY: M.E. Sharpe, 1996), 56–58; Cynthia Whittaker, "The Reforming Tsar: The Redefinition of Autocratic Duty in Eighteenth-Century Russia," *Slavic Review*51, no. 1 (1992), 83. For lengthier discussions of Peter I's reforms, see James Cracraft, *The Petrine Revolution in Russian Culture* (Cambridge, MA: Belknap Press of Harvard University Press, 2004); Lindsey Hughes, *Russia in the Age of Peter the Great* (New Haven, CT: Yale University Press, 1998).

4. Whittaker, "Reforming Tsar," 78.

5. Ragsdale, *Russian Tragedy*, 58.

6. Even Catherine's record as a reformer is mixed. Ragsdale notes that the empress lost her zeal for reform after the outbreak of the French Revolution, which "sealed the fate of the process of Westernization and the idea of progress in Russia"(ibid., 70). For a fuller discussion of Catherine's reign see Isabel de Madariaga, *Russia in the Age of Catherine the Great* (New Haven, CT: Yale University Press, 1981).

7. Thornton Anderson characterizes the reigns prior to and after Catherine's as times of "drunken stupor, imbecility, and madness" (Anderson, *Russian Political Thought: An Introduction* [Ithaca, NY: Cornell University Press, 1967], 141). Ragsdale refers to the period between Peter and Catherine as "the era of cretins and freaks," adding that "Alexander [the first] was the only sovereign of Russia between Catherine and the end of the empire who had genuinely progressive sentiments and harbored enthusiastic intentions of reform" (Ragsdale, *Russian Tragedy*, 62, 74). Exceptions might include Ivan III (ibid., 17) and Ivan IV (Anderson, *Russian Political Thought*, 123). Even the "Tsar-Liberator," Alexander II, "was a reluctant reformer at best" (Ragsdale, *Russian Tragedy*, 84).

8. Andrzej Walicki, "Russian Philosophers of the Silver Age as Critics of Marxism," in *Russian Thought After Communism: The Recovery of a Philosophical Heritage*, ed. James P. Scanlan (Armonk, NY: M.E. Sharpe, 1994), 81.

9. Peter Chaadayev, "Philosophical Letters," in Edie, Scanlan, and Zeldin, *The Beginnings of Russian Philosophy*, 116.

10. James Edie, James Scanlan, and Mary-Barbara Zeldin, "Peter Yakovlevich Chaadayev," in Edie, Scanlan, and Zeldin, *The Beginnings of Russian Philosophy*, 102; Anderson, *Russian Political Thought*, 197.

11. Chaadayev, "Philosophical Letters," 140.

12. Ibid., 115.

13. Ibid., 111.

14. Ibid., 118.

15. Ibid., 133.

16. Ibid., 141.

17. Walicki writes that, "in the dispute between Slavophiles and Westernizers, Chaadaev's position was . . . untypical. He was an ardent Westernizer; but the Western Europe he admired was not that of the democratic Westernizers of the 1840's, but that of the old aristocratic order before the age of revolutions" (Andrzej Walicki, *A History of Russian Thought: From the Enlightenment to Marxism* [Oxford: Clarendon, 1988], 91.

18. Ibid., 113.

19. Ibid., 151.

20. Ibid., 144.

21. Ibid., 114.

22. Ibid., 112.

23. Ibid., 120.

24. Ibid., 149.

25. Ibid., 122.

26. Ibid., 118.

27. In contrast with most of his countrymen, Chaadaev supported Catholicism.

28. Ivan Kireevsky, "On the Nature of European Culture and on Its Relationship to Russian Culture: Letter to Count E. E. Komarovsky," in *On Spiritual Unity: A Slavophile Reader*, trans. and ed. Boris Jakim and Robert Bird (Hudson, NY: Lindisfarne, 1998), 192.

29. Ibid., 193–194. With two unsatisfactory options before them, many Western thinkers escaped into their own minds, where each began to develop new "common" principles to guide the world, with each thinker contradicting the others (ibid.).

30. Aleksei Khomiakov, "On Humboldt," in *Russian Intellectual History: An Anthology*, ed. Marc Raeff (New York: Harcourt Brace and World, 1966), 213.

31. Ibid., 215. The term Kireevsky, Khomiakov, and other Slavophiles used to denote this sort of harmonious coupling of unity and freedom was *sobornost'*.

32. "In this way, having subordinated faith to the logical conclusions of rationalistic understanding, the Western Church, already in the ninth century, sowed within itself the inescapable seed of the Reformation" (Kireevsky, "European Culture," 203).

33. Ibid., 211.

34. Khomiakov, "On Humboldt," 229.

35. Ibid., 215.

36. Given the unique features of Slavophile thought, Walicki's assertion that "Slavophile criticism of Western Europe was . . . essentially, though not solely, a critique of capitalist civilization from a romantic conservative point of view" seems inapt; see Walicki, *History of Russian Thought*, 107.

37. Frederick C. Copleston, *Philosophy in Russia: From Herzen to Lenin and Berdyaev* (Notre Dame, IN: University of Notre Dame Press, 1986), 46.

38. Khomiakov, "On Humboldt," 227.

39. Ibid., 229.

40. Patrick Lally Michelson, "Slavophile Religious Thought and the Dilemma of Russian Modernity, 1830–1860," *Modern Intellectual History* 7, no. 2 (2010), 244.

41. N. O. Lossky notes that Khomiakov, in particular, "attached the greatest value to the Russian village commune, the *mir*, with its meetings that passed unanimous decisions and its traditional justice in accordance with custom, conscience, and inner truth" (Lossky, *History of Russian Philosophy* [New York: International Universities Press, 1951], 39). In his discussion of the *mir*, Richard Pipes notes that the *mir* tempered the antisocial behaviors of the peasants. Pipes quotes Khomiakov: "a Russian, taken individually, will not get into heaven, but there is no way of keeping out an entire village" (cited in Pipes, *Russia Under the Old Regime* [London: Weidenfeld and Nicolson, 1974], 158).

42. Copleston, *Philosophy in Russia*, 46.

43. Khomiakov, "On Humboldt," 215.

44. Kireevsky, "European Culture," 218.

45. Ibid., 206.

46. Khomiakov, "On Humboldt," 229.

47. Ibid., 226.

48. Susanna Rabow-Edling, *Slavophile Thought and the Politics of Cultural Nationalism* (Albany: State University of New York Press, 2006), 83. Anderson notes that the Slavophiles' critiques "had little or no effect on the government's course of action" and "serve most clearly to illustrate the impotence of the Moscow Slavophils' approach, of their rejection of political methods in their effort to influence the formal government by informal moral suasion" (Anderson, *Russian Political Thought*, 226). But the attempt to influence government through apolitical means is but one of example of the "self-contradictory and chimerical qualities" of Slavophile thought: "These men thought the West to be decadent and fundamentally misguided in religion and philosophy, yet they derived their basic notions from the West. They believed in the superiority of autocracy yet they wanted the tsar to act as an agent of the people. They admired local autonomy in the peasant commune yet they defended autocracy, which is necessarily centralized. They insisted upon freedom of opinion and of expression yet they denied the validity of individual thought and held only community opinion to be true" (ibid., 230).

49. James Edie, James Scanlan, and Mary-Barbara Zeldin, "The Westernizers," in Edie, Scanlan, and Zeldin, *The Beginnings of Russian Philosophy*, 274–275.

50. Michael Bakunin, "The Reaction in Germany," in Edie, Scanlan, and Zeldin, *The Beginnings of Russian Philosophy*, 390.

51. Ibid., 400.

52. V. G. Belinsky, "To V. P. Botkin. 8 September, 1841," in *Selected Philosophical Works* (Moscow: Foreign Language Publishing, 1948), 164.

53. Bakunin, "Reaction," 406.

54. Ibid., 387.

55. "And so, I am now at a new extreme, which is the idea of socialism, that has become for me the idea of ideas, the being of beings, the question of questions, the alpha and omega of belief and knowledge. It is the be all and end all. It is the question and its solution. It has (for me) engulfed history and religion and philosophy" (Belinsky, "To V. P. Botkin," 159).

56. V. G. Belinsky, "Review of *A Guide to the Study of Modern History*, by S. Smaragdov," in *Selected Philosophical Works*, 304.

57. Ibid., 301, 311.

58. Michael Bakunin, "The Paris Commune and the Idea of the State," in Edie, Scanlan, and Zeldin, *The Beginnings of Russian Philosophy*, 413.

59. Michael Bakunin, "God and the State," in ibid., 419.

60. Ibid.

61. Belinsky, "To V. P. Botkin," 164.

62. Belinsky, "Review," 308.

63. Belinsky, "To V. P. Botkin," 165.

64. Bakunin, "God and the State," 416.

65. Bakunin, "Reaction," 387.

66. Ibid., 386. Belinsky echoes: "the general trend of history, the sum-total of historic events, knows neither accidents nor hazards" (V. G. Belinsky, "Review of *The History of Malorussia*, by Nikolai Markevich," in *Selected Philosophical Works*, 290).

67. Bakunin, "God and the State," 416–417.

68. Vissarion Grigor'evich Belinskii, "Letter to N. V. Gogol," in Raeff, *Russian Intellectual History*, 256.

69. Bakunin, "God and the State," 418.

70. Ibid., 415.

71. "We recognize, then, the absolute authority of science. . . . Outside of this only legitimate authority, legitimate because rational and in harmony with human liberty, we declare all other authorities false, arbitrary and fatal" (ibid., 416).

72. Ibid., 419.

73. Belinsky, "Review," 297–298.

74. Belinsky, "To V. P. Botkin," 165–166.

75. I have focused on the shared beliefs of Belinsky and Bakunin. But an important difference must be noted. Though they both had socialism as a goal, they disagreed on how that goal would be achieved. Belinsky thought it would be brought about by

elites on behalf of the masses, while Bakunin believed the masses would organize themselves.

76. Aleksandr Herzen, *From the Other Shore*, in *From the Other Shore and The Russian People and Socialism: An Open Letter to Jules Michelet* (New York: Braziller, 1956), 36–37.

77. Ibid., 38.

78. For a detailed account of this period in Herzen's life, see "The Crucial Year— 1847" and "The Revolution of 1848" in Martin Malia, *Alexander Herzen* (New York: Grosset and Dunlap, 1965), 335–368, 369–387.

79. Ibid., 48–49.

80. Ibid., 49.

81. Aleksandr Herzen, "Author's Introduction," in *From the Other Shore*, 5.

82. Aileen Kelly, "Herzen Versus Schopenhauer: An Answer to Pessimism," *Journal of European Studies* 26, no. 1 (1996): 54.

83. Herzen, *From the Other Shore*, 103.

84. Herzen, "Author's Introduction," 16.

85. Herzen, *From the Other Shore*, 66.

86. Aleksandr Herzen, "The Russian People and Socialism: An Open Letter to Jules Michelet," in ibid., 166.

87. Ibid., 201.

88. Ibid., 205.

89. Ibid., 201.

90. Ibid., 175.

91. Ibid., 205.

92. Ibid., 193.

93. Ibid., 190. As Malia points out, this is a key difference between Russian socialism and Western socialism. As theorized by Westerners, including Karl Marx, socialism would be the outcome of class conflict between an urban proletariat and their capitalist overlords, the bourgeoisie. But until the 1890s Russia had no industrial base of which to speak. Thus, as envisioned by Russian theorists, socialism could emerge in Russia only from the peasantry; peasant socialism, Malia argues, was the unique theoretical contribution of Russian thinkers after 1848. Only after industrialization took off could Marxism make inroads in Russia. And Herzen himself, Malia writes, "simply never made intellectual contact with Marx" (Martin Malia, *Alexander Herzen and the Birth of Russian Socialism, 1812–1855* [Cambridge, MA: Harvard University Press, 1961], 3, 105, 324).

94. Isaiah Berlin writes that "compared to Bakunin's doctrines, Herzen's views are a model of dry realism," and yet "Herzen was himself, at times, Utopian enough" (Berlin, "Herzen and Bakunin on Individual Liberty," in *Russian Thinkers*, ed. Henry Hardy and Aileen Kelly [New York, 1978], 104–105. Anderson echoes this sentiment: "Herzen, the most clear-sighted of the Westerners, shared, at times, the messianic dream" (Anderson, *Russian Political Thought*, 202).

95. Dostoevsky presents an anecdote in *Diary of a Writer*: "On one occasion, conversing with the late Hertzen, I gave high praise to one of his books—*From the Other Shore*. . . . The book is written in the form of a dialogue between Hertzen and his opponent. / 'And what I like most,' I remarked *inter alia*, 'is the fact that your opponent is also very clever. You must concede that many a time he has pinned you to the wall' " (Dostoievsky, *The Diary of a Writer*, trans. Boris Brasol, vol. 1 (New York: Charles Scribner's Sons, 1949), 4.

96. Andrew Wachtel writes that, "while the assertion that *War and Peace* is about history is unlikely to surprise scholars or general readers, the same assertion made about *The Brothers Karamazov* is sure to raise eyebrows." Nevertheless, he argues that Dostoevsky's novel should be read in just such a way (Wachtel, *An Obsession with History: Russian Writers Confront the Past* [Stanford, CA: Stanford University Press, 1994)], 124). I concur.

97. Fyodor Dostoevsky, *The Brothers Karamazov*, trans. Richard Pevear and Larissa Volokhonsky (New York: Farrar, Straus and Giroux, 2002), 237.

98. Ibid., 235.

99. Ibid., 243.

100. Ibid., 235.

101. Ibid., 234.

102. Ibid., 241.

103. Ibid., 238.

104. Ibid., 243.

105. Ibid., 238–240.

106. In *Fathers and Sons*, Ivan Turgenev famously depicts nihilism as the rejection of all values. The character Arkady says that "a nihilist is a person who does not take any principle for granted" (Turgenev, *Fathers and Sons*, trans. Rosemary Edmonds [New York: Penguin, 1975], 94). Arkady's nihilist friend Bazarov consistently maintains that "I don't believe in anything" (ibid., 98). Pessimism ought not to be conflated with nihilism: the pessimist has values, he just finds what he values—whether human decency, or beauty, or happiness—to be in short supply.

107. Dostoevsky, *Brothers Karamazov*, 230.

108. Joshua Foa Dienstag, *Pessimism: Philosophy, Ethic, Spirit* (Princeton, NJ: Princeton University Press, 2006), 183.

109. David Walsh, "Dostoevsky's Discovery of the Christian Foundation of Politics," *Religion and Literature* 19, no. 2 (1987): 50.

110. Konstantin Leont'ev, *Against the Current: Selections from the Novels, Essays, Notes, and Letters of Konstantin Leontiev*, ed. George Ivask, trans. George Reavey (New York: Weybright and Talley, 1969), 244.

111. See Dostoevsky, *Brothers Karamazov*, 299.

112. Walsh, "Dostoevsky's Discovery," 60.

113. Fyodor Dostoyevsky, *Letters of Fyodor Michailovitch Dostoevsky to His Family and Friends*, trans. Ethel C. Mayne (New York: Horizon, 1961), 239.

114. Feodor M. Dostoievsky, *The Diary of a Writer*, trans. Boris Brasol, vol. 1 (New York: Charles Scribner's Sons,, 1949), 189.

115. Richard Pipes, *Russian Conservatism and Its Critics* (New Haven, CT: Yale University Press, 2005), 137.

116. Cited in Anderson, *Russian Political Thought*, 227 and Alexander Obolonsky, *The Drama of Russian Political History: System Against Individuality* (College Station: Texas A&M University Press, 2003), 94–95.

117. John D. Simons, "The Myth of Progress in Schiller and Dostoevsky," *Comparative Literature* 24, no. 4 (1972): 336. Simons supports his argument by pointing to "The Legend of the Grand Inquisitor" in *Brothers Karamazov*. The Grand Inquisitor offers harmony, but at the price of enslavement.

118. Obolonsky quotes from Dostoevsky's *Diary*: "We ourselves need this war; not merely because our Slavic brethren have been oppressed by the Turks. We are also rising for our own salvation. The war will clear the air which we breathe and in which we have been suffocating, closeted in spiritual narrowness and stricken with impotent decay" (cited in Obolonsky, *Drama*, 95).

119. Rabow-Edling, *Slavophile Thought*, 81.

120. Hans Kohn, *Pan-Slavism: Its History and Ideology* (New York: Vintage, 1960), 161–162.

121. Anderson, *Russian Political Thought*, 211.

122. Martin Malia argues that Nicholas I justifiably regarded the Slavophiles with suspicion: "the Slavophiles proper . . . were by no means unconditional supporters of the existing state of affair," and "Nicholas quite rightly sensed a significant difference between the Slavophiles and . . . idolators of autocracy." The state, to the Slavophiles, was nothing better than a necessary evil (Malia, *Alexander Herzen*, 284–286). Walicki echoes this point: "Nicholas rightly sensed that there was a difference between his own conservatism and that of the Slavophiles" (Walicki, *History of Russian Thought*, 110).

123. Cited in Anderson, *Russian Political Thought*, 177.

124. The Tolstoy-Buddha comparison is inexact. Whereas the Buddha had not known about suffering or death until early adulthood, Tolstoy experienced the loss of his parents at a young age. And whereas Buddhism became a world religion, Tolstoyism attracted comparatively few adherents. Moreover, Tolstoy had foibles and more serious faults not attributable to the Buddha.

125. A. N. Wilson, *Tolstoy* (New York: Norton, 1988), 15.

126. Wilson contrasts Tolstoy's (uncompleted) university education with that of Herzen. Where the atmosphere at the University of Moscow nurtured a political interest in men like Herzen, the University of Kazan inspired no great political debates (ibid., 41–42).

127. The Decembrist uprising would be foreshadowed at the end of *War and Peace*.

128. Leo Tolstoy, *A Confession*, in *A Confession, The Gospel in Brief, and What I Believe*, trans. Aylmer Maude (London: Oxford University Press, 1967), 8.

129. Wilson, *Tolstoy*, 97. Wilson notes that Tolstoy's later work, *Anna Karenina*, was released by a conservative publisher (177).

130. See ibid., 102, 112, 126.

131. Cited in ibid., 190.

132. Ibid.

133. Henri Troyat, *Tolstoy* (New York: Grove, 2001), 343. For short comparisons of Tolstoy and the Slavophiles, see Andrzej Walicki, *The Slavophile Controversy* (Oxford: Clarendon, 1975), 279–283 and Isaiah Berlin, "Tolstoy and Enlightenment," in *Russian Thinkers*, ed. Hardy and Kelly, 239–240.

134. Wilson, *Tolstoy*, 63.

135. Ibid., 77.

136. Tolstoy, *Confession*, 11.

137. Troyat, *Tolstoy*, 162–164.

138. Tolstoy, *Confession*, 12.

139. Ibid.

140. Isaiah Berlin, "The Hedgehog and the Fox," in Hardy and Kelly, *Russian Thinkers*, 28.

141. Leo Tolstoy, "A Few Words Apropos of the Book *War and Peace*," in *War and Peace*, trans. Richard Pevear and Larissa Volokhonsky (New York, 2007), 1217. Tolstoy says that *War and Peace* departs from European conventions, but that it has precedents in Russian literature.

142. Leo Tolstoy, *War and Peace*, trans. Richard Pevear and Larissa Volokhonsky (New York: Knopf, 2007), 1182.

143. Ibid., 604–605. Without the French Revolution and the turmoil it produced, there would have been no need for a General Bonaparte to restore order and thus no opportunity for Napoleon's becoming emperor. If Russia had lacked a tradition of autocracy, it might not have resisted Napoleon's advances. Had the various field commanders not given orders to fight, or had men ignored those orders, battle could not have happened. The Napoleonic Wars, like any other historical event, issued not from the will of one man alone, but occurred when a multitude of interrelated circumstances conspired.

144. Tolstoy, *War and Peace*, 605. Elsewhere in the novel, "Napoleon, during all this time of his activity, was like a child who, holding the straps tied inside a carriage, fancies that he is driving it" (1008).

145. Berlin, "Hedgehog," 26–27.

146. Tolstoy, "A Few Words," 1224.

147. Tolstoy, *War and Peace*, 605.

148. Again, Tolstoy's views and those of the narrator are one and the same: "Why did millions of men set about killing each other, if it has been known ever since the world began that it is both physically and morally bad? Because it was so inevitably necessary that, in fulfilling it, men were fulfilling that elementary zoological law which the bees fulfill by exterminating each other in the fall" ("A Few Words," 1222).

149. Tolstoy, *War and Peace*, 1138.

150. Troyat, *Tolstoy*, 342.

151. Ibid., 316. Tolstoy recounts his exposure to Schopenhauer in *A Confession*.

152. Tolstoy, *War and Peace*, 1208.

153. See Arthur Schopenhauer, *The World as Will and Representation*, trans. E. F. J. Payne, vol. 1 (New York, 1969). G. W. Spence describes Tolstoy's position: "the question arises whether we have any freewill at all. Our actions seem to be the result of our freewill only when we do not know by what they are conditioned or caused, but the more we know of the circumstances of an action, the less degree of freewill do we ascribe to it. No human action, in fact, can be completely dissociated from the conditions of place, time and cause" (G. W. Spence, "Tolstoy's Dualism," *Russian Review* 20, no. 3 [1961]: 220).

154. Tolstoy, "A Few Words," 1217.

155. Schopenhauer, *The World as Will and Representation*, 2:442, 444.

156. Elisabeth Stenbock-Fermor, *The Architecture of Anna Karenina: A History of Its Writing, Structure and Message* (Lisse: Peter de Ridder Press, 1975), 20.

157. Sigrid McLaughlin, "Some Aspects of Tolstoy's Intellectual Development: Tolstoy and Schopenhauer," *California Slavic Studies* 5 (1970).

158. Stenbock-Fermor, *Architecture*, 66.

159. Schopenhauer, *WWR:II*, 443.

160. Tolstóy, "Progress and the Definition of Education," 176.

161. Jean-Jacques Rousseau, *Discourse on the Origin and Foundation of Inequality Among Mankind*, in *The Social Contract and Discourse on the Origin and Foundation of Inequality Among Mankind*, ed. Lester G. Crocker (New York: Washington Square Press, 1967), 183.

162. Tolstóy, "Progress and the Definition of Education," 177.

163. Berlin, "Tolstoy and Enlightenment," 240.

164. Even Berlin acknowledges that Rousseau's influence "does not account for Tolstoy's theory of history, of which little trace can be found in the profoundly unhistorical Rousseau" (Berlin, "Hedgehog," 53).

165. Ibid., 162.

166. Ibid., 163.

167. Ibid., 167–168.

168. Ibid., 162.

169. Ibid., 173.

170. Ibid., 165.

171. Rene Fueloep-Miller, "Tolstoy the Apostolic Crusader," *Russian Review* 19, no. 2 (1960): 99.

172. See Leo Tolstoy, *What Is Art?: And Essays on Art*, trans. Aylmer Maude (New York: Oxford University Press, G. Cumberlege, 1930).

173. Spence, "Tolstoy's Dualism," *Russian Review* 20, no. 3 (1961): 217.

174. Tolstoy, "Progress and the Definition of Education," 163.

175. Tolstoy, *Confession*, 12.

176. Ibid., 65.

177. Alexandre Christoyannopoulos, "Turning the Other Cheek to Terrorism: Reflections on the Contemporary Significance of Leo Tolstoy's Exegesis of the Sermon on the Mount," *Politics and Religion* 1, no. 1 (2008): 34. Copleston makes a similar suggestion; see Copleston, *Philosophy in Russia*, 175.

178. Lev N. Tolstóy, *The Kingdom of God Is Within You*, in *The Kingdom of God Is Within You; Christianity and Patriotism; Miscellanies*, vol. 20 of *The Complete Works of Count Tolstóy*, trans. Leo Wiener (Boston, Dana Estes, 1905), 87.

179. Ibid., 35–36.

180. Desiderius Erasmus, *The Education of a Christian Prince*, trans. Neil M. Cheshire and Michael J. Heath (Cambridge: Cambridge University Press, 1997).

181. Max Weber, "Politics as a Vocation," in *From Max Weber: Essays in Sociology*, trans. Hans Gerth and C. Wright Mills (New York: Oxford University Press, 1946).

182. Tolstoy, *Kingdom of God*, 242.

183. Copleston, *Philosophy in Russia*, 176.

184. Janko Lavrin, "Tolstoy and Gandhi," *Russian Review* 19, no. 2 (1960): 136.

185. Berlin observes that "Tolstoy rejected political reform because he believed that ultimate regeneration could come only from within" (Berlin, "Hedgehog," 67).

186. Tolstoy, "Progress and the Definition of Education," 169. As Andreas Schönle notes, Tolstoy *wants* people to be self-reliant (Schönle, "Modernity as a 'Destroyed Anthill': Tolstoy on the History and Aesthetics of Ruins," in *Ruins of Modernity*, ed. Julia Hell and Andreas Schönle [Durham, NC: Duke University Press, 2010], 99).

187. Tolstoy, *Kingdom of God*, 236.

188. James Billington, *The Icon and the Axe* (New York: Knopf, 1966), 314.

189. Marc Raeff, *Understanding Imperial Russia*, trans. Arthur Goldhammer (New York: Columbia University Press, 1984), 35, 37. For more on the development of the "well-ordered police state," see Marc Raeff, *The Well-Ordered Police State: Social and Institutional Change Through Law in the Germanies and Russia; 1600–1800* (New Haven, CT.: Yale University Press, 1983).

190. Anderson, *Russian Political Thought*, 124–125.

191. Evgenii Anisimov, *The Reforms of Peter the Great: Progress Through Coercion in Russia*, trans. John T. Alexander (Armonk, NY: M.E. Sharpe, 1993), 298.

192. Evgenii Anisimov, "Progress Through Violence from Peter the Great to Lenin and Stalin," *Russian History* 17, no. 4 (1990): 409.

193. Raeff, *Understanding*, 96–97. Nicholas I, by contrast, did not have the same totalitarian bent or aggressive way of dealing with non-Russians in Russia's vicinity or Russia proper. "Nicholas lacked the one essential ingredient of every totalitarian system, namely, an ideology. Admittedly, the government did make some feeble attempts, none very successful, to elaborate a sort of theory or, rather, a legitimating rationale for its rule" (Raeff, *Understanding*, 148). In foreign policy, "the government of Nicholas I was primarily concerned with preserving the status quo, and not with cultural

and linguistic russification"; Andreas Kappeler, *The Russian Empire: A Multiethnic History* (Harlow: Longman, 2001), 250.

194. Cited in L. V. Cherepnin, "Tolstoy's Views on History," *Soviet Studies in History* 4, no. 2 (1965): 17.

195. Cited in Wilson, *Tolstoy*, 43.

196. Christoyannopoulos writes that Tolstoy "believed that, democratic or not, the state is a violent and deceitful institution. . . . Indeed, he was particularly suspicious of democratic states because of the aura of legitimacy which they claim for themselves" (Christoyannopoulos, "Tolstoy's Anarchist Denunciation of State Violence and Deception," in *Anti-Democratic Thought*, ed. Erich Kofmel [Charlottesville, VA: Imprint Academic, 2008], 85). See also Anderson, *Russian Political Thought*, 240.

197. Even Pierre Bezukhov, the Decembrist Tolstoy modeled after himself, calls for a "society of true conservatives" who will seek the reform of the tsarist system rather than pursue its violent overthrow (Tolstoy, *War and Peace*, 1169).

198. Tomáš Masaryk goes so far as to suggest similarities between Tolstoy and the man who ordered his excommunication, Konstantin Pobedonostsev, a latter-day defendant of Orthodoxy, autocracy, and nationality (Thomas Garrigue Masaryk, *The Spirit of Russia*, trans. Eden Paul and Cedar Paul (New York: Macmillan, 1955), 2: 205.

199. Wilson, *Tolstoy*, 191.

200. Nicholas V. Riasanovsky, *Nicholas I and Official Nationality in Russia, 1825–1855* (Berkeley: University of California Press, 1959), 226.

201. Slavenka Drakulić, *Café Europa* (New York: Norton, 1996), 30.

202. Gandhi, however, drew from Tolstoy.

203. Anderson, *Russian Political Thought*, 214.

204. Robert MacMaster, *Danilevsky: A Russian Totalitarian Philosopher* (Cambridge, MA: Harvard University Press, 1967), 18–20.

205. Nikolai I. Danilevskii, *Russia and Europe: The Slavic World's Political and Cultural Relations with the Germanic-Roman West*, trans. Stephen M. Woodburn (Bloomington, IN: Slavica, 2013), 73–74.

206. Ibid., 61.

207. Ibid., 71–72.

208. Danilevsky's thoughts on universal progress are actually mixed. He does suggest that one people can build off of another. But he is against the Western theory of progress that puts Europe at the vanguard, leading the rest of the world on a forward march. See ibid., 56–57, 72.

209. Ibid., 342, 435.

210. Ibid., 412.

211. Ibid., 420.

212. This "all-Slavic" union would also include non-Slavic peoples like Greeks, Romanians, and Hungarians.

213. Ibid., 291.

214. Ibid., 369.

215. He himself writes that for all the work's literary merits, the philosophical aspects of *War and Peace* are "irrelevant" but easy enough to "slough off" (432).

216. Ibid., 234.

## Chapter 3. "The Path to Hell"

Note to epigraph: Brooks Adams's wife suggested "The Path to Hell: A Story Book" as a title for what would be called instead *The Law of Civilization and Decay*, Brooks Adams's best-known work. As will be shown, Henry Adams shared his brother's belief that the United States was headed straight to perdition. Arthur F. Beringause, *Brooks Adams: A Biography* (New York: Knopf, 1955), 115.

Epigraph: Henry Adams, *Henry Adams and His Friends; A Collection of His Unpublished Letters*, Comp. Harold Dean Cater, (Boston: Houghton Mifflin, 1947), 529.

1. Rutherford E. Delmage, "The American Idea of Progress, 1750–1800," *Proceedings of the American Philosophical Society* 91, no. 4 (1947): 313.

2. Robert A. Nisbet, *History of the Idea of Progress* (New Brunswick, NJ: Transaction, 1994), 193.

3. Ibid., 198. For Adams's sometimes favorable and occasionally skeptical comments on Turgot, Condorcet, and other "prophets of progress," see Zoltán Haraszti, *John Adams and the Prophets of Progress* (Cambridge, MA: Harvard University Press, 1952).

4. Margarita Mathiopoulos, *History and Progress: In Search of the European and American Mind* (New York: Praeger, 1989), 109.

5. As Hannah Arendt notes, the founders viewed themselves as such: not as constructors of something that would be unchanging, but as beginners of a project who knew that their creation (the Constitution) would develop further (Arendt, *On Revolution* [New York: Penguin, 2006], 194–196).

6. The idea of progress in American thought both postdates and antedates the founding. See Delmage, "American Idea," for examples of pre-independence promulgations of the idea.

7. Dorothy Ross, "Historical Consciousness in Nineteenth-Century America," *American Historical Review* 89, no. 4 (1984): 912.

8. Warren I. Susman, "History and the American Intellectual: Uses of a Usable Past," *American Quarterly* 16, no. 2 (1964): 252–253.

9. Thomas L. Pangle, *The Spirit of Modern Republicanism: The Moral Vision of the American Founders and the Philosophy of Locke* (Chicago: University of Chicago Press, 1990), 7, 104.

10. Ernst Breisach, *American Progressive History: An Experiment in Modernization* (Chicago: University of Chicago Press, 1993), 20.

11. The themes of Bancroft's 1854 speech are present, as well, in his monumental *History of the United States* (1834–1874). There, Bancroft tells his reader that "the

inference that there is progress in human affairs" is justified (Bancroft, *History of the United States: From the Discovery of the American Continent*, 19th ed., vol. 3 [Boston: Little and Brown, 1841], 398).

12. George Bancroft, *The Necessity, the Reality and the Promise of the Progress of the Human Race; Oration Delivered Before the New-York Historical Society*, November 20, 1854 (New York: New-York Historical Society, 1854), 13.

13. Ibid., 17.

14. Ibid., 21–23, 35.

15. Ibid., 34.

16. Ibid., 36.

17. John Lothrop Motley, *Historic Progress and American Democracy: An Address Delivered Before the New-York Historical Society at Their Sixty-Fourth Anniversary* (New York: Scribner, 1869), 6.

18. Ibid., 16–17.

19. Ibid., 29.

20. Ibid., 44. Motley also writes: "The effect of the triumph of freedom in this country on the cause of progress in Europe is plain" (39). He makes similar assertions in other writings, such as "Polity of the Puritans," where he suggests that the United States is a country "in whose progress the general cause of humanity is benefited" (Motley, "Review: *Geschichte der Colonisation von Neu-England: Von den Ersten Niederlassungen Daselbst im Jahre 1607, bis zur Einführung der Provinzialverfassung von Massachusetts im Jahre 1692* by Talvj [Polity of the Puritans]," *North American Review* 69, no. 145 (1849): 496. He argues further that the conclusion of the American Civil War meant that "the standing reproach to Democracy" had been removed and that the basis of American institutions was generally recognized as "an everlasting truth" (Motley, *Historic Progress*, 69).

21. David D. Van Tassel, "From Learned Society to Professional Organization: The American Historical Association, 1884–1900," *American Historical Review* 89, no. 4 (1984): 933; Michael Kraus and Davis D. Joyce, *The Writing of American History* (Norman: University of Oklahoma Press, 1985), 136; Gerald N. Grob and George Athan Billias, *Interpretations of American History: Patterns and Perspectives*, vol. 1, *To 1877* (New York: Free Press, 1992), 6.

22. W. Stull Holt, "The Idea of Scientific History in America," *Journal of the History of Ideas* 1, no. 3 (1940): 355; Georg G. Iggers, "The Image of Ranke in American and German Historical Thought," *History and Theory* 2, no. 1 (1962): 18.

23. Holt, "Idea of Scientific History," 352–353.

24. John Fiske, "Manifest Destiny," in *American Political Ideas Viewed from the Standpoint of Universal History: Three Lectures Delivered at the Royal Institution of Great Britain in May, 1880* (New York: Houghton Mifflin, 1911), 95.

25. Ibid., 99. In addition to authoring many historical works, Fiske wrote extensively on Darwinism. See, for instance, John Fiske, *Darwinism and Other Essays* (Boston: Houghton Mifflin, 1879/1885).

26. Fiske, "Manifest Destiny," 98–99, 128, 142.

27. Ibid., 99.

28. Ibid., 143. Fiske asks: "does it not seem very probable that in due course of time Europe—which has learned some valuable lessons from America already—will find it worth while to adopt the lesson of federalism?" (136). Here he sounds reminiscent of Immanuel Kant, who likewise endorsed the federative principle and who asserted that peace was a prerequisite for other types of improvement. Kant argued that "wars by which states in turn try to encroach upon or subjugate one another [must] at last bring them, even against their will, to enter into a *cosmopolitan constitution*." (Kant, "On the Common Saying: That May Be Correct in Theory, But It Is of No Use in Practice," in *Practical Philosophy*, ed. Mary J. Gregor [New York: Cambridge University Press, 1996], 307). Their having joined together allows states to coexist peacefully, and, having attained such peace, "progress toward the better is assured humanity" (Kant, "An Old Question Raised Again: Is the Human Race Constantly Progressing," in *Religion and Rational Theology*, ed. Allen W. Wood and George di Giovanni, trans. Mary J. Gregor and Robert Anchor [New York: Cambridge University Press, 1996], 302).

29. Fiske, "Manifest Destiny," 142.

30. Herbert Baxter Adams, *The Germanic Origin of New England Towns: Read Before the Harvard Historical Society, May 9, 1881* (Baltimore: Johns Hopkins University Press, 1882), 8.

31. Ibid., 23. Elsewhere, he writes that "the most striking indication of historic connection between the village communities of New England and those of the Old World lies in the sovereignty of the people" (33).

32. As Dorothy Ross puts it, Adams harbored "a conservative attachment to liberal democracy" (Ross, "Historical Consciousness," 924). For more on how the idea of progress was used for conservative ends in the United States, see Welter, "Idea of Progress in America: An Essay in Ideas and Method," *Journal of the History of Ideas* 16, no. 3 (1955).

33. Frederick Jackson Turner, "The Significance of the Frontier in American History," in *The Frontier in American History* (New York: Henry Holt, 1921), 2.

34. Ibid., 3.

35. Ibid., 30.

36. Ibid., 32, 37.

37. Ibid., 30.

38. Lloyd E. Ambrosius, *Wilsonian Statecraft: Theory and Practice of Liberal Internationalism During World War I* (Wilmington, DE: SR Books, 1991), 8.

39. Ralph Henry Gabriel and Robert Harris Walker, *The Course of American Democratic Thought* (New York: Greenwood, 1986), 319.

40. Bancroft, *Necessity*, 36.

41. Richard Hofstadter, *The Progressive Historians: Turner, Beard, Parrington* (New York: Knopf, 1968), 85, 106.

42. As Christopher Lasch puts it: "American historical writing . . . takes little account of the possibility of tragedy—missed opportunities, fatal choices, conclusive and irrevocable defeats. History has to have a happy ending" (Lasch, *The True and Only Heaven: Progress and Its Critics* [New York: Norton, 1991], 221).

43. Henry Adams, *The Education of Henry Adams*, in *Novels; Mont Saint Michel; The Education*, comp. Ernest Samuels and Jayne N. Samuels (New York: Library of America, 1983), 734.

44. In the course of his career as a historian, Adams would also come to know Frederick Jackson Turner, a native Midwesterner.

45. Edward Chalfant, *Better in Darkness: A Biography of Henry Adams; His Second Life, 1862–1891* (Hamden, CT: Archon, 1994), 786. Adams taught at Harvard from 1870 to 1877.

46. Garry Wills writes: "In the *Education*, astonishingly, Adams would claim that he never accepted the Teutonic thesis, though his writings and those of his students prove that this is false" (Wills, *Henry Adams and the Making of America* [Boston: Houghton Mifflin, 2005], 93).

47. Kraus and Joyce, *Writing*, 152.

48. Jurgen Herbst, *The German Historical School in American Scholarship: A Study in the Transfer of Culture* (Ithaca, NY: Cornell University Press, 1965), 35.

49. Grob and Billias, *Interpretations*, 7.

50. Ernest Samuels, *The Young Henry Adams* (Cambridge, MA: Harvard University Press, 1965), 267.

51. Gabriel and Walker, *Course*, 328.

52. Hofstadter writes of Adams: "Others might see scientific history as a surer way of plotting the advance of mankind toward some freer or better state of things—and there are in fact a few passages even in Adams that suggest a momentary concurrence with the idea. But more often than not, his native mordant alienation asserted itself, and then one sees his essential view of the matter: scientific history shows man in the grip of natural impulsions that carry him to ends determined neither by ideals nor by anyone's well-formulated purposes but to a destiny of nature's own" (*Progressive*, 32–33).

53. Adams, *Education*, 945.

54. Ibid., 959.

55. Wills, *Henry Adams*, 5.

56. Ernest Samuels writes of *Democracy*'s reception: "The book provoked an angry and baffled clamor from American reviewers, and an occasional grudging admission that it hit the mark, but in general they played down the sensational implications." In England, "all the periodicals treated it as a major literary event and devoted column after column to praise the force of its satire and literary artistry" (Samuels, *Henry Adams: The Middle Years* [Cambridge, MA: Belknap Press of Harvard University Press, 1958], 86–87).

57. Henry Adams, *Democracy*, in *Novels*, comp. Samuels and Samuels, 7.

58. Ibid., 12.

59. Ibid., 39.

60. Ibid., 182.

61. Catherine Zuckert, "On Reading Classic American Novelists as Political Thinkers," *Journal of Politics* 43, no. 3 (1981): 686.

62. Elisha Greifer, "The Conservative Pose in America: The Adamses' Search for a Pre-Liberal Past," *Western Political Quarterly* 15, no. 1 (1962): 10.

63. Michael Colacurcio, "Democracy and Esther: Henry Adams's Flirtation with Pragmatism," in *A Political Companion to Henry Adams*, ed. Natalie F. Taylor (Lexington: University Press of Kentucky, 2010), 69.

64. Samuels, *Henry Adams*, 69–70.

65. B. H. Gilley, "Democracy: Henry Adams and the Role of Political Leader," in Taylor, *Political Companion to Henry Adams*, 49.

66. Denise Dutton offers an interesting alternative interpretation of *Democracy*. She argues that readers ought to "resist this temptation to assume that Adams endorses Mrs. Lee's resignation from democracy and that he shares her disparaging judgment of it" (Dutton, "Henry Adams's Democracy: Novel Sources of Democratic Virtues," in Taylor, *Political Companion to Henry Adams*, 83). In her heterodox reading, Dutton argues that readers tend to overlook the novel's secondary characters, who "affirm the moral promise of democracy" (84). While I agree that characters other than Mrs. Lee sometimes speak for Adams, I reject the view that the takeaway message of *Democracy* is that "the realization of democracy's morally distinctive promise depends on our willingness to believe in its promise" (103).

67. Ernest Samuels and Jayne Samuels, "Notes," in Adams, *Novels*, 1229.

68. Vernon Louis Parrington, *Main Currents in American Thought: An Interpretation of American Literature from the Beginnings to 1920*, vol. 3 (New York: Harcourt Brace, 1930), 170.

69. Adams, *Democracy*, 12.

70. Ibid., 91.

71. Ibid., 74.

72. Ibid., 169.

73. Ibid., 42.

74. Ibid., 76.

75. Ibid., 95.

76. Ibid., 17.

77. Ibid., 58.

78. Ibid., 162.

79. Ibid., 37.

80. Ibid., 184.

81. Ibid., 91.

82. Ibid., 18.

83. Ibid., 52.

84. Ibid., 56.

85. Ibid., 44.

86. Ibid., 44.

87. Ibid., 55.

88. Ibid., 168.

89. Alexis de Tocqueville, *Democracy in America: And Two Essays on America*, trans. Gerald E. Bevan (London: Penguin, 2003), 229.

90. John Stuart Mill, *On Liberty* (Mineola, NY: Dover, 2002), 17.

91. Cited in Samuels, *Young Henry*, 136.

92. Robert Dawidoff observes that "Henry Adams borrowed a Tocquevillian attitude that . . . claimed a detachment from what it observed and never acknowledged kinship with what it described. His writing was distinguished and cosmopolitan, deliberately meant to stand apart from the rest of America" (Dawidoff, *The Genteel Tradition and the Sacred Rage: High Culture Vs. Democracy in Adams, James, and Santayana* [Chapel Hill: University of North Carolina Press 1992], 38). Matthew J. Mancini, however, argues that parallels between Adams and Tocqueville are largely superficial: "it is difficult to detect overt signs in the forms of concepts, themes or methods of Tocqueville that appeared in the later work of the great American pessimist" (Mancini, *Alexis de Tocqueville and American Intellectuals: From His Times to Ours* [Lanham, MD: Rowman & Littlefield, 2006], 128).

93. Alan S. Kahan notes that Tocqueville later tempered his optimistic views (Kahan, *Alexis de Tocqueville* [New York: Continuum 2010], 42). Aurelian Craiutu and Jeremy Jennings likewise observe of Tocqueville at the time he composed Volume 1 of *Democracy in America*, that "in spite of his musings about the tyranny of the majority," his "words offered a reassuring confidence in the future of the country, based on his image of America as an accomplished and mature democracy, capable of overcoming its challenges" (Craiutu and Jennings, "The Third Democracy: Tocqueville's Views of America After 1840," *American Political Science Review* 98, no. 3 [2004], 396). They note that Tocqueville later qualified his favorable outlook for America and democracy: "As he neared the end of his time, there appeared little cause for optimism that the cause of liberty would triumph and now not even the inspiration derived from America remained" (403).

94. Mill, *On Liberty*, 1, 9, 29.

95. Ibid., 95.

96. Adams, *Democracy*, 39.

97. Ibid., 45.

98. Ibid., 178.

99. Arthur Herman, *The Idea of Decline in Western History* (New York: Free Press, 1997), 158.

100. Brooks D. Simpson, *The Political Education of Henry Adams* (Columbia: University of South Carolina Press, 1996), xiv; Chalfant, *Better*, 164.

101. Grob and Billias refer to Adams's *History* as "one of the classics of American historical literature" (Grob and Billias, *Interpretations*, 7). Kraus and Joyce suggest that Adams's writings "mark one of the highest achievements in American historiography" (Kraus and Joyce, *Writing*, 163). Thomas Bender refers to Adams as "the greatest American historian of the nineteenth century and perhaps the finest ever" (Bender, "Writing American History: 1789–1945," in *The Oxford History of Historical Writing*, vol. 4, ed. Stuart Macintyre, Juan Maiguascha, and Attila Pók [Oxford: Oxford University Press, 2011], 376).

102. Henry Steele Commager goes so far as to credit Adams as "the only American historian who has ever seriously attempted to formulate a philosophy of history" (cited in Kraus and Joyce, *Writing*, 160–161).

103. Adams, *Education*, 1090.

104. Henry Adams, "A Letter to American Teachers of History," in Brooks Adams, ed., *The Degradation of the Democratic Dogma* (New York, P. Smith, 1949), 191.

105. Ibid., 231.

106. Ibid., 186. Adams was almost assuredly correct in his belief that the idea of progress was gaining ever greater currency. Pangle suggests that the idea was more attractive in the nineteenth century than the century it followed; Pangle, *Spirit*, 7, 104. Warren Wagar notes that "the belief in progress reached its apogee just before 1914," i.e., on the eve of World War I (Wagar, *Good Tidings: The Belief in Progress from Darwin to Marcuse* [Bloomington: Indiana University Press, 1972], 9).

107. Adams, "Letter," 228.

108. Henry Adams, "The Rule of Phase Applied to History," in Brooks Adams, *Degradation of the Democratic Dogma*, 283.

109. William H. Jordy, *Henry Adams: Scientific Historian* (New Haven, CT: Yale University Press, 1953), 132.

110. Adams, "Letter," 156. Judith N. Shklar declares Adams's decision to model his philosophy of history on physics to have been "disastrous." Her reading of Adams is far less charitable than most, however: she refers to him as "an ill-tempered bigot" with a case of "sour grapes" (Shklar, " 'The Education of Henry Adams' by Henry Adams," *Daedalus* 103, no. 1 [1974]: 65–66).

111. Adams, "Letter," 148.

112. Adams, "Rule," 270.

113. Adams, "Letter," 148.

114. Adams, "Rule," 282.

115. Adams, "Letter," 191.

116. Ibid., 157.

117. Ibid., 218.

118. Ibid., 157.

119. Adams, *Education*, 963.

120. Henry Adams, *Selected Letters*, ed. Ernest Samuels (Cambridge, MA: Belknap Press of Harvard University Press, 1992), 309.

121. Francis G. Wilson, "Pessimism in American Politics," *Journal of Politics* 7, no. 2 (1945): 138, 140. Andrew R. Murphy writes about the tradition of the jeremiad in American thought from colonial times to the present. Individuals who issued jeremiads, like Wilson's contingent pessimists, warned of doom unless their fellows reformed themselves and/or institutions (Murphy, *Prodigal Nation: Moral Decline and Divine Punishment from New England to 9/11* [Oxford: Oxford University Press, 2009]).

122. Roger V. Shumate, "The Political Philosophy of Henry Adams," *American Political Science Review* 28, no. 4 (1934): 608.

123. Daniel Aaron, *Men of Good Hope: A Story of American Progressives* (New York: Oxford University Press, 1961), 276.

124. Henry's essays, in turn, led Brooks to refine his ideas. Thornton Anderson, *Brooks Adams: Constructive Conservative* (Ithaca, NY: Cornell University Press, 1951), 166. See also Beringause, *Brooks Adams*.

125. Henry Adams, letter to Elizabeth Cameron, October 4, 1895, in *The Letters of Henry Adams, Vol. IV, 1892–1899*, ed. J.C. Levenson, Ernest Samuels, Charles Vandersee, and Viola H. Winner (Cambridge, MA: Belknap Press of Harvard University Press, 1988), 335–336.

126. Henry Adams, *Education*, 1030.

127. James P. Young, for instance, argues that Henry "did not subscribe to a theory of the 'degradation of the democratic dogma,'" and that Brooks was reading his own opinions into his brother's work (Young, *Henry Adams: The Historian as Political Theorist* [Lawrence: University Press of Kansas, 2001], 203).

128. Adams, *Education*, 1035. Private letters reveal Henry's preoccupation with the unhealthy influence of capitalism on democracy. In a letter to Brooks, for instance, he laments that he has "ceased even to be shocked at the corruption of money" (Adams, *Selected Letters*, 386). In his later life, he could no longer idolize Mill, to whom he disparagingly referred as "his Satanic free trade majesty" (Adams, *Education*, 786).

129. Brooks Adams, "The Heritage of Henry Adams," in Adams, *Degradation of the Democratic Dogma* 78.

130. Ibid., 121.

131. Brooks Adams, "Introductory Note," in Adams, *Degradation of the Democratic Dogma*, viii. Decades prior to penning his essays on history, Henry suggested (through the heroine of his first novel) that "the end of American society" entails that "there will be no order" (Adams, *Democracy*, 45). To Brooks, such an end is part and parcel to democracy, which he defines as "an infinite mass of conflicting minds and of conflicting interests" (Adams, "Heritage," 109).

132. "The relationship between industrialism and democracy," a more contemporary critic writes, "looks more and more tenuous and problematical." Greater productivity, Lasch observes, in no way guarantees a more equitable society; resources may, in fact, become ever more concentrated in the hands of the few (Lasch, *True and Only*, 157).

133. Cited in Benjamin R. Barber, "Three Scenarios for the Future of Technology and Strong Democracy," *Political Science Quarterly* 113, no. 4 (1998): 574. See this same article for Barber's thoughts on the possible effects of technological change on democratic governance.

134. Patrick J. Deneen argues that, rather than fearing that the dynamo would bring about a new multiplicity, Adams actually worried that technological advances would erase real differences: "he detected the evisceration of actual diversity and distinctive cultures before the leveling power of the machine" (Deneen, "Mont-Saint-Michel and Chartres: From Unity to Multiplicity," in Taylor, *Political Companion to Henry Adams*, 177).

135. Adams, "Heritage," 109. See Jordy, *Henry Adams*, for a more in-depth discussion of Henry's idea of phase. Jordy notes that Adams predicted "oblivion" by 1921, a year we have since passed (154).

136. Brooks Adams, "The Revolt of Modern Democracy Against Standards of Duty," in *The Portable Conservative Reader*, ed. Russell Kirk (New York: Viking, 1982), 355.

137. Adams, *Education*, 1124.

138. Ibid., 1126.

139. Ibid., 1124–1125.

140. Pierre Manent highlights this same passage from *The Education* to show another similarity between Tocqueville and his later American follower (Manent, *Tocqueville and the Nature of Democracy* [Lanham, MD, Rowman & Littlefield, 1996], 84, 143).

141. William A. Williams, "Brooks Adams and American Expansion," *New England Quarterly* 25, no. 2 (1952): 218.

142. Brooks Adams, *The Law of Civilization and Decay: An Essay on History* (New York: Macmillan, 1895), iv–vi.

143. During the long period of their collaboration, Arthur Beringause writes, "Henry remained the diagnostician, while Brooks gradually became convinced that he could and should act as physician to the ailing world" (Beringause, *Brooks Adams*, 133).

144. Brooks Adams, *America's Economic Supremacy* (New York: Macmillan, 1900), 12.

145. Ibid., 18.

146. Ibid., 12.

147. Adams, *Law of Civilization*, vi.

148. Adams, *America's Economic Supremacy*, 50.

149. Ibid., 12.

150. Ibid., 51–52.

151. Ibid., 24.

152. Ibid., 24–25.

153. Cited in Beringause, *Brooks Adams*, 208–209.

154. Anderson says that Brooks himself ultimately reversed course: "from the high point of his optimism, which was probably reached shortly after the annexation of the Philippines and which sustained him during his career at Boston University, he underwent a progressive and complete surrender to a pessimism matching that of his brother Henry" (Anderson, *Brooks Adams*, 166).

155. Arthur Schopenhauer, *The World as Will and Representation*, vol. 2, trans. E. F. J. Payne (New York: Dover, 1969), 442.

156. Cited in Adams, "Heritage," 99.

157. Adams, *Democracy*, 178.

158. Hofstadter, *Progressive*, 30.

159. Cited in Natalie F. Taylor, "Introduction: The Literary Statesmanship of Henry Adams," in Taylor, *A Political Companion to Henry Adams*, 2.

160. Adams, "Heritage," 6.

161. The exact phrase appears in Adams, *Education*, 1090–1093, while variants appear in private letters.

162. Ibid., 1027.

163. Ibid., 751.

164. For more on Adams's anarchism, see J. C. Levenson, *The Mind and Art of Henry Adams* (Boston: Houghton Mifflin, 1957), 296–302, and Caroline V. Hamilton, "Henry Adams and Andrei Bely: The Explosive Mind," *Anarchist Studies* 18, no. 2 (2010): 58–84. For a related discussion of Adams's resistance to social legislation, see Jordy, *Henry Adams*, 136–137.

165. Cited in Adams, "Heritage," 99.

166. In *Education*, Henry acknowledges having paid special attention to the conclusions Brooks reached in *The Law of Civilization and Decay* (Adams, *Education*, 1030).

167. "Marcus Aurelius would have been my type of highest human attainment" (Adams, *Selected Letters*, 542).

168. Russell L. Hanson and W. Richard Merriam, "Henry Adams and the Decline of the Republican Tradition," in Taylor, *Political Companion to Henry Adams*, 22.


Chapter 4. Critics of the Idea of Progress in an Age of Extremes

1. Oswald Spengler, *The Decline of the West*, vol. 2, trans. Charles F. Atkinson (New York: Knopf, 1992), 398. Hereafter cited as *DOW:II*.

2. Ibid., 440.

3. Ibid., 441.

4. Ibid., 369.

5. Oswald Spengler, *The Decline of the West*, vol. 1, trans. Charles F. Atkinson (New York: Knopf, 1992), 4. Hereafter cited as *DOW:I*.

6. Ibid., 32.

7. Plato, *The Republic*, ed. G. R. F. Ferrari, trans. Tom Griffith (Cambridge: Cambridge University Press, 2000), 269–270.

8. Spengler, *DOW:I*, 26.

9. Ibid. 44.

10. Plato, *Republic*, 269.

11. Spengler, *DOW:I*, 44.

12. Ibid., 40. Compare with Brooks Adams: "as consolidation apparently nears its climax, art seems to presage approaching disintegration. The architecture, the sculpture, and the coinage of London at the close of the nineteenth century, when compared with those of the Paris of Saint Louis, recall the Rome of Caracalla as contrasted with the Athens of Pericles, save that we lack the stream of barbarian blood which made the Middle Age" (Adams, *Law of Civilization*, 383).

13. Ibid., 41.

14. "Spengler Speaks," *Time* 23, no. 7 (1934): 69.

15. Georg Iggers, *The German Conception of History: The National Tradition of Historical Thought from Herder to the Present* (Middletown, CT: Wesleyan University Press, 1968), 241.

16. H. Stuart Hughes, *Oswald Spengler: A Critical Estimate* (New York: Scribner, 1952), 97.

17. Oswald Spengler, "Pessimism?," in *Selected Essays*, trans. Donald O. White (Chicago: Regnery, 1967), 154.

18. "Spengler Speaks," 69.

19. Hans W. Weigert, "The Future in Retrospect: Oswald Spengler Twenty-Five Years After," *Foreign Affairs* 21, no. 1 (1942): 123. Weigert did, however, acknowledge that Spenglerism and Hitlerism were not one and the same.

20. Cited in Arthur Herman, *The Idea of Decline in Western History* (New York: Free Press, 1997), 250.

21. Cited in Hughes, *Oswald Spengler*, 127.

22. Cited in John Farrenkopf, *Prophet of Decline: Spengler on World History and Politics* (Baton Rouge: Louisiana State University Press, 2001), 238.

23. Ibid., 237.

24. Herman, *Idea*, 251.

25. Farrenkopf, *Prophet*, 239.

26. Cited in Hughes, *Oswald Spengler*, 133.

27. Alfred Rosenberg, *The Myth of the Twentieth Century: An Evaluation of the Spiritual-Intellectual Confrontations of Our Age* (Torrance, CA: Noontide, 1982), 424.

28. Farrenkopf, *Prophet*, 264.

29. John J. Reilly, "Review: John Farrenkopf, *Prophet of Decline: Spengler on World History and Politics*," *Comparative Civilizations Review* 49 (2003): 152.

30. Northrop Frye, "*The Decline of the West* by Oswald Spengler," *Daedalus* 103, no. 1 (1974): 8.

31. Hughes, *Oswald Spengler*, 132. Take, for instance, Spengler's claim that "war is the creator of all great things. All that is meaningful in the stream of life has emerged through victory and defeat" (Spengler, *DOW:II*, 363). Consider too the claims that "imperialism is so necessary a product of any Civilization that when a people refuses to assume the rôle of master, it is seized and pushed into it" and that "life if it would be great, is hard; it lets choose *only* between victory and ruin, not between war and peace, and to the victory belong the sacrifices of victory" (422, 429).

32. Farrenkopf, *Prophet*, 240.

33. Spengler, *DOW:II*, 431.

34. Ibid., 442.

35. Ibid., 445. There is a curious parallel with Joseph de Maistre, who was also preoccupied with war. Maistre writes in *Considerations on France*: "Mankind may be considered as a tree which and invisible hand is continually pruning and which often profits from the operation. . . . Moreover, following the same comparison, we may observe that the skillful gardener directs the pruning less towards lush vegetation than towards the fructification of the tree; he wants fruit, not wood or leaves" (de Maistre, *Considerations on France* [Cambridge: Cambridge University Press, 1994], 28–29).

36. Cited in Hughes, *Oswald Spengler*, 129.

37. Farrenkopf, *Prophet*, 186.

38. Ibid., 246.

39. Ibid., 240.

40. Hughes, *Oswald Spengler*, 132.

41. Oswald Spengler, *Man and Technics: A Contribution to a Philosophy of Life* (London: Allen & Unwin), 1932.

42. Spengler, *DOW:II*, 435.

43. Ibid., 370.

44. Moreover, Spengler thought that Burckhardt and Nietzsche erred by focusing only on the best of Greek culture, not the culture in its entirety (*DOW:I*, 28).

45. Spengler, *DOW:I*, 18.

46. Spengler, *DOW:II*, 430.

47. "Short" when measured against the eternity of world history.

48. Oswald Spengler, *Prussianism and Socialism*, in *Selected Essays* (Chicago: Regnery, 1967), 78.

49. Ibid., 72.

50. Ibid., 44.

51. Ibid., 67.

52. Ibid., 44.

53. Ibid., 40.

54. Ibid., 47.

55. Ibid., 122. The "socialism" Spengler describes would be termed "corporatism" today. Spengler takes great pains to differentiate his true socialism from the false socialism peddled by Marx, whom he repeatedly brands as an "English" thinker (see, for

instance, 42, 95, 97–98, 100, 102). To Spengler, Marxism is an egoistic philosophy that rests on class antagonisms, stokes resentment and reprisals, and exalts sloth. Proper socialism, by contrast, "does not mean nationalization by expropriation or theft. It is not at all concerned with nominal property, but rather with the techniques of administration. . . . Socialization means the slow, decades-long transformation of the worker into an economic civil servant, of the employer into a responsible administrative official with extensive powers of authority, and of property into a kind of old-style hereditary fief to which a certain number of rights and privileges are attached" (120).

56. Spengler dismisses out of hand the philosophical traditions emanating from non-Teutonic countries of Europe. "Of all Western nations," he writes, "France and Italy have not brought forth a single political idea" (ibid., 79). He is particularly mocking of the "anarchic" French (111). Drawing inferences from the sartorial habits of West Europeans, he observes that "the Frenchman gives his creative attention to women's fashion rather than the uniforms of profession and success. In France, business and civic duty have had to give way to *l'amour*" (49).

57. Ibid., 67.

58. Ibid., 69.

59. See Paul Gottfried for more on Spengler's Sparta-Prussia comparison; Paul Gottfried, "Oswald Spengler and the Inspiration of the Classical Age," *Modern Age* 26, no. 1 (1982): 68–75.

60. Ibid., 20.

61. Ibid., 89.

62. Ibid., 67, 90.

63. Ibid., 70.

64. Theodor Adorno, "Spengler After the Decline," in Theodor Adorno, *Prisms*, trans. Samuel Weber and Shierry Weber (Cambridge: Cambridge University Press, 1981), 54.

65. Spengler makes his wishes perfectly clear to his German audience, ending his political tract by stating: "We are socialists. Let us hope that it will not have been in vain" (*Prussianism and Socialism*, 131).

66. Spengler, *DOW:I*, xiv.

67. Ibid., 16.

68. Spengler, *DOW:II*, 196.

69. Aleksandr Solzhenitsyn, "Templeton Lecture," in *The Solzhenitsyn Reader: New and Essential Writings, 1947–2005*, ed. Edward E. Ericson, Jr., and Daniel J. Mahoney (Wilmington, DE: ISI, 2006), 581.

70. Cited in Hilton Kramer, "A Talk with Solzhenitsyn," *New York Times Book Review*, May 1, 1980, 3.

71. Aleksandr I. Solzhenitsyn, "A World Split Apart," in *Solzhenitsyn at Harvard: The Address; Twelve Early Responses, and Six Later Reflections*, ed. Ronald Berman (Washington, DC: Ethics and Public Policy Center, 1980), 12.

72. Ibid., 19.

73. Ibid., 13.

74. Ibid., 5–7.

75. Ibid., 16.

76. Solzhenitsyn, "Templeton Lecture," 584.

77. Aleksandr Solzhenitsyn, "A Reflection on the Vendée Uprising," in *The Sol-zhenitsyn Reader: New and Essential Writings, 1947–2005*, ed. Edward E. Ericson, Jr., and Daniel J. Mahoney (Wilmington, DE: 2006), 605.

78. Aleksandr Solzhenitsyn, "We Have Ceased to See the Purpose," in Ericson, Jr., and Mahoney, *The Solzhenitsyn Reader*, 594.

79. Ibid., 598.

80. Ibid., 595.

81. Ibid., 594.

82. Aleksandr I. Solzhenitsyn, "Letter to the Soviet Leaders," trans. Hilary Stern-berg, in *East and West* (New York: Harper & Row, 1980), 94–95.

83. Ibid., 98.

84. Solzhenitsyn writes about post-communism: "The environs of our cities are befouled by the effluents of our primitive industry, we have poisoned our rivers, lakes, and fish, and today we are obliterating our last resources of clean water, air, and soil. . . . Depleting our natural wealth for the sake of grandiose future conquests under a crazed leadership, we have . . . plundered our earth of its incomparable riches" (Solzhenitsyn, *Rebuilding Russia*, trans. Alexis Klimoff [New York: Farrar, Straus and Giroux1991], 4).

85. Solzhenitsyn, "World Split," 13. Solzhenitsyn says, as well, that "different parts of the world have followed different paths, but today they are all approaching the threshold of a common ruin" (Solzhenitsyn, "Templeton Lecture," 579).

86. James Reston, "A Russian at Harvard," in *Solzhenitsyn at Harvard: The Address; Twelve Early Responses, and Six Later Reflections*, ed. Ronald Berman (Washington, DC: Ethics and Public Policy Center, 1980), 38.

87. *Washington Post*, "Mr. Solzhenitsyn as Witness," in ibid., 26.

88. Mary McGrory, "Solzhenitsyn Doesn't Love Us," in ibid., 61.

89. Charles Kessler, "Up from Modernity," in ibid., 48.

90. Ibid., 56.

91. George Will, "Solzhenitsyn's Critics," in ibid., 34. The political right in the United States did not accept all Solzhenitsyn's ideas. According to a *National Review* editorial, for instance: "surrounding these core assertions [of Solzhenitsyn's] are others, arguable, dubious, or self-evidently false" (*National Review*, "Thoughts on Sol-zhenitsyn," in ibid., 31).

92. Arthur Schlesinger, Jr., "The Solzhenitsyn We Refuse to See," in ibid., 68.

93. Ibid., 66–67.

94. Jack Fruchtman, Jr., "A Voice from Russia's Past at Harvard," in ibid., 44.

95. Daniel Mahoney, *The Other Solzhenitsyn: Telling the Truth* (South Bend, IN: St. Augustine's Press, 2014), 192. Solzhenitsyn saw truth in religions other than Christianity, too.

96. Cited in Joseph Pearce, *Solzhenitsyn: A Soul in Exile* (Grand Rapids, MI: Baker Books, 2001), 278.

97. Solzhenitsyn, *Rebuilding*, 60.

98. Cited in James Pontuso, *Solzhenitsyn's Political Thought* (Charlottesville, VA: University of Virginia Press, 1990), 210.

99. Solzhenitsyn, "We Have Ceased," 599.

100. Solzhenitsyn, *Rebuilding*, 82.

101. Marcus G. Raskin associates Solzhenitsyn with "pan-Slav nationalism" (Raskin, *Liberalism: The Genius of American Ideals* [Lanham, MD: Rowman & Littlefield, 2004], 216). Tim McDaniel counts him as one of the "neo-Slavophile dissidents of the Brezhnev period" who "passionately insisted on the uniqueness and superiority of Russia" (McDaniel, *The Agony of the Russian Idea* [Princeton, NJ: Princeton University Press, 1996], 10).

102. Solzhenitsyn, *Rebuilding*, 10.

103. Aleksandr Solzhenitsyn, "Repentance and Self-Limitation in the Life of Nations," in Ericson and Mahoney, *The Solzhenitsyn Reader*, 539.

104. Solzhenitsyn, *Rebuilding*, 21.

105. Ibid., 17–18.

106. Edward E. Ericson, Jr., and Alexis Klimoff, *The Soul and Barbed Wire: An Introduction to Solzhenitsyn* (Wilmington, DE: ISI, 2008), 197.

107. Andrew Wachtel, *An Obsession with History: Russian Writers Confront the Past* (Stanford, CA: Stanford University Press, 1994), 205.

108. Cited in Ericson and Klimoff, *Soul*, 197.

109. Lev N. Tolstóy, "Progress and the Definition of Education," *in Pedagogical Articles; Linen-Measurer*, vol. 4 of *The Complete Works of Count Tolstóy*, trans. Leo Wiener (Boston: Colonial Press, 1904), 163.

110. Solzhenitsyn, "We Have Ceased," 601. Francis Fukuyama, following Hegel, famously advanced the idea of an "end of history" in a 1989 piece for *National Interest*; he expanded on his thesis in a book three years later. That thesis, which Solzhenitsyn casually dismisses, posits that the telos of history draws near: "the end point of mankind's ideological evolution and the universalization of Western liberal democracy as the final form of human government" (Fukuyama, "The End of History?" in *National Interest* 16 [1989], 4). Fukuyama's argument is certainly optimistic, but Fukuyama has never been as Pollyannaish as Solzhenitsyn or later detractors have caricatured him. In his article, Fukuyama acknowledges that events on the ground have not kept pace with changes in the realm of ideas; liberal democracy has bested all rival ideologies, even though this may not be apparent from the current political landscape. "Russia and China are not likely to join the developed nations of the West as liberal societies any time in the foreseeable future," he notes (15). Religious fundamentalism poses some challenge to the liberal ideal, but "only Islam has offered a theocratic state as a political alternative to both liberalism and communism," and theocracy "has little appeal for non-Muslims" (14). Nationalist movements likewise "may constitute a source of

conflict for liberal societies" (15). Indeed, Fukuyama expects that "terrorism and wars of national liberation will continue to be an important item on the international agenda." Fukuyama concludes his article by calling the triumph of liberal democracy an "inevitability." At the same time, he muses that perhaps the "prospect of centuries of boredom" brought about by the end of history "will serve to get history started once again" (18). Fukuyama's thesis, thus, is not nearly as utopian as Solzhenitsyn or others would have it. Nevertheless, given all the caveats to it, that thesis is of dubious worth— the West has won, except where it has not; the end of history has been reached, but that could change.

111. Solzhenitsyn, "World Split," 13. Perhaps Solzhenitsyn would be more amenable to Samuel Huntington's ideas than to Fukuyama's. Writing in response to Fukuyama, Huntington posited a "clash of civilizations" thesis, first in a 1993 article for *Foreign Affairs* and then in greater detail in his 1996 book. In the earlier piece, Huntington writes that "with the end of the Cold War, international politics moves out of its Western phase, and its centerpiece becomes the interaction between the West and non-Western civilizations and among non-Western civilizations. In the politics of civilizations, the peoples and governments of non-Western civilizations no longer remain the objects of history as targets of Western colonialism but join the West as movers and shapers of history" (Huntington, "The Clash of Civilizations?" *Foreign Affairs* 72, no. 3 [1993]: 23).

112. Tolstoy, "Progress," 163.

113. Solzhenitsyn, "We Have Ceased," 600.

114. Tolstoy, *Kingdom of God*, 236.

115. Solzhenitsyn, *Rebuilding*, 47.

116. Solzhenitsyn, "World Split," 19.

117. Solzhenitsyn, *Rebuilding*, 49.

118. Pontuso, *Solzhenitsyn's Political Thought*, 209. This is not to say Solzhenitsyn lacks political preferences or has absolutely no use for the state. He declares his support for such things as federalism and localism, rights to private property, and (wading into more specific measures) funding for libraries and museums (Solzhenitsyn, *Rebuilding*, 31–32, 34, 40, 45, 83).

119. Edward E. Ericson, Jr., and Daniel J. Mahoney, "Editors' Introduction," in *The Solzhenitsyn Reader*, xliii.

120. Solzhenitsyn, "World Split," 20.

121. Solzhenitsyn, "Repentance," 532.

122. Solzhenitsyn, "We Have Ceased," 601.

123. Christopher Lasch, *The True and Only Heaven: Progress and Its Critics* (New York: Norton, 1991), 529.

124. Ibid., 530.

125. "As a corrective to the idea of progress, the 'imagination of disaster,' as Sontag refers to it elsewhere, leaves a good deal to be desired. All too obviously, it simply inverts the idea of progress, substituting irresistible disintegration for irresistible

advance.... A sober assessment of our predicament, one that would lead to action instead of paralyzing despair, has to begin by calling into question the fatalism that informs the whole discourse of progress and disaster" (ibid., 169–170).

126. Ibid., 54.

127. Ibid., 46, 52.

128. Ibid., 52.

129. Ibid., 531.

130. Ibid., 529.

131. Ibid., 52.

132. Ibid., 48.

133. Ibid., 78.

134. Ibid., 45.

135. Ibid., 76.

136. Ibid., 52.

137. Ibid., 33.

138. Christopher Lasch, *The Culture of Narcissism: American Life in an Age of Diminishing Expectations* (New York: Norton, 1978), 8.

139. Lasch, *True*, 13.

140. Lasch, *Culture*, 4.

141. Lasch, *True*, 82; Lasch, *Culture*, 53.

142. Eric Miller, "The Need for Roots," in Miller, *Hope in a Scattering Time* (Grand Rapids, MI: Eerdmans, 2010), 239–267.

143. Cited in ibid., 243.

144. Jimmy Carter, "Crisis of Confidence," July 15, 1969, WGBH *American Experience*, PBS.

145. Miller, *Hope*, 243–244. Lasch would not speak as glibly as he had in *The Culture of Narcissism*. In *The True and Only Heaven*, he is clear about who the heroes and villains are: the book offers a defense of "lower middle-class culture" (Lasch, *True*, 17).

146. Ronald Beiner, "Left-Wing Conservatism: The Legacy of Christopher Lasch," in *Philosophy in a Time of Lost Spirit: Essays on Contemporary Theory* (Toronto: University of Toronto Press, 1997), 150.

147. Carter, "Crisis of Confidence."

148. Lasch, *True*, 221.

149. Cited in Miller, *Hope*, 269. Carter's successor had two terms to change both the direction of the country and Lasch's opinion of him. Whether Reagan successfully helmed the United States through troubled waters is debatable. Whether he managed to impress Lasch is not: "after a decade of Reaganism, everything is worse than before" (ibid., 317).

150. Lasch, *True*, 226.

151. Ibid., 530. Lasch again finds common cause with Solzhenitsyn, who writes: "The time is urgently upon us to limit our wants. It is difficult to bring ourselves to practice sacrifice and self-denial, because in political, public, and private life we have

long since dropped the golden key of self-restraint to the ocean floor" (Solzhenitsyn, "We Have Ceased," 599). To Jean-Bethke Elshtain, Lasch's "populism" sounds remarkably similar to the communitarianism professed by other contemporary writers (Elshtain, "The Life and Work of Christopher Lasch: An American Story," *Salmagundi* 106/107 [1995]: 150).

152. When Lasch does discuss other historians, they are his contemporaries (including Lawrence Goodwyn and Richard Hofstadter).

153. Miller, *Hope*, xv.

## Conclusion

1. Louis Hartz, *The Liberal Tradition in America: An Interpretation of American Political Thought Since the Revolution* (New York: Harcourt Brace, 1955).

2. Barack Obama, "State of the Union Address" White House, Office of the Press Secretary (speech, Washington, DC, January 24, 2012).

3. Jeffrey M. Jones, *U.S. Satisfaction Up Slightly at Start of 2012, to 18%: Percentage Satisfied Is Lower Than in January of Other Presidential Election Years*, Gallup, January 11, 2012.

4. Joy Wilke, *Americans' Satisfaction with U.S. Gov't Drops to New Low: Democrats Remain Most Likely to Be Satisfied, But Much Less So Than in September*, Gallup, October 10, 2013.

5. Pew, *Supreme Court's Favorability Edges Below 50%: Blacks' Views of Court Turn More Negative*, Pew Research Center for the People and the Press, July 24, 2013; Rob Asghar, *The 3 Reasons Congress' Approval Rating Is at 10%*, Forbes, October 1, 2013.

6. "For First Time, Americans Say U.S. Power in the World Is Declining," interview by Robert Siegel, NPR, December 3, 2013.

7. John McCormick, "72 Percent of Americans Think Their Country Isn't as Great as It Once Was," *Bloomberg*, September 24, 2015.

8. For a discussion of the appropriateness of grouping thinkers according to particular national traditions, see Mark Bevir, "National Histories: Prospects for Critique and Narrative," *Journal of the Philosophy of History* 1, no. 3 (2007): 293–317; and Bevir "On Tradition," *Humanitas* 13, no. 2 (2000): 28–53. Bevir argues that being part of a tradition shapes one's thoughts, but that individuals are able to challenge and change the traditions into which they are born.

9. Arthur Schopenhauer, "Ethical Reflections," in *Schopenhauer: Essays*, trans. T. Baily Saunders (London: Allen and Unwin, 1951), 75.

10. Whether Vico could be considered a critic of progress is debatable. Charles Van Doren suggests that while Vico did not believe in *linear* progress, he did consent that one culture could build off of a declining culture's achievements. That is, progress occurred not in a straight line, but in the shape of a spiral (Van Doren, *The Idea of*

*Progress* [New York: Praeger, 1967]). For more on Vico, see Isaiah Berlin, *Vico and Herder: Two Studies in the History of Ideas* (London: Hogarth, 1992); Mark Lilla, *G. B. Vico: The Making of an Anti-Modern* (Cambridge, MA: Harvard University Press), 1993; Donald P. Verene, *Vico's Science of Imagination* (Ithaca, NY: Cornell University Press), 1981.

11. See Roger Scruton, *The Uses of Pessimism: And the Danger of False Hope* (New York: Oxford University Press, 2010).

12. Joshua Foa Dienstag, "Tragedy, Pessimism, Nietzsche," *New Literary History* 35, no. 1 (2004): 84.

13. John Kekes and John Derbyshire do equate pessimism and conservatism. But to both, "pessimism" goes beyond mere criticism of the idea of progress. To them it means as well the mistrust of human nature, which I would suggest is an issue altogether different from the belief that history's unfolding does not yield progress. See John Kekes, *A Case for Conservatism* (Ithaca, NY: Cornell University Press, 1998) and John Derbyshire, *We Are Doomed: Reclaiming Conservative Pessimism* (New York: Crown Forum, 2009).

14. Don Gonyea, "'How's That Hopey, Changey Stuff?' Palin Asks," *NPR*, February 7, 2010.

15. Mitt Romney, "Transcript: Mitt Romney's Acceptance Speech," NPR, August 31, 2012.

16. Christopher Lasch, *The True and Only Heaven: Progress and Its Critics* (New York: Norton, 1991).

17. Mark Lilla, *The Shipwrecked Mind: On Political Reaction* (New York: New York Review of Books, 2016), 2.

18. Ibid.

19. Spengler, *DOW:I*, 44.

20. There is a difference between building an inner citadel, that is, the response of certain critics of the idea of progress, and being completely aloof. Schopenhauer encouraged the retreat from direct political involvement, but even he still advocated some engagement with the world, for example, through practicing altruism. Henry Adams, for all his daydreaming about medieval Chartres, still had an active social life. Jacob Burckhardt deplored politics, but sought to give back to his native Basel in ways that he could.

21. Vladimir V. Putin, "Presidential Address to the Federal Assembly," *Kremlin. ru*, December 12, 2013.

22. Spengler combined pessimistic long-term visions for the West with short-term optimism for Germany; many of his German readers put into power a man with grievances about the present but hopes for a "thousand-year reich." Time will tell whether any of the present-day nationalist movements, arising as they do in a period of tumult, are bound to take similarly sinister turns.

23. Leo Strauss, "What Is Political Philosophy?" in *What Is Political Philosophy? And Other Studies* (Glencoe, IL: Free Press, 1959), 12.

24. See John G. Gunnell, *The Descent of Political Theory: The Genealogy of an American Vocation* (Chicago: University of Chicago Press), 1993.

25. For more on comparative political theory as a subdiscipline, see Melissa S. Williams and Mark E. Warren, "A Democratic Case for Comparative Political Theory," *Political Theory* 41, no. 1 (2014): 36; Antony Black, "The Way Forward in Comparative Political Thought," *Journal of International Political Theory.* 7, no. 2 (2011): 221–228; Andrew F. March, "What Is Comparative Political Theory?," *Review of Politics* 71, no. 4 (2009): 531–565; Fred Dallmayr, "Introduction: Toward a Comparative Political Theory," *Review of Politics* 59 no. 3 (1997): 421–428.

26. Voltaire, *Philosophical Dictionary*, trans. Theodore Besterman (Harmondsworth: Penguin, 1971).

27. Raymond Williams, *Keywords: A Vocabulary of Culture and Society*, rev ed. (New York: Oxford University Press, 1985).

28. Robert A. Nisbet, *Prejudices: A Philosophical Dictionary* (Cambridge, MA: Harvard University Press, 1982).

29. On "contested concepts," see Walter B. Gallie, "Essentially Contested Concepts," *Proceedings of the Aristotelian Society* 56 (1955): 167–198; John Gray, "On the Contestability of Social and Political Concepts," *Political Theory* 5, no. 3 (1977): 331–348; Alasdair MacIntyre, "The Essential Contestability of Some Social Concepts," *Ethics* 84, no. 1 (1973): 1–9.

30. William E. Connolly, *The Terms of Political Discourse*, 2nd ed. (Princeton, NJ: Princeton University Press, 1983), 180.

31. What Russell L. Hanson says of "democracy" could also be said about "progress": "it is evident that political science has not removed the confusion surrounding this concept. If anything, it might be argued that political scientists have merely added to that confusion by promulgating still more definitions" (Hanson, *The Democratic Imagination in America: Conversations with Our Past* [Princeton, NJ: Princeton University Press, 1985], 11).

32. James Farr, "Understanding Conceptual Change Politically," in *Political Innovation and Conceptual Change*, ed. Terence Ball, James Farr, and Russell Hanson (Cambridge: Cambridge University Press, 1989), 33.

33. See Dienstag, *Pessimism*, for a discussion of how pessimism differs from nihilism, cynicism, and other "isms."

34. Schopenhauer was famously misanthropic. Solzhenitsyn was a bit reclusive. *Asocial* they might have been; *antisocial* they were not.

35. See, for instance, Paul Howe, *Citizens Adrift* (Vancouver: UBC Press, 2010), 261; and Robert Putnam, *Bowling Alone: The Collapse and Revival of American Community* (New York: Simon and Schuster, 2000). For theoretical treatments of political cynicism and civic engagement, see David R. Hiley, *Doubt and the Demands of Democratic Citizenship* (New York: Cambridge University Press, 2006), and Ben Berger, *Attention Deficit Democracy: The Paradox of Citizenship* (Princeton, NJ: Princeton University Press, 2011).

36. John Gray, *Straw Dogs: Thought on Humans and Other Animals* (London: Granta, 2002), 29. See also John Gray, *The Silence of Animals: On Progress and Other Modern Myths* (New York: Farrar, Strauss and Giroux, 2013) and the discussion of Gray's ideas in the special issue of *Critical Review of International Social and Political Philosophy* 9, no. 2 (2006), "The Political Theory of John Gray."

37. Terry Eagleton, "Review: Straw Dogs by John Gray," *Guardian News and Media*, September 6, 2002.

38. Danny Postel, "Gray's Anatomy," *Nation*, December 4, 2003.

39. Herzen, "Author's Introduction," in *From the Other Shore and The Russian People and Socialism: An Open Letter to Jules Michelet* (New York: Braziller, 1956), 3.

40. Aristotle, *Nicomachean Ethics*, trans. Terence Irwin (Indianapolis: Hackett, 1999), 29.

41. Lasch, *True and Only*, 45.

# BIBLIOGRAPHY

Aaron, Daniel. *Men of Good Hope: A Story of American Progressives*. New York: Oxford University Press, 1961.

Abbey, Ruth. *Nietzsche's Middle Period*. Oxford: Oxford University Press, 2000.

Adams, Brooks. *America's Economic Supremacy*. New York: Macmillan, 1900.

———. "The Heritage of Henry Adams." In Henry Adams, *The Degradation of the Democratic Dogma*, ed. Brooks Adams. New York: P. Smith, 1949. 1–122.

———. "Introductory Note." In Henry Adams, *The Degradation of the Democratic Dogma*, ed. Brooks Adams. New York: P. Smith, 1949. v–xiii.

———. *The Law of Civilization and Decay: An Essay on History*. New York: Macmillan, 1895.

———. "The Revolt of Modern Democracy Against Standards of Duty." In *The Portable Conservative Reader*, ed. Russell Kirk. New York: Viking, 1982. 350–359.

Adams, Henry. *Democracy*. In *Novels; Mont Saint Michel; The Education*, comp. Ernest Samuels and Jayne N. Samuels. New York: Library of America, 1983. 1–184.

———. *The Education of Henry Adams*. In *Novels; Mont Saint Michel; The Education*, comp. Ernest Samuels and Jayne N. Samuels. New York: Library of America, 1983. 715–1181.

———. *Henry Adams and His Friends: A Collection of His Unpublished Letters*. Comp. Harold Dean Cater. Boston: Houghton Mifflin, 1947.

———. "A Letter to American Teachers of History." In *The Degradation of the Democratic Dogma*, ed. Brooks Adams. New York: P. Smith, 1949. 137–263.

———. *The Letters of Henry Adams*. Vol. 4, *1892–1899*. Ed. J. C. Levenson, Ernest Samuels, Charles Vandersee, and Viola H. Winner. Cambridge, MA: Belknap Press of Harvard University Press, 1988.

———. "The Rule of Phase Applied to History." In *The Degradation of the Democratic Dogma*, ed. Brooks Adams. New York: P. Smith, 1949. 267–311.

———. *Selected Letters*. Ed. Ernest Samuels. Cambridge, MA: Belknap Press of Harvard University Press, 1992.

Adams, Herbert Baxter. *The Germanic Origin of New England Towns: Read before the Harvard Historical Society, May 9, 1881*. Baltimore: Johns Hopkins University Press, 1882.

Adorno, Theodor. "Spengler After the Decline." In Theodor Adorno, *Prisms*, trans. Samuel Weber and Sherry Weber. Cambridge, MA: MIT Press, 1981. 51–72.

Ambrosius, Lloyd E. *Wilsonian Statecraft: Theory and Practice of Liberal Internationalism During World War I.* Wilmington, DE: SR Books, 1991.

Anderson, Benedict. *Imagined Communities: Reflections on the Origin and Spread of Nationalism.* London: Verso, 1991.

Anderson, Thornton. *Brooks Adams: Constructive Conservative.* Ithaca, NY: Cornell University Press, 1951.

———. *Russian Political Thought: An Introduction.* Ithaca, NY: Cornell University Press, 1967.

Anisimov, Evgenii. "Progress Through Violence from Peter the Great to Lenin and Stalin." *Russian History* 17, no. 4 (1990): 409–418.

———. *The Reforms of Peter the Great: Progress Through Coercion in Russia.* Trans. John T. Alexander. Armonk, NY: M.E. Sharpe, 1993.

Ankersmit, Frank, Mark Bevir, Paul Roth, Aviezer Tucker, and Alison Wylie. "The Philosophy of History: An Agenda." *Journal of the Philosophy of History* 1, no. 1 (2007): 1–9.

Arendt, Hannah. *On Revolution.* New York: Penguin, 2006.

Aristotle. *Nicomachean Ethics.* Trans. Terence Irwin. Indianapolis: Hackett, 1999.

Asghar, Rob. *The 3 Reasons Congress' Approval Rating Is at 10%.* Forbes, October 1, 2013.

Atkinson, Simon, and Bobby Duffy. "What Worries the World—October 2016." *Ipsos*, November 15, 2016.

Ausmus, Harry. "Schopenhauer's View of History: A Note." *History and Theory* 15, no. 2 (1976): 141–145.

Avineri, Shlomo. "Hegel and Nationalism." *Review of Politics* 24, no. 4 (1962): 461–484.

Bakunin, Michael. "God and the State." In *The Beginnings of Russian Philosophy; The Slavophiles; The Westernizers*, vol. 1 of *Russian Philosophy*, ed. James Edie, James Scanlan, and Mary-Barbara Zeldin. Knoxville: University of Tennessee Press, 1976. 415–423.

———. "The Paris Commune and the Idea of the State." In *The Beginnings of Russian Philosophy; The Slavophiles; The Westernizers*, vol. 1 of *Russian Philosophy*, ed. James Edie, James Scanlan, and Mary-Barbara Zeldin. Knoxville: University of Tennessee Press, 1976. 407–414.

———. "The Reaction in Germany." In *The Beginnings of Russian Philosophy; The Slavophiles; The Westernizers*, vol. 1 of *Russian Philosophy*, ed. James Edie, James Scanlan, and Mary-Barbara Zeldin. Knoxville: University of Tennessee Press, 1976. 385–406.

Bancroft, George. *History of the United States: From the Discovery of the American Continent*, 19th ed. Vol. 3. Boston: Little and Brown, 1841.

———. *The Necessity, the Reality and the Promise of the Progress of the Human Race; Oration Delivered Before the New-York Historical Society.* New York: New-York Historical Society, 1854.

Barber, Benjamin R. "Three Scenarios for the Future of Technology and Strong Democracy." *Political Science Quarterly* 113, no. 4 (1998), 573–589.

Beiner, Ronald. "Left-Wing Conservatism: The Legacy of Christopher Lasch." In *Philosophy in a Time of Lost Spirit: Essays on Contemporary Theory.* Toronto: University of Toronto Press, 1997. 139–150.

Belinskii, Vissarion G. "Letter to N. V. Gogol." In *Russian Intellectual History: An Anthology*, ed. Marc Raeff. New York: Harcourt Brace & World, 1966. 253–261.

Belinsky, Vissarion G. "Review of *A Guide to the Study of Modern History*, by S. Smaragdov." In Belinsky, *Selected Philosophical Works.* Moscow: Foreign Language Publishing, 1948. 293–319.

———. "To V. P. Botkin. 8 September, 1841." In Belinsky, *Selected Philosophical Works.* Moscow: Foreign Language Publishing, 1948. 158–167.

Bender, Thomas. "Writing American History: 1789–1945." In *The Oxford History of Historical Writing*, vol. 4, ed. Stuart Macintyre, Juan Maiguascha, and Attila Pók. Oxford: Oxford University Press, 2011. 369–389.

Berger, Ben. *Attention Deficit Democracy: The Paradox of Citizenship.* Princeton, NJ: Princeton University Press, 2011.

Beringause, Arthur F. *Brooks Adams: A Biography.* New York: Knopf, 1955.

Berlin, Isaiah. "The Hedgehog and the Fox." In *Russian Thinkers*, ed. Henry Hardy and Aileen Kelly. New York: Viking, 1978. 22–81.

———. "Herzen and Bakunin on Individual Liberty." In *Russian Thinkers*, ed. Henry Hardy and Aileen Kelly. New York: Viking, 1978. 82–113.

———. "Tolstoy and Enlightenment." In *Russian Thinkers*, ed. Henry Hardy and Aileen Kelly. New York: Viking, 1978. 238–260.

———. *Vico and Herder: Two Studies in the History of Ideas.* London: Hogarth, 1992.

Bevir, Mark. "National Histories: Prospects for Critique and Narrative." *Journal of the Philosophy of History*, no. 31 (2007): 293–317.

———. "On Tradition," *Humanitas* 13, no. 2 (2000): 28–53.

Billington, James. *The Icon and the Axe.* New York: Knopf, 1966.

Black, Antony. "The Way Forward in Comparative Political Thought." *Journal of International Political Theory* 7, no. 2 (2011): 221–228.

Breisach, Ernst. *American Progressive History: An Experiment in Modernization.* Chicago: University of Chicago Press, 1993.

Burckhardt, Jacob. *The Civilization of the Renaissance in Italy: An Essay.* Trans. S. G. C. Middlemore. New York: Phaidon, 1951.

———. *Force and Freedom: Reflections on History.* Ed. James H. Nichols. New York: Pantheon, 1943.

———. *Judgments on History and Historians.* Trans. Harry Zohn. Boston: Beacon, 1958.

Burke, Edmund. "Thoughts and Details on Scarcity." In *The Writings and Speeches of Edmund Burke*, ed. Paul Langford and William B. Todd. Oxford: Clarendon, 1981. 119–145.

Bury, J. B. *The Idea of Progress: An Inquiry into Its Origin and Growth.* New York: Dover, 1955.

Carter, Jimmy. "Crisis of Confidence," July 15, 1969, WGBH "American Experience," PBS.

Cartwright, David. *Schopenhauer: A Biography.* Cambridge: Cambridge University Press, 2010.

Chaadayev, Peter. "Philosophical Letters." In *The Beginnings of Russian Philosophy: The Slavophiles; The Westernizers*, vol. 1 of *Russian Philosophy*, ed. James M. Edie, James P. Scanlan, and Mary-Barbara Zeldin. Knoxville: University of Tennessee Press, 1976. 106–154.

Chalfant, Edward. *Better in Darkness: A Biography of Henry Adams: His Second Life, 1862–1891.* Hamden, CT: Archon, 1994.

Cherepnin, L. V. "Tolstoy's Views on History." *Soviet Studies in History* 4, no. 2 (1965): 3–29.

Christoyannopoulos, Alexandre. "Tolstoy's Anarchist Denunciation of State Violence and Deception." In *Anti-Democratic Thought*, ed. Erich Kofmel. Charlottesville, VA: Imprint Academic, 2008. 85–100.

———. "Turning the Other Cheek to Terrorism: Reflections on the Contemporary Significance of Leo Tolstoy's Exegesis of the Sermon on the Mount." *Politics and Religion* 1, no. 1 (2008): 27–54.

Colacurcio, Michael. "Democracy and Esther: Henry Adams's Flirtation with Pragmatism." In *A Political Companion to Henry Adams*, ed. Natalie F. Taylor. Lexington: University Press of Kentucky, 2010. 61–80.

Condorcet, Marquis de. *The Progress of the Human Mind.* In *The Idea of Progress Since the Renaissance*, ed. Warren W. Wagar. New York: Wiley, 1969.

Connolly, William E. *The Terms of Political Discourse.* 2nd ed. Princeton, NJ: Princeton University Press, 1983.

Constantinidès, Yannis. "Two Great Enemies of the Enlightenment: Joseph de Maistre and Schopenhauer." In *Joseph de Maistre and the Legacy of the Enlightenment*, ed. Carolina Armenteros and Richard Lebrun. Oxford: Voltaire Foundation, 2011. 105–122.

Copleston, Frederick C. *Philosophy in Russia: From Herzen to Lenin and Berdyaev.* Notre Dame, IN: University of Notre Dame Press, 1986.

Cracraft, James. *The Petrine Revolution in Russian Culture.* Cambridge, MA: Belknap Press of Harvard University Press, 2004.

Craiutu, Aurelian, and Jeremy Jennings. "The Third Democracy: Tocqueville's Views of America After 1840." *American Political Science Review* 98, no. 3 (2004): 391–404.

Dallmayr, Fred. "Introduction: Toward a Comparative Political Theory." *Review of Politics* 59, no. 3 (1997): 421–428.

Danilevskii, Nikolai I. *Russia and Europe: The Slavic World's Political and Cultural Relations with the Germanic-Roman West*. Trans. Stephen M. Woodburn. Bloomington, IN: Slavica, 2013.

Dawidoff, Robert. *The Genteel Tradition and the Sacred Rage: High Culture Vs. Democracy in Adams, James, and Santayana*. Chapel Hill: University of North Carolina Press, 1992.

Delmage, Rutherford E. "The American Idea of Progress, 1750–1800." *Proceedings of the American Philosophical Society* 91, no. 4 (1947): 307–14.

Deneen, Patrick J. "Mont-Saint-Michel and Chartres: From Unity to Multiplicity," in Natalie Fuehrer Taylor, *A Political Companion to Henry Adams*. Lexington: University Press of Kentucky, 2010. 171–89.

Derbyshire, John. *We Are Doomed: Reclaiming Conservative Pessimism*. New York: Crown Forum, 2009.

Detwiler, Bruce. *Nietzsche and the Politics of Aristocratic Radicalism*. Chicago: University of Chicago Press, 1990.

Dienstag, Joshua Foa. *Pessimism: Philosophy, Ethic, Spirit*. Princeton, NJ: Princeton University Press, 2006.

———. "Tragedy, Pessimism, Nietzsche." *New Literary History* 35, no. 1 (2004): 83–101.

Dostoevsky, Fyodor. *The Brothers Karamazov*. Trans. Richard Pevear and Larissa Volokhonsky. New York: Farrar, Straus and Giroux, 2002.

Dostoievsky, Feodor M. *Letters of Fyodor Michailovitch Dostoevsky to His Family and Friends*. Trans. Ethel C. Mayne. New York: Horizon, 1961.

———. *The Diary of a Writer*. Trans. Boris Brasol. Vol. 1. New York: Charles Scribner's Sons, 1949.

Drakulić, Slavenka. *Café Europa*. New York: Norton, 1996.

Dutton, Denise. "Henry Adams's Democracy: Novel Sources of Democratic Virtues." In *A Political Companion to Henry Adams*, ed. Natalie F. Taylor. Lexington: University Press of Kentucky, 2010. 81–110.

Eagleton, Terry. "Review: Straw Dogs by John Gray." *Guardian News and Media*, 6 September 6, 2002.

Edie, James, James Scanlan, and Mary-Barbara Zeldin. "Peter Yakovlevich Chaadayev." In *The Beginnings of Russian Philosophy; The Slavophiles; The Westernizers*, vol. 1 of *Russian Philosophy*, ed. James Edie, James Scanlan, and Mary-Barbara Zeldin. Knoxville: University of Tennessee Press, 1976. 101–105.

———. "Preface." In *The Beginnings of Russian Philosophy; The Slavophiles; The Westernizers*, vol. 1 of *Russian Philosophy*, ed. James Edie, James Scanlan, and Mary-Barbara Zeldin. Knoxville: University of Tennessee Press, 1976. ix–xiv.

———. "The Westernizers." In *The Beginnings of Russian Philosophy; The Slavophiles; The Westernizers*, vol. 1 of *Russian Philosophy*, ed. James Edie, James Scanlan, and Mary-Barbara Zeldin. Knoxville: University of Tennessee Press, 1976. 273–279.

Elshtain, Jean Bethke. "The Life and Work of Christopher Lasch: An American Story." *Salmagundi* 106/107 (1995): 146–161.

Erasmus, Desiderius. *The Education of a Christian Prince*. Trans. Neil M. Cheshire and Michael J. Heath. Cambridge: Cambridge University Press, 1997.

Ericson, Edward E., Jr., and Alexis Klimoff, *The Soul and Barbed Wire: An Introduction to Solzhenitsyn*. Wilmington, DE: ISI Books, 2008.

Ericson, Edward E., Jr., and Daniel J. Mahoney. "Editors' Introduction," in *The Solzhenitsyn Reader: New and Essential Writings*, 1947–2005, ed. Edward E. Ericson, Jr., and Daniel J. Mahoney. Wilmington, DE: ISI Books, 2006. xv–xliv.

Farr, James. "Understanding Conceptual Change Politically." In *Political Innovation and Conceptual Change*, ed. Terence Ball, James Farr, and Russell Hanson. Cambridge: Cambridge University Press, 1989. 24–49.

Farrenkopf, John. *Prophet of Decline: Spengler on World History and Politics*. Baton Rouge: Louisiana State University Press, 2001.

Fichte, Johann. *Addresses to the German Nation*. Trans. Isaac Nakhimovsky, Béla Kapossy, and Keith Tribe. Indianapolis: Hackett, 2013.

———. *The Characteristics of the Present Age*. Trans. William E. Smith. London: John Chapman, 1847.

Fiske, John. *Darwinism and Other Essays*. Boston: Houghton, Mifflin, 1879/1885.

———. "Manifest Destiny." In *American Political Ideas Viewed from the Standpoint of Universal History: Three Lectures Delivered at the Royal Institution of Great Britain in May, 1880*. New York: Houghton Mifflin, 1911. 93–144.

"For First Time, Americans Say U.S. Power in the World Is Declining." Interview by Robert Siegel. *NPR*, December 3, 2013.

Forster, Michael N. "Introduction." In *Johann Gottfried von Herder: Philosophical Writings*, ed. Michael N. Forster. Cambridge: Cambridge University Press, 2002. vii–xxxv.

Fruchtman, Jack, Jr. "A Voice from Russia's Past at Harvard." In *Solzhenitsyn at Harvard: The Address; Twelve Early Responses, and Six Later Reflections*, ed. Ronald Berman. Washington, DC: Ethics and Public Policy Center, 1980. 43–47.

Frye, Northrop. "*The Decline of the West* by Oswald Spengler." *Daedalus* 103, no. 1 (1974): 1–13.

Fueloep-Miller, Rene. "Tolstoy the Apostolic Crusader." *Russian Review* 19, no. 2 (1960): 99–121.

Fukuyama, Francis. "The End of History?" *National Interest* 16 (1989): 3–18.

Gabriel, Ralph Henry, and Robert Harris Walker. *The Course of American Democratic Thought*. New York: Greenwood, 1986.

Gallie, Walter Bryce. "Essentially Contested Concepts." *Proceedings of the Aristotelian Society* 56 (1955): 167–198.

Gardiner, Patrick. *Schopenhauer*. Baltimore: Penguin, 1963.

Gilley, B. H. "Democracy: Henry Adams and the Role of Political Leader." In *A Political Companion to Henry Adams*, ed. Natalie F. Taylor. Lexington: University Press of Kentucky, 2010. 43–60.

Glueck, Katie. "Clinton Decries Trump's 'Midnight in America.'" *POLITICO*, July 28, 2016.

Gonyea, Don. "'How's That Hopey, Changey Stuff?' Palin Asks." *NPR*, February 7, 2010.

Gottfried, Paul. "Arthur Schopenhauer as a Critic of History." *Journal of the History of Ideas* 36, no. 2 (1975): 331–338.

———. "Oswald Spengler and the Inspiration of the Classical Age." *Modern Age* 26. no. 1 (1982): 68–75.

Gray, John. "On the Contestability of Social and Political Concepts." *Political Theory* 5, no. 3 (1977): 331–348.

———. *The Silence of Animals: On Progress and Other Modern Myths*. New York: Farrar, Strauss and Giroux, 2013.

———. *Straw Dogs: Thoughts on Humans and Other Animals*. London: Granta, 2002.

Greifer, Elisha. "The Conservative Pose in America: The Adamses' Search for a Pre-Liberal Past." *Western Political Quarterly* 15, no. 1 (1962): 5–16.

Grob, Gerald N. and George A. Billias. *Interpretations of American History: Patterns and Perspectives*. Vol. 1, *To 1877*. New York: Free Press, 1992.

Gunnell, John G. *The Descent of Political Theory: The Genealogy of an American Vocation*. Chicago: University of Chicago Press, 1993.

Hamilton, Caroline V. "Henry Adams and Andrei Bely: The Explosive Mind." *Anarchist Studies* 18, no. 2 (2010): 58–84.

Hanson, Russell L. *The Democratic Imagination in America: Conversations with Our Past*. Princeton, NJ: Princeton University Press, 1985.

Hanson, Russell L., and W. Richard Merriam. "Henry Adams and the Decline of the Republican Tradition." In *A Political Companion to Henry Adams*, ed. Natalie F. Taylor. Lexington: University Press of Kentucky, 2010. 17–42.

Haraszti, Zoltán. *John Adams and the Prophets of Progress*. Cambridge, MA: Harvard University Press, 1952.

Hartz, Louis. *The Liberal Tradition in America: An Interpretation of American Political Thought Since the Revolution*. New York: Harcourt Brace, 1955.

Hegel, G. W. F. *Elements of the Philosophy of Right*. Trans. H. B. Nisbet. Cambridge: Cambridge University Press, 1991.

———. *Lectures on the Philosophy of World History*. Trans. H. B. Nisbet. New York: Cambridge University Press, 1975.

Heilke, Thomas. *Nietzsche's Tragic Regime: Culture, Aesthetics, and Political Education*. Dekalb: Northern Illinois University Press, 1998.

Heller, Erich. "Burckhardt and Nietzsche." In *The Importance of Nietzsche*. Chicago: University of Chicago Press, 1988. 39–54.

Herbst, Jurgen. *The German Historical School in American Scholarship: A Study in the Transfer of Culture*. Ithaca, NY: Cornell University Press, 1965.

Herder, Johann Gottfried von. *Reflections on the Philosophy of the History of Mankind*. Comp. Frank Edward Manuel. Chicago: University of Chicago Press, 1968.

———. *This Too a Philosophy of History for the Formation of Humanity*. In *Johann Gottfried von Herder: Philosophical Writings*, ed. Michael N. Forster. Cambridge: Cambridge University Press, 2002. 272–358.

Herman, Arthur. *The Idea of Decline in Western History*. New York: Free Press, 1997.

Herzen, Aleksandr. "Author's Introduction." In *From the Other Shore and The Russian People and Socialism: An Open Letter to Jules Michelet*. New York: Braziller, 1956. 3–17.

———. *From the Other Shore*. In *From the Other Shore and The Russian People and Socialism: An Open Letter to Jules Michelet*. New York: Braziller, 1956. 19–162.

———. "The Russian People and Socialism: An Open Letter to Jules Michelet." in *From the Other Shore and The Russian People and Socialism: An Open Letter to Jules Michelet*. New York: Braziller, 1956. 165–208.

Hiley, David R. *Doubt and the Demands of Democratic Citizenship*. New York: Cambridge University Press, 2006.

Hinde, John R. "The Development of Jacob Burckhardt's Early Political Thought." *Journal of the History of Ideas* 53, no. 3 (1992): 425–436.

Hofstadter, Richard. *The Progressive Historians: Turner, Beard, Parrington*. New York: Knopf, 1968.

Holborn, Hajo. "Origins and Political Character of Nazi Ideology." *Political Science Quarterly* 79, no. 4 (1964): 542–554.

Holt, W. Stull. "The Idea of Scientific History in America." *Journal of the History of Ideas* 1, no. 3 (1940): 352–362.

Horkheimer, Max. "Schopenhauer and Society (1955)." Trans. Todd Cronan. *Qui Parle* 15, no. 1 (2004): 85–96.

Howe, Paul. *Citizens Adrift*. Vancouver: UBC Press, 2010.

Hübscher, Arthur. *The Philosophy of Schopenhauer in Its Intellectual Context: Thinker Against the Tide*. Trans. Joachim T. Baer and David E. Cartwright. Lewiston, NY: Edwin Mellen, 1989.

Hughes, H. Stuart. *Oswald Spengler: A Critical Estimate*. New York: Scribner, 1952.

Hughes, Lindsey. *Russia in the Age of Peter the Great*. New Haven, CT: Yale University Press, 1998.

Iggers, Georg G. *The German Conception of History: The National Tradition of Historical Thought from Herder to the Present*. Middletown, CT: Wesleyan University Press, 1968.

———. "The Image of Ranke in American and German Historical Thought." *History and Theory* 2, no. 1 (1962): 17–40.

Jacquette, Dale. *The Philosophy of Schopenhauer*. Chesham, UK: Acumen, 2005.

Janaway, Christopher. *Self and World in Schopenhauer's Philosophy*. Oxford: Clarendon, 1989.

Jones, Jeffrey M. *U.S. Satisfaction Up Slightly at Start of 2012, to 18%: Percentage Satisfied Is Lower Than in January of Other Presidential Election Years*. Gallup, January 11, 2012.

Jordan, Neil. "Schopenhauer's Politics: Ethics, Jurisprudence, and the State." In *Better Consciousness: Schopenhauer's Philosophy of Value*, ed. Alex Neill and Christopher Janaway. Chichester: Wiley-Blackwell, 2009. 171–88.

Jordy, William H. *Henry Adams: Scientific Historian*. New Haven, CT: Yale University Press, 1953.

Kahan, Alan S. *Alexis de Tocqueville*. New York: Continuum, 2010.

———. *Aristocratic Liberalism: The Social and Political Thought of Jacob Burckhardt, John Stuart Mill, and Alexis de Tocqueville*. New York: Oxford University Press, 1992.

Kant, Immanuel. *Groundwork of the Metaphysics of Morals*. In *Practical Philosophy*, ed. Mary J. Gregor. New York: Cambridge University Press, 1996. 41–108.

———. "Idea for a Universal History with a Cosmopolitan Aim.'" In *Anthropology, History, and Education*, ed. Günter Zöller and Robert B. Louden, trans. Allen Wood. Cambridge: Cambridge University Press, 2007. 107–20.

———. "An Old Question Raised Again: Is the Human Race Constantly Progressing." In *Religion and Rational Theology*, ed. Allen W. Wood and George di Giovanni, trans. Mary J. Gregor and Robert Anchor. New York: Cambridge University Press, 1996. 297–309.

———. "On the Common Saying: That May Be Correct in Theory, But It Is of No Use in Practice." In *Practical Philosophy*, ed. Mary J. Gregor. New York: Cambridge University Press, 1996. 277–309.

———. "Toward Perpetual Peace." In *Practical Philosophy*, ed. Mary J. Gregor. New York: Cambridge University Press, 1996. 317–351.

Kappeler, Andreas. *The Russian Empire: A Multiethnic History*. Harlow: Longman, 2001.

Kaufmann, Walter A. *Nietzsche: Philosopher, Psychologist, Antichrist*. New York: Meridian, 1956.

Kekes, John. *A Case for Conservatism*. Ithaca, NY: Cornell University Press, 1998.

Kelly, Aileen. "Herzen Versus Schopenhauer: An Answer to Pessimism." *Journal of European Studies* 26, no. 1 (1996): 37–59.

Kessler, Charles. "Up from Modernity." In *Solzhenitsyn at Harvard: The Address; Twelve Early Responses, and Six Later Reflections*, ed. Ronald Berman. Washington, DC: Ethics and Public Policy Center, 1980. 48–56.

Khomiakov, Aleksei. "On Humboldt." In *Russian Intellectual History: An Anthology*, ed. Marc Raeff. New York: Harcourt Brace & World, 1966. 209–229.

Kireevsky, Ivan. "On the Nature of European Culture and on Its Relationship to Russian Culture: Letter to Count E. E. Komarovsky." In *On Spiritual Unity: A*

*Slavophile Reader*, trans. and ed. Boris Jakim and Robert Bird. Hudson, NY: Lindisfarne, 1998. 189–232.

Kohn, Hans. *The Idea of Nationalism: A Study in Its Origins and Background*. New Brunswick, NJ: Transaction, 2005.

———. *Pan-Slavism: Its History and Ideology*. New York: Vintage, 1960.

Kramer, Hilton. "A Talk with Solzhenitsyn." *New York Times Book Review*, May 1, 1980, 3, 30–31.

Kraus, Michael, and Davis D. Joyce. *The Writing of American History*. Norman: University of Oklahoma Press, 1985.

Lasch, Christopher. *The Culture of Narcissism: American Life in an Age of Diminishing Expectations*. New York: Norton, 1978.

———. *The True and Only Heaven: Progress and Its Critics*. New York: Norton, 1991.

Lavrin, Janko. "Tolstoy and Gandhi." *Russian Review* 19, no. 2 (1960): 132–139.

Leont'ev, Konstantin. *Against the Current: Selections from the Novels, Essays, Notes, and Letters of Konstantin Leontiev*. Ed. George Ivask, trans. George Reavey. New York: Weybright and Talley, 1969.

Levenson, J. C. *The Mind and Art of Henry Adams*. Boston: Houghton Mifflin, 1957.

Lilla, Mark. *G. B. Vico: The Making of an Anti-Modern*. Cambridge, MA: Harvard University Press, 1993.

———. *The Shipwrecked Mind: On Political Reaction*. New York: New York Review of Books, 2016.

Lossky, N. O. *History of Russian Philosophy*. New York: International Universities Press, 1951.

Lukács, György. *The Destruction of Reason*. London: Merlin, 1981.

MacIntyre, Alasdair. "The Essential Contestability of Some Social Concepts." *Ethics* 84. no. (1973): 1–9.

MacMaster, Robert. *Danilevsky: A Russian Totalitarian Philosopher*. Cambridge, MA: Harvard University Press, 1967.

Madariaga, Isabel de. *Russia in the Age of Catherine the Great*. New Haven, CT: Yale University Press, 1981.

Magee, Bryan. *The Philosophy of Schopenhauer*. Oxford: Clarendon, 1983.

Mahoney, Daniel. *The Other Solzhenitsyn: Telling the Truth About a Misunderstood Writer and Thinker*. South Bend, IN: St. Augustine's Press, 2014.

Maistre, Joseph de. *Considerations on France*. Cambridge: Cambridge University Press, 1994.

Malia, Martin. *Alexander Herzen*. New York: Grosset & Dunlap, 1965.

———. *Alexander Herzen and the Birth of Russian Socialism, 1812–1855*. Cambridge, MA: Harvard University Press, 1961.

Mancini, Matthew J. *Alexis de Tocqueville and American Intellectuals: From His Times to Ours*. Lanham, MD: Rowman & Littlefield, 2006.

Manent, Pierre. *Tocqueville and the Nature of Democracy*. Lanham, MD: Rowman & Littlefield, 1996.

March, Andrew F. "What Is Comparative Political Theory?" *Review of Politics* 71, no. 4 (2009):531–565.

Marcin, Raymond. *In Search of Schopenhauer's Cat: Arthur Schopenhauer's Quantum-Mystical Theory of Justice.* Washington, DC: Catholic University of America Press, 2006.

Masaryk, Thomas G. *The Spirit of Russia.* Trans. Eden Paul and Cedar Paul. 3 vols. New York: Macmillan, 1955.

Mathiopoulos, Margarita. *History and Progress: In Search of the European and American Mind.* New York: Praeger, 1989.

McCormick, John. "72 Percent of Americans Think Their Country Isn't as Great as It Once Was." *Bloomberg*, September 24, 2015.

McDaniel, Tim. *The Agony of the Russian Idea.* Princeton, NJ: Princeton University Press, 1996.

McGrory, Mary. "Solzhenitsyn Doesn't Love Us." In *Solzhenitsyn at Harvard: The Address; Twelve Early Responses, and Six Later Reflections*, ed. Ronald Berman. Washington, DC: Ethics and Public Policy Center, 1980. 60–62.

McLaughlin, Sigrid. "Some Aspects of Tolstoy's Intellectual Development: Tolstoy and Schopenhauer." *California Slavic Studies* 5 (1970): 187–245.

Michelson, Patrick Lally. "Slavophile Religious Thought and the Dilemma of Russian Modernity, 1830–1860." *Modern Intellectual History* 7, no. (2010): 239–267.

Mill, John Stuart. *On Liberty.* Mineola, NY: Dover, 2002.

Miller, Eric. *Hope in a Scattering Time.* Grand Rapids, MI: Eerdmans, 2010.

Motley, John Lothrop. *Historic Progress and American Democracy: An Address Delivered Before the New-York Historical Society at Their Sixty-Fourth Anniversary.* New York: Charles Scribner, 1869.

———. "Review: *Geschichte der Colonisation von Neu-England: Von den Ersten Niederlassungen Daselbst im Jahre 1607, bis zur Einführung der Provinzialverfassung von Massachusetts im Jahre 1692 by Talvj* [Polity of the Puritans]." *North American Review* 69, no. 145 (1849): 470–98.

Murphy, Andrew R. *Prodigal Nation: Moral Decline and Divine Punishment from New England to 9/11.* Oxford: Oxford University Press, 2009.

Nakhimovsky, Isaac. "Introduction." In Johann Fichte, *Addresses to the German Nation*, trans. Isaac Nakhimovsky, Béla Kapossy, and Keith Tribe. Indianapolis: Hackett, 2013. ix–xxx.

*National Review.* "Thoughts on Solzhenitsyn." In *Solzhenitsyn at Harvard: The Address; Twelve Early Responses, and Six Later Reflections*, ed. Ronald Berman. Washington, DC: Ethics and Public Policy Center, 1980. 30–32.

Nietzsche, Friedrich. *The Birth of Tragedy.* Trans. Shaun Whiteside. New York: Penguin, 1993.

———. "Schopenhauer as Educator." In *Unfashionable Observations*, trans. Richard T. Gray. Stanford, CA: Stanford University Press, 1995. 171–255.

————. "The Utility and Liability of History." In *Unfashionable Observations*, trans. Richard T. Gray. Stanford, CA: Stanford University Press, 1995. 83–168.

Nipperdey, Thomas. *Germany from Napoleon to Bismarck: 1800–1866*. Dublin: Gill and Macmillan, 1996.

Nisbet, Robert A. *History of the Idea of Progress*. New Brunswick, NJ: Transaction, 1994.

————. *Prejudices: A Philosophical Dictionary*. Cambridge, MA: Harvard University Press, 1982.

Obama, Barack. "Remarks by the President at Hillary for America Rally in Ann Arbor, Michigan." White House, Office of the Press Secretary. Speech, University of Michigan, Ann Arbor, November 7, 2016.

————. "State of the Union Address." White House, Office of the Press Secretary. Speech, Washington, DC, January 24, 2012.

Obolonsky, Alexander. *The Drama of Russian Political History: System Against Individuality*. College Station: Texas A&M University Press, 2003.

Pangle, Thomas L. *The Spirit of Modern Republicanism: The Moral Vision of the American Founders and the Philosophy of Locke*. Chicago: University of Chicago Press, 1990.

Parrington, Vernon L. *Main Currents in American Thought: An Interpretation of American Literature from the Beginnings to 1920*. Vol. 3. New York: Harcourt Brace, 1930.

Patten, Allen. *Hegel's Idea of Freedom*. New York: Oxford University Press, 1999.

PBS. "Gwen Ifill Interviews President Obama on Trump, Economic Recovery." June 1, 2016.

————. "Shields and Brooks on Obama's NewsHour Interview, Presidential Legacy." June 1, 2016.

Pearce, Joseph. *Solzhenitsyn: A Soul in Exile*. Grand Rapids, MI: Baker, 2001.

Pew. *Supreme Court's Favorability Edges Below 50%: Blacks' Views of Court Turn More Negative*. Pew Research Center for the People and the Press, July 24, 2013.

Pipes, Richard. *Russian Conservatism and Its Critics*. New Haven, CT: Yale University Press, 2005.

————. *Russia Under the Old Regime*. London: Weidenfeld and Nicolson, 1974.

Plato. *The Republic*. Ed., G. R. F. Ferrari, trans. Tom Griffith. Cambridge: Cambridge University Press, 2000.

"The Political Theory of John Gray." *Critical Review of International Social and Political Philosophy* 9, no. 2 (2006): 107–347.

Pontuso, James. *Solzhenitsyn's Political Thought*. Charlottesville, VA: University of Virginia Press, 1990.

Popper, Karl. *The Open Society and Its Enemies*. London: Routledge and Kegan Paul, 1962.

Postel, Danny. "Gray's Anatomy." *The Nation*. Nation Company, L.P., December 4, 2003.

Putin, Vladimir V. "Presidential Address to the Federal Assembly." *Kremlin.ru.*, December 12, 2013.

Putnam, Robert. *Bowling Alone: The Collapse and Revival of American Community.* New York: Simon and Schuster, 2000.

Rabow-Edling, Susanna. *Slavophile Thought and the Politics of Cultural Nationalism.* Albany: State University of New York Press, 2006.

Raeff, Marc. *Understanding Imperial Russia.* Trans. Arthur Goldhammer. New York: Columbia University Press, 1984.

——. *The Well-Ordered Police State: Social and Institutional Change Through Law in the Germanies and Russia, 1600–1800.* New Haven, CT: Yale University Press, 1983.

Ragsdale, Hugh. *The Russian Tragedy: The Burden of History.* Armonk, NY: M.E. Sharpe, 1996.

Raskin, Marcus G. *Liberalism: The Genius of American Ideals.* Lanham, MD: Rowman & Littlefield, 2004.

Regent, Nikola. "A 'Wondrous Echo': Burckhardt, Renaissance and Nietzsche's Political Thought." In *Nietzsche, Power and Politics: Rethinking Nietzsche's Legacy for Political Thought*, ed. Herman W. Siemens and Vasti Roodt. New York: De Gruyter, 2008. 629–665.

Reilly, John J. "Review: John Farrenkopf, *Prophet of Decline: Spengler on World History and Politics." Comparative Civilizations Review* 49 (2003): 146–154.

Reston, James. "A Russian at Harvard." In *Solzhenitsyn at Harvard: The Address; Twelve Early Responses, and Six Later Reflections*, ed. Ronald Berman. Washington, DC: Ethics and Public Policy Center, 1980, 36–38.

Riasanovsky, Nicholas V. *Nicholas I and Official Nationality in Russia, 1825–1855.* Berkeley: University of California Press, 1959.

Romney, Mitt. "Transcript: Mitt Romney's Acceptance Speech." NPR, August 31, 2012.

Rosenberg, Alfred. *The Myth of the Twentieth Century: An Evaluation of the Spiritual-Intellectual Confrontations of Our Age.* Torrance, CA: Noontide, 1982.

Ross, Dorothy. "Historical Consciousness in Nineteenth-Century America." *American Historical Review* 89, no. 4 (1984): 909–28.

Rousseau, Jean-Jacques. *Discourse on the Origin and Foundation of Inequality Among Mankind.* In *The Social Contract and Discourse on the Origin and Foundation of Inequality Among Mankind*, ed. Lester G. Crocker. New York: Washington Square Press, 1967. 151–252.

Sabine, George H. *A History of Political Theory.* Ed. Thomas Landon Thorson. Hinsdale, IL: Dryden, 1973.

Safranski, Rudiger. *Schopenhauer and the Wild Years of Philosophy.* Trans. Ewald Osers. Cambridge, MA: Harvard University Press, 1990.

Samuels, Ernest. *Henry Adams: The Middle Years.* Cambridge, MA: Belknap Press of Harvard University Press, 1958.

——. *The Young Henry Adams.* Cambridge, MA: Harvard University Press, 1965.

Samuels, Ernest, and Jayne N. Samuels. "Notes." In Henry Adams, *Novels; Mont Saint Michel; The Education*, comp. Ernest Samuels and Jayne N. Samuels. New York: Library of America, 1983. 1229–1246.

Schlesinger, Arthur, Jr. "The Solzhenitsyn We Refuse to See." In *Solzhenitsyn at Harvard: The Address; Twelve Early Responses, and Six Later Reflections*, ed. Ronald Berman. Washington, DC: Ethics and Public Policy Center, 1980. 63–71.

Schönle, Andreas. "Modernity as a 'Destroyed Anthill': Tolstoy on the History and Aesthetics of Ruins." In *Ruins of Modernity*, ed. Julia Hell and Andreas Schönle. Durham, NC: Duke University Press, 2010. 89–103.

Schopenhauer, Arthur. "Ethical Reflections." In *Schopenhauer: Essays*, trans. T. Baily Saunders. London: Allen and Unwin, 1951. 75–87.

———. "On Jurisprudence and Politics." In *Parerga and Paralipomena*, vol. 2, trans. E. F. J. Payne. Oxford: Oxford University Press, 2000. 240–266.

———. *On the Basis of Morality*. Trans. E. F. J. Payne. Indianapolis: Bobbs-Merrill, 1965.

———. *Spicilegia*. In *Arthur Schopenhauer: Manuscript Remains in Four Volumes*, ed. Arthur Hübscher, vol. 4,trans. E. F. J. Payne. New York: St. Martin's, 1990. 271–351.

———. "What a Man Represents." In *Parerga and Paralipomena*, vol. 1, trans. E. F. J. Payne. Oxford: Oxford University Press, 2000. 353–403.

———. *The World as Will and Representation*. 2 vols. Trans. E. F. J. Payne. New York: Dover, 1969.

Scruton, Roger. *The Uses of Pessimism: And the Danger of False Hope*. New York: Oxford University Press, 2010.

Shaw, Tamsin. *Nietzsche's Political Skepticism*. Princeton, NJ: Princeton University Press, 2007.

Sheehan, James J. *German History, 1770–1866*. Oxford: Clarendon, 1989.

Sherman, Jake. "Poll: Voters Liked Trump's 'America First' Address." *POLITICO*, January 25, 2017.

Shklar, Judith N. *After Utopia: The Decline of Political Faith*. Princeton, NJ: Princeton University Press, 1957.

———. "'The Education of Henry Adams' by Henry Adams." *Daedalus* 103, no. 1 (1974): 59–66.

Shumate, Roger V. "The Political Philosophy of Henry Adams." *American Political Science Review* 28, no. 4 (1934): 599–610.

Sigurdson, Richard. *Jacob Burckhardt's Social and Political Thought*. Toronto: University of Toronto Press, 2004.

Simons, John D. "The Myth of Progress in Schiller and Dostoevsky." *Comparative Literature* 24, no. 4 (1972): 328–337.

Simpson, Brooks D. *The Political Education of Henry Adams*. Columbia: University of South Carolina Press, 1996.

Skinner, Gideon. "EU Citizens Think Things Across the Union Heading in the Wrong Direction—But Committed to Membership." *Ipsos in North America*, August 31, 2015.

Solzhenitsyn, Aleksandr I. "Letter to the Soviet Leaders." Trans. Hilary Sternberg in *East and West*. New York: Harper & Row, 1980. 73–142.

———. *Rebuilding Russia*. Trans. Alexis Klimoff. New York: Farrar, Straus and Giroux, 1991.

———. "A Reflection on the Vendée Uprising." In *The Solzhenitsyn Reader: New and Essential Writings, 1947–2005*, ed. Edward E. Ericson, Jr., and Daniel J. Mahoney. Wilmington, DE: ISI, 2006. 602–605.

———. "Repentance and Self-Limitation in the Life of Nations." In *The Solzhenitsyn Reader: New and Essential Writings, 1947–2005*, ed. Edward E. Ericson, Jr., and Daniel J. Mahoney. Wilmington, DE: ISI, 2006. 527–555.

———. "Templeton Lecture." In *The Solzhenitsyn Reader: New and Essential Writings, 1947–2005*, ed. Edward E. Ericson, Jr., and Daniel J. Mahoney. Wilmington, DE: ISI, 2006. 576–584.

———. "We Have Ceased to See the Purpose." In *The Solzhenitsyn Reader: New and Essential Writings, 1947–2005*, ed. Edward E. Ericson, Jr., and Daniel J. Mahoney. Wilmington, DE: ISI, 2006. 591–601.

———. "A World Split Apart." In *Solzhenitsyn at Harvard: The Address; Twelve Early Responses, and Six Later Reflections*, ed. Ronald Berman. Washington, DC: Ethics and Public Policy Center, 1980. 3–20.

Spence, G. W. "Tolstoy's Dualism." *Russian Review* 20, 3 (1961): 217–231.

Spengler, Oswald. *The Decline of the West*. Trans. Charles F. Atkinson. 2 vols. New York: Knopf, 1992.

———. *Man and Technics: A Contribution to a Philosophy of Life*. London: Allen & Unwin, 1932.

———. "Pessimism?" In *Selected Essays*, trans. Donald O. White. Chicago: Regnery, 1967. 133–154.

———. *Prussianism and Socialism*. In *Selected Essays*, trans. Donald O. White. Chicago: Regnery, 1967. 1–131.

"Spengler Speaks." *Time* 23, no. 7 (1934).

Stenbock-Fermor, Elisabeth. *The Architecture of Anna Karenina: A History of Its Writing, Structure and Message*. Lisse: Peter de Ridder Press, 1975.

Strauss, Leo. "What Is Political Philosophy?" In *What Is Political Philosophy? And Other Studies*. Glencoe, IL: Free Press, 1959. 9–55.

Strong, Tracy. *Friedrich Nietzsche and the Politics of Transfiguration*. Berkeley: University of California Press, 1975.

Susman, Warren I. "History and the American Intellectual: Uses of a Usable Past." *American Quarterly* 16, no. 2 (1964): 243–263.

Tamir, Yael. *Liberal Nationalism*. Princeton, NJ: Princeton University Press, 1995.

Taylor, Charles. *Hegel*. Cambridge: Cambridge University Press, 1975.

Taylor, Natalie F. "Introduction: The Literary Statesmanship of Henry Adams." In *A Political Companion to Henry Adams*, ed. Natalie F. Taylor. Lexington: University Press of Kentucky, 2010. 1–14.

Tocqueville, Alexis de. *Democracy in America: And Two Essays on America*. Trans. Gerald E. Bevan. London: Penguin, 2003.

Tolstoy, Leo. *A Confession*. In *A Confession, The Gospel in Brief, and What I Believe*, trans. Aylmer Maude. London: Oxford University Press, 1967. 3–84.

———. "A Few Words Apropos of the Book *War and Peace*." In *War and Peace*, trans. Richard Pevear and Larissa Volokhonsky. New York: Knopf, 2007. 1217–1224.

———. *War and Peace*. Trans. Richard Pevear and Larissa Volokhonsky. New York: Knopf, 2007.

———. *What Is Art?: And Essays on Art*. Trans. Aylmer Maude. New York: Oxford University Press, G. Cumberlege, 1930.

Tolstóy, Lev N. *The Kingdom of God Is Within You*. In *The Kingdom of God Is Within You; Christianity and Patriotism; Miscellanies*, vol. 20 of *The Complete Works of Count Tolstóy*, trans. Leo Wiener. Boston: Dana Estes, 1905. 1–380.

———. "Progress and the Definition of Education." In *Pedagogical Articles; Linen-Measurer*, vol. 4 of *The Complete Works of Count Tolstóy*, trans. Leo Wiener. Boston: Colonial Press, 1904. 152–190.

Troyat, Henri. *Tolstoy*. New York: Grove, 2001.

Trump, Donald J. "Inaugural Address." White House, January 20, 2017.

Turgenev, Ivan. *Fathers and Sons*. Trans. Rosemary Edmonds. New York: Penguin, 1975.

Turner, Frederick Jackson. "The Significance of the Frontier in American History." In *The Frontier in American History*. New York: Henry Holt, 1921. 1–38.

Van Doren, Charles L. *The Idea of Progress*. New York: Praeger, 1967.

Van Tassel, David D. "From Learned Society to Professional Organization: The American Historical Association, 1884–1900." *American Historical Review* 89, no. 4 (1984): 929–956.

Verene, Donald Phillip. *Vico's Science of Imagination*. Ithaca, NY: Cornell University Press, 1981.

Voltaire. *Candide*. Trans. Lowell Bair. New York: Bantam, 1981.

———. *Philosophical Dictionary*. Trans. Theodore Besterman. Harmondsworth: Penguin, 1971.

Wachtel, Andrew. *An Obsession with History: Russian Writers Confront the Past*. Stanford, CA: Stanford University Press, 1994.

Wagar, Warren. *Good Tidings: The Belief in Progress from Darwin to Marcuse*. Bloomington: Indiana University Press, 1972.

Walicki, Andrzej. *A History of Russian Thought: From the Enlightenment to Marxism*. Oxford: Clarendon, 1988.

———. "Russian Philosophers of the Silver Age as Critics of Marxism." In *Russian Thought After Communism: The Recovery of a Philosophical Heritage*, ed. James P. Scanlan. Armonk, NY: M.E. Sharpe, 1994. 81–103.

———. *The Slavophile Controversy*. Oxford: Clarendon, 1975.

Walsh, David. "Dostoevsky's Discovery of the Christian Foundation of Politics." *Religion and Literature* 19, no. 2 (1987): 49–72.

*Washington Post*. "Mr. Solzhenitsyn as Witness." In *Solzhenitsyn at Harvard: The Address; Twelve Early Responses, and Six Later Reflections*, ed. Ronald Berman. Washington, DC: Ethics and Public Policy Center, 1980. 25–26.

Weber, Max. "Politics as a Vocation." In *From Max Weber: Essays in Sociology*, trans. Hans Gerth and C. Wright Mills. New York: Oxford University Press, 1946.

Weigert, Hans W. "The Future in Retrospect: Oswald Spengler Twenty-Five Years After." *Foreign Affair* 21, no. 1 (1942): 120–131.

Welter, Rush. "The Idea of Progress in America: An Essay in Ideas and Method." *Journal of the History of Ideas* 16, no. 3 (1955): 401–415.

White, Hayden. "The Politics of Historical Interpretation: Discipline and De-Sublimation." *Critical Inquiry* 9, no. 1 (1982): 113–137.

Whittaker, Cynthia. "The Reforming Tsar: The Redefinition of Autocratic Duty in Eighteenth-Century Russia." *Slavic Review* 51, no. 1 (1992): 77–98.

Wilke, Joy. *Americans' Satisfaction with U.S. Gov't Drops to New Low: Democrats Remain Most Likely to Be Satisfied, But Much Less So Than in September*. Gallup, October 10, 2013.

Will, George. "Solzhenitsyn's Critics." In *Solzhenitsyn at Harvard: The Address; Twelve Early Responses, and Six Later Reflections*, ed. Ronald Berman. Washington, DC: Ethics and Public Policy Center, 1980. 33–35.

Williams, Melissa S., and Mark E. Warren. "A Democratic Case for Comparative Political Theory." *Political Theory* 41, no. 1 (2014): 26–57.

Williams, Raymond. *Keywords: A Vocabulary of Culture and Society*. Rev. ed. New York: Oxford University Press, 1985.

Williams, William A. "Brooks Adams and American Expansion." *New England Quarterly* 25, no. 2 (1952): 217–232.

Wills, Garry. *Henry Adams and the Making of America*. Boston: Houghton Mifflin, 2005.

Wilson, A. N. *Tolstoy*. New York: Norton, 1988.

Wilson, Francis G. "Pessimism in American Politics." *Journal of Politics* 7, no. 2 (1945): 125–44.

Wilson, James. "Oration Delivered on the 4th of July, 1788, at the Procession Formed at Philadelphia to Celebrate the Adoption of the Constitution of the United States (1787)." In *Collected Works of James Wilson*, vol. 1, ed. Kermit L. Hall and Mark David Hall. Indianapolis: Liberty Fund, 2007. 285–293.

Winkler, Robin. "Schopenhauer's Critique of Moralistic Theories of the State." *History of Political Thought* 34, no. 2 (2013): 296–323.

Wood, Allen. "Herder and Kant on History: Their Enlightenment Faith." In *Metaphysics and the Good: Themes from the Philosophy of Robert Merrihew Adams*, ed. Samuel Newlands and Larry M. Jorgensen Oxford: Oxford University Press, 2009. 313–472.

Young, James P. *Henry Adams: The Historian as Political Theorist*. Lawrence: University Press of Kansas, 2001.

Young, Julian. *Schopenhauer*. London: Routledge, 2005.

Zuckert, Catherine. "On Reading Classic American Novelists as Political Thinkers." *Journal of Politics* 43, no. 3 (1981): 683–706.

# INDEX

Adams, Brooks, 6, 65, 89, 100, 111–114, 143n, 153n12; Henry Adams and, 66, 68, 82–88, 150n124, 150nn127–128, 151n143, 152n154, 152n166; cyclical theory of, 84–86; *The Degradation of the Democratic Dogma*, 73–74, 82, 83, 150n127; democracy and, 83–84, 150n131; *The Law of Civilization and Decay*, 82, 85, 89, 143n, 152n166

Adams, Charles Francis, 73, 78

Adams, Henry, 4, 6, 89, 111–118 passim, 143n, 149n106, 151n134, 161n20; Brooks Adams and, 66, 68, 82–88, 150n124, 150nn127–128, 151n143, 152n154, 152n166; biography of, 71–73; capitalism and, 83, 108,150n128; "conservative Christian anarchism" of, 86–88, 152n164; *Democracy*, 72–78, 81, 87, 146n56, 147n66; democracy and, 73–79, 83–84, 147n66, 150n128, 150n131; *The Education of Henry Adams*, 72–73, 79, 81–82, 84, 146n46, 151n140, 152n166; *Essays in Anglo-Saxon Law*, 72; *Esther*, 72; *History of the United States During the Administrations of Thomas Jefferson and James Madison*, 72, 79; "A Letter to American Teachers of History," 79; John Stuart Mill and, 77–78, 150n128; relationship with and views of other historians, 67–68, 79–81, 146n44, 146n46, 149n102; "The Rule of Phase Applied to History," 7; Schopenhauer and, 8, 79; Tocqueville and, 77–78, 100, 148n92, 151n140; views on physical and social sciences, 79–81, 146n52, 149n110, 151n135

Adams, Herbert Baxter, 68, 70–72, 108, 145nn30–32

Adams, John, 67, 71, 143n3

Adams, John Quincy, 71, 73

Adams, Marian Hooper, 74

Aesthetics, 7, 114, 117; Burckhardt and, 30, 32, 94, 117–118, 129–130n151; Nietzsche and, 32, 94, 131n167; Schopenhauer and, 9, 24, 29, 32, 94, 117, 122n4, 129–130n151; Spengler and, 90, 94. *See also* Art

Alexander I, 35, 55, 132n7

Alexander II, 51, 132n7

Alexander III, 51

Alexander the Great, 94

Altruism, 117, 161n20

America. *See* United States

American Academy of Arts and Letters, 84

American Historical Association, 67, 70

Analogy, 63, 90

Anarchism, 24, 103; Henry Adams and, 86–88, 152n164; Tolstoy and, 59–62, 112, 142n196

Ancient Greece, 14, 17, 32, 39, 63, 89, 91, 154n44

Ancient Rome, 17, 32, 46, 63, 86, 89, 91, 153n12

Antiquity, 27. *See also* Ancient Greece; Ancient Rome; Classical culture

Aphorism, 92

Apollonian culture. *See* Classical culture

Art, 1, 68–69, 76, 81, 85, 99, 153n12; Burckhardt and, 29–30, 94, 117, 129n147; Nietzsche and, 32, 131n169; Schopenhauer and, 24, 94; Spengler and, 90–91, 94; Tolstoy and, 52–53, 59, 140n172. *See also* Aesthetics

Asceticism, 23, 51

Athens, 91, 95, 153n12

Augustine, 100

Authoritarianism, 16, 26, 62, 100–101, 94, 109, 128n123. *See also* Totalitarianism

Autocracy, 6, 36, 61; Slavophiles and, 41, 134n48, 138n122; Solzhenitsyn and, 100–101; Tolstoy and, 36, 52–53, 112, 139n143, 142n198; Westernizers and, 42, 50. *See also* Monarchism; Tsarism

Babylon, 90, 94
Bakunin, Mikhail, 42–44, 46, 63, 135–136n75, 136n94
Bancroft, George, 68–73, 108, 143–144n11
Basel, 27, 30–31, 128n126, 129n142, 161n20
Belinsky, Vissarion, 42–44, 46, 135n55, 135n66, 135–136n75
Biology, 69–70, 79–80. *See also* Physics; Science
Bonaparte, Napoleon, 35–36, 55, 139nn143–144
Borgia, Cesare, 131n182
Brexit, 3, 114
Brezhnev, Leonid, 157
Brownson, Orestes, 108
Buddha, 51, 138n124
Burckhardt, Jacob, 112, 114, 117–118, 128n126, 129n132, 129n144, 129n150, 130nn155–156; aesthetics and, 29–30, 129n147, 129–130n151; Basel and, 27–28, 30, 129n142, 161n20; *The Civilization of the Renaissance in Italy*, 29, 32; happiness and, 27–28, 130n152; ideology of, 28–29, 129n143; *Judgments on History and Historians*, 27; nationalism and, 28; Nietzsche and, 30–33, 130n161, 131n166, 131n177, 131n183; *Reflections on History*, 27; Schopenhauer and, 5, 7, 11, 26–29, 128n125, 128n127, 128n130; Spengler and, 94, 154n44
Burke, Edmund, 4, 19, 100
Bury, John Bagnell, 5

Caesar, Julius, 91–92, 94, 112
Caesarism, 96
Cameron, Elizabeth Sherman, 82
Capitalism, 6; Adams brothers on, 83, 108, 150n128; Lasch on, 108–109, 118. *See also* Economics; Free trade
Carter, Jimmy, 107, 159n149
Categorical imperative, 126n61
Catherine II, 35, 51, 61–62, 132n7
Censorship, 24, 93, 97. *See also* Freedom: of expression

Centralization: Brooks Adams on, 85; Henry Adams on, 85, 87; Burckhardt on, 28, 32; Lasch and, 108; Slavophiles and, 41, 134n48
Chaadaev, Petr, 36–41, 133n17, 133n27
Chartres, 88, 114, 161n20
China, 34, 39, 90, 94, 157n110
Christ, 43, 60
Christianity: Henry Adams and, 87; Bancroft and, 69; Chaadaev and, 39; Dostoevsky and, 48; Schopenhauer and, 127n105; Slavophiles and, 40, 100; Solzhenitsyn and, 97, 100, 156n95; Tolstoy and, 60; Westernizers and, 43. *See also* Orthodox Christianity; Protestantism; Religion; Roman Catholicism
Cicero, Marcus Tullius, 100
Civilization, 37, 46, 48, 77, 112, 116; Brooks Adams and, 84–86; Danilevsky and, 63–65; Fiske and, 70; Solzhenitsyn and, 99; Spengler and, 90–92, 95, 97, 114, 154n31; Tolstoy and, 57–59, 61; Western, 134n36
Civil War (U.S.), 67, 144n20
Clash of civilizations, 158n111
Classical culture, 89–91, 94–95
Clinton, Hillary, 1–2
Cold War, 158n111
Colonial America, 69, 150n121
Colonization, 158n111. *See also* Empire; Imperialism
Communism, 3, 6, 157–158n110; Schopenhauer and, 25–26; Solzhenitsyn and, 97–99, 101, 109; Tolstoy and, 63
Communitarianism, 160n151
Comparative political theory, 115, 162n25
Compassion, 23
Compromise, 42
Condorcet (Marie Jean Antoine Nicolas de Caritat), 3–5, 104, 143n3
Congress (U.S.), 73, 75–76, 111
Conservatism: Henry Adams and, 87; American, 71, 108, 113, 145n32; Burckhardt and, 28–29, 129n143; historical pessimism and, 113, 161n13; Russian, 36, 134n36; Schopenhauer and, 25–26; Solzhenitsyn and, 100; Spengler and, 94; Tolstoy and, 139n129, 142n197
Constitutions: American, 143n5; cosmopolitan, 15, 145n28; Schopenhauer and, 20, 24–25, 128n116; Spengler and, 90

Consumerism, 98, 107, 109. *See also*
Materialism
Contested concepts, 115–116, 162n29
Corporatism, 154n55. *See also* Socialism:
Spengler and
Corruption, 76–77, 87, 109, 150n128
Cosmopolitanism, 13–15, 17, 22, 148n92.
*See also* Globalization; Universalism
Crimean War, 51–53, 58
Culture, 5–6; Henry Adams and, 151n134;
Burckhardt and, 30, 32; Danilevsky
and, 65; Egyptian, 14, 94; middle-class,
159n145; Nietzsche and, 32; Russian, 34,
41, 49, 96–97; Solzhenitsyn and, 98–99,
101; Spengler and, 89–91, 94–96, 154n44;
Tolstoy and, 53; Vico and, 160–161n10;
Western, 30, 34, 94–95, 98
Cyclical theory, 5, 7, 111–114; Brooks Adams
and, 84–86; Danilevsky and, 63–65;
Spengler and, 89–91, 94–96

Danilevsky, Nikolai, 63–65, 89–90, 112–114,
142n208; *Russia and Europe*, 63, 89
Darwin, Charles, 79, 81. *See also* Darwinism
Darwinism, 63, 70–71, 79–80, 129n32,
144n25. *See also* Darwin, Charles
*Darwinism and Other Essays* (Fiske), 144n25
Decembrist uprising, 46, 51–52, 138n127,
142n197
Declaration of Independence, 1, 67
Democracy, 16, 115–116, 118, 155n133,
157–158n110, 162n31; Brooks Adams and,
83, 150n131; Henry Adams and, 72–79,
83–84, 147n66, 150n128; American, 6, 67,
69–71, 77–78, 108–109, 144n20, 145n32,
148n93; Athenian, 91, 95; British, 96;
Chaadaev and, 133n17; Lasch and, 109,
150n132; Solzhenitsyn and, 101, 109;
Tolstoy on, 62, 142n196. *See also* Majority
rule; Majority tyranny; Parliamentarism;
Republicanism
Democrats, 1
Desire: Burckhardt on, 27; Lasch on,
104–106, 118; Schopenhauer on, 18, 20,
24, 56–57; Solzhenitsyn on, 159–160n151
Despotism, 24, 28, 112
Determinism: Fichte and, 16; Lasch and,
104; Solzhenitsyn and, 102; Tolstoy and,
55–56, 102. *See also* Necessity (historical)
Diversity, 99, 151n134

Dostoevsky, Fyodor, 46–49, 100, 137nn95–96,
138nn117–118; *The Brothers Karamazov*,
46, 48, 137n96, 138n117; *The Diary of a
Writer*, 48, 137n95
Duty, 21; Brooks Adams on, 84; Belinsky
and, 43; Hegel and, 17; Nietzsche and,
130–131n165; Slavophiles and, 43; Spengler and, 155n56; Tolstoy and, 53

Ecology: Lasch on, 105–106; Solzhenitsyn
on, 99, 156n84
Economics: Brooks Adams and, 82, 85;
American founders and, 67; contemporary
conservatism and, 113; Lasch and, 104–105;
Solzhenitsyn and, 97–99; Spengler and,
90, 97; Turner and, 70. *See also* Capitalism;
Communism; Corporatism; Socialism
Education: American historians' expecta-
tions of, 79; Bakunin on, 44; competition
and, 83; Fichte and, 125n51; Lasch and,
106; in nineteenth-century Germany,
21–22; Schopenhauer on, 15, 20; Tolstoy
and, 51; tsarist Russia and, 35
Egypt, 63, 74, 90, 94
Eighteenth century, 4, 13, 17, 34, 87, 98, 106,
115. *See also* Enlightenment
Elections, 1–2, 92, 108, 114. *See also* Voting
Empire: Brooks Adams on, 83, 85–86; Rus-
sian, 62, 101; Spengler on, 91, 96, 154n31.
*See also* Colonization; Imperialism
"End of history," 6, 102, 157–158n110
England, 22, 73, 78, 95, 146n56
Enlightenment, 31; Burckhardt on, 27;
French, 105; Russian rulers and, 35–36;
Schopenhauer and, 10; Scottish, 104;
Slavophiles, Solzhenitsyn, and, 98–99;
Spengler and, 91; United States and, 1,
6, 111; Westernizers and, 38. *See also*
Eighteenth century
Entropy, 80–81
Environment: Lasch and, 105–106;
Solzhenitsyn and, 99, 156n84
Epistemology, 91, 116
Equality: Burckhardt on, 118; Christian-
ity ideal of, 43; as a contested concept,
115–116; education and, 21–22; in
international affairs, 15, 90, 94; social, 69;
women's, 68
Eudemonism: Burckhardt and, 27; Schopen-
hauer and, 19. *See also* Happiness

Europe: Adams brothers and, 78, 85; American historians and, 69–71, 144n20, 145n28; Burckhardt and, 30, 130n156; Chaadaev and, 37–39, 133n17; contemporary, 3; Danilevsky and, 64–65, 142n208; Dostoevsky and, 48–49; eighteenth-century, 4, 13, 28; Herder and, 125n43; Herzen and, 45–46; Kant and, 15; medieval, 40, 83, 88–91, 153n12; nineteenth-century, 13, 22, 28; Russia and, 34–36; Slavophiles and, 40–41, 134n36; Solzhenitsyn and, 98, 102; Spengler and, 92, 155n56; Tolstoy and, 57–59. *See also* European Union; The West; *and specific countries*
European Union, 3, 114

Faith: Henry Adams and, 87; Chaadaev and, 38; Slavophiles and, 133n32; Tolstoy and, 59. *See also* Mysticism; Religion; Spirituality
Family: Adams brothers and, 83–84; Lasch and, 108
Fascism, 3, 6, 105; Schopenhauer and, 25; Spengler and, 92–94, 109. *See also* Nazism
Fatalism: Fichte and, 16; Lasch and, 104; Solzhenitsyn and, 102; Tolstoy and, 55–56, 102. *See also* Necessity (historical)
Faustian culture. *See* The West: Spengler and
Federalism, 30, 70, 145n28, 158n118
Fichte, Johann, 10–13, 15–17, 20, 33, 96, 125n44, 125n48, 125n51; *Addresses to the German Nation*, 15–16; *The Characteristics of the Present Age*, 15–16
Fiske, John, 68–72, 108, 144n25, 145n28
Foreign affairs, 89, 111; American, 76–77; clash of civilizations and, 158n111; Danilevsky and, 63, 113; economy and, 85; Kant and, 15; nationalism and, 28, 158n110; Russian, 62, 141–142n193; Spengler and, 90, 94, 113
Founders (American), 4, 66–67, 143n5
Freedom, 21, 49, 50, 105, 146n52; and duty, 17, 43; and equality, 69, 94; of expression, 50; of religion, 98; of thought, 27, 100, 134n48; United States and, 69, 71, 84, 144n20; and unity, 40, 133n31. *See also* Liberty; Rights
Freedom Party of Austria, 114
Free trade, 150n128. *See also* Capitalism
Free will, 55–57, 102, 112, 140n153

French Revolution, 22, 28, 132n6, 139n143
Freud, Sigmund, 10
Fukuyama, Francis, 157–158nn110–111

Genocide, 3, 105
George, Henry, 81
*The Germanic Origin of New England Towns* (Herbert Baxter Adams), 70
Germans, 3; ancient, 70, 88; philosophy of, 10–11, 15–17, 20, 25, 124n27; Schopenhauer on, 22–23; social scientific methods of, 69; Spengler and, 92, 93, 96, 114, 155n65, 161n22. *See also* Germany
Germany, 3, 5, 13, 21, 59, 98, 113; Fichte and, 125n44; Herder and, 125n44; Schopenhauer and, 22, 128n123; Spengler and, 88, 92, 94–96, 112, 161n22. *See also* Germans
Germ theory, 70, 72, 145n31, 146n46
Gilded Age, 81. *See also* Reconstruction
Globalization, 30, 114. *See also* Cosmopolitanism; Universalism
Goebbels, Joseph, 92
Goethe, Johann Wolfgang von, 92
Gogol, Nikolai, 52
Government, 4, 111–112; Henry Adams and, 72, 74–78, 81, 83–84; Burckhardt and, 32; Kant and, 15; Nicholas I and, 36, 50, 141–142n193; Schopenhauer and, 19–22, 122n4; Slavophiles and, 134n48; Solzhenitsyn and, 101, 157–158n110, 158n111; Spengler and, 95–96; Tolstoy and, 52–53, 59–62, 103; Westernizers and, 42. *See also* The State; Statism
Grant, Ulysses, 73, 78–79, 81
Gray, John, 117–118
"Great man" theory of history, 55, 102
Greece (ancient), 14, 17, 32, 39, 63, 89, 91, 154n44
*Groundwork of the Metaphysics of Morals*, 126n61

Happiness, 1, 14, 19, 42, 45, 100, 125n43; Burckhardt and, 27; desire and, 18, 104, 118; Schopenhauer and, 18–20, 123n12. *See also* Eudemonism
Hegel, Georg Wilhelm Friedrich, 4–5, 33, 157–158n110; Henry Adams and, 8, 79; Burckhardt and, 29, 129n144; nationalism and, 16–17, 96, 125n56; Nietzsche and, 17, 31; Russian thought and, 39, 53; Scho-

penhauer and, 10–13, 19–20, 23, 25–26, 124n26; the state and, 17, 29, 96

Herder, Johann Gottfried von, 11, 13–15, 17, 23, 125nn43–44; *Reflections on the Philosophy of the History of Mankind*, 13–14; *This Too a Philosophy of History for the Formation of Humanity*, 13

Herzen, Alexander, 44–47, 63, 118, 136n78, 136nn93–94, 138n126; *From the Other Shore*, 44–46; "Open Letter to Jules Michelet," 46

Historical laws: Brooks Adams and, 84–86; Henry Adams and, 78, 80–81, 84, 89, 118; American thinkers and, 67, 69; Chaadaev and, 37–38; Danilevsky and, 64; Tolstoy and, 55–58, 60, 102

Historical methods, 55, 67, 69–70, 72–73, 148n92. *See also* Historiography

*Historic Progress and American Democracy* (John Lothrop Motley), 69

Historiography, 29, 68–69, 72–73, 108, 149n101. *See also* Historical methods

*History of the United States* (Bancroft), 73, 143–144n11

Hitler, Adolf, 92–93, 153n19

Hobbes, Thomas, 19, 116

Homogeneity, 30

Hope, contrasted with optimism, 45–46, 103–104

Human nature, 15, 23, 105, 116, 128n116, 128n125, 161n13

Huntington, Samuel, 158n111

Imperialism, 62, 83, 91, 154n31. *See also* Colonization; Empire

India, 63, 90

Individualism, 38–39, 71, 84. *See also* Individuality

Individuality, 22. *See also* Individualism

Industry, 1, 3, 27, 58, 65, 70, 83–84, 150n132; Russian and Soviet, 62–63, 99, 136n93, 156n84

Intellectual history, 11, 68, 115

International relations. *See* Foreign affairs

Italy, 3, 93, 114, 155n56

Ivan III, 132n7

Ivan IV, 132n7

Jefferson, Thomas, 67

Jeremiad, 150

Jesus, 43, 60

John Paul II, 100

Juries, 24, 128n123

Justice, 10, 14, 134n41

Kant, Immanuel, 4, 11–15, 17, 33, 126n61, 145n28

Kazan, 51, 138n126

Khomiakov, Alexei, 39–41, 49, 63, 133n31, 134n41

Khrushchev, Nikita, 97

Kireevsky, Ivan, 39–41, 49, 63, 133nn31–32

Korean War, 3

Lamar, Lucius, 75

Lasch, Christopher, 4, 104–110, 112, 113, 118, 146n42, 150n132, 160n152; Jimmy Carter and, 107–108, 159n149; *The Culture of Narcissism*, 106–107, 159n145; Solzhenitsyn and, 104, 109, 159–160n151; *The True and Only Heaven*, 106, 108, 110, 159n145

Leers, Johann von, 93

Leibniz, Gottfried Wilhelm von, 3, 5, 18–19

Lenin, Vladimir, 63, 97, 101

Leontiev, Konstantin, 48

Lermontov, Mikhail, 52

Liberalism: American political development and, 67, 70, 110, 145n32; Burckhardt and, 129n143; contemporary, 1, 108, 114, 157–158n110; nineteenth-century German, 16–17; Schopenhauer and, 22, 24; Spengler and, 95; Tolstoy and, 53; Westernizers and, 50, 61

Liberty, 1, 4, 112, 115–116; Henry Adams and, 79; American historians and, 69–70; Lasch and, 105; John Stuart Mill and, 77, 79; Tocqueville and, 148n93; Westernizers and, 43, 135n71. *See also* Freedom; Rights

Lichtenstein, Martin Hinrich Carl, 126n78

Limits, 43, 62, 81, 105–106, 108, 110, 159–160n151

Linguistic rights, 101–102

Localism, 30, 71, 108, 134n48, 158n118

Locke, John, 24, 116

Lord Kelvin (William Thomson), 80

Luxury, 104–105

Lyell, Charles, 79

Machiavelli, Niccolò, 29

Magian culture, 89

Maistre, Joseph de, 4, 10, 154n35
Majority rule, 76. *See also* Democracy; Majority tyranny
Majority tyranny, 109, 116, 148n93
"Manifest Destiny" (Fiske), 69
Marcus Aurelius, 88, 152n167
Marx, Karl, 4, 136n93, 154–155n55. *See also* Marxism
Marxism, 99, 136n93, 154–155n55. *See also* Marx, Karl
Materialism, 4, 27, 39, 42, 49, 57–58; Henry Adams and, 76, 81, 84; Solzhenitsyn and, 99, 102; Lasch and, 105–106, 113. *See also* Consumerism
Medieval Europe, 40, 83, 88–91, 153n12
Mesoamerica, 90
Messianism, 136n94
Mexico, 94
Middle class, 92, 159n145
Mill, John Stuart, 4, 77–79, 150n128
Millennialism, 2, 26, 67
*Mir*, 134n41. *See also* Village commune
Modernity: Brooks Adams and, 83; Henry Adams and, 67, 83–84; Burckhardt and, 27–29; China and, 39; Danilevsky and, 64; Dostoevsky and, 48; Herzen and, 45, 118; Lasch and, 105–106; Nietzsche and, 32; philosophical trends of, 3, 5, 111; political development and, 21; Russia and, 35, 62; Solzhenitsyn and, 98; Spengler and, 95; Tolstoy and, 55, 58
Monarchism, 46, 62, 93, 112. *See also* Autocracy; Tsarism
Morality, 4, 7, 62, 118; Adams brothers and, 83, 147n66; Burckhardt and, 29; Chaadaev and, 37–38; Hegel and, 17; Herzen and, 46; Kant and, 15, 126n61; Lasch and, 104–106; Schopenhauer and, 12, 20–21, 23, 112, 117; Slavophiles and, 134n48; Solzhenitsyn and, 98–100; Spengler and, 90; Tolstoy and, 60–61, 139n148; Westernizers and, 42, 44
Moscow, 35–36, 134n48, 138n126
Motley, John Lothrop, 68–72, 108, 144n20
Mussolini, Benito, 25, 93–94
Mysticism, 43, 67, 127n105

Napoleonic Wars, 35–36, 54–55, 57, 139n143
*Nation* (magazine), 78, 117

National Front, 1
Nationalism, 109, 113, 116; American, 71; Burckhardt and, 28, 30; contemporary, 3, 30, 114–115, 118, 157–158n110, 161n22; Fichte and, 13, 15–16, 96; Hegel and, 13, 16–17, 96, 125n56; Herder and, 15; linguistic, 15, 28, 141–142n193; Nietzsche and, 130–131n165; Russian, 36, 49, 61, 100, 142n198, 157n101; Schopenhauer and, 13, 19, 22–23, 25–26; Spengler and, 94, 96. *See also* Patriotism
"On the Nature of European Culture and Its Relationship to Russian Culture" (Kireevsky), 39
Nazism, 105; Schopenhauer and, 25; Spengler and, 92–93. *See also* Fascism
Necessity (historical), 55–57, 68. *See also* Fatalism
*The Necessity, the Reality and the Promise of the Progress of the Human Race* (Bancroft), 68
New-York Historical Society, 68–69
Nicholas I, 41, 46, 50, 132n2, 138n122, 141–142n193; Tolstoy and, 36–37, 51, 61–63
Nicholas II, 62
Nietzsche, Friedrich, 112, 130–131n165, 131n169, 131n182; *The Birth of Tragedy*, 32; Burckhardt and, 30–33, 130nn161–162, 131n166, 131n177, 131n183; Hegel and, 17, 31; Nazism and, 25, 92–93; Schopenhauer and, 5, 7, 10–11, 25–26, 130n158, 130n162, 131n177; "Schopenhauer as Educator," 31, 130n158; Spengler and, 94, 154n44; *Unfashionable Observations*, 31
Nihilism, 47, 117–118, 137n106, 162n33
Nisbet, Robert, 5, 115
Nonparticipation, 117
Nonresistance, 51, 60. *See also* Nonviolence; Pacifism
Nonviolence, 60, 64, 65. *See also* Nonresistance; Pacifism
*North American Review* (magazine), 78

Obama, Barack, 1–2, 110, 113
Ochlocracy, 109, 116, 148n93
October Revolution, 51, 97, 103
Opinion polls, 2–3, 110–111

Orthodox Christianity, 39–41, 49–50, 61–62, 100
"Orthodoxy, Autocracy, and Nationality," 36, 61, 100, 142n198

Pacifism, 54, 58–59, 61, 118. *See also* Nonresistance; Nonviolence
Palin, Sarah, 113
Pan-Slavism, 49, 65, 100, 102, 157n101
Parkman, Francis, 69
Parliamentarism, 92, 96. *See also* Democracy; Republicanism
Partisanship, 75–76
Party for Freedom, 114
Patriotism, 69, 101, 125n51. *See also* Nationalism
Peace, 3, 14–15, 70, 80, 90, 103, 145n28, 154n31
Peasantry, 46, 51, 53, 58, 61–62, 134n41, 134n48, 136n93
Pericles, 91, 153n12
Peter I, 35, 36, 42, 51, 61–62, 96–97, 101, 132n7
Petrashevsky Circle, 42
Petrine reforms, 35–36, 42, 132n3. *See also* Peter I
Phase, 80, 86, 151n135
*Phenomenology of the Mind* (Hegel), 12
Philippines, 152n154
*Philosophical Letters* (Chaadaev), 37–38
Physics, 80–81, 149n110
Plato, 11–12, 77, 91
Pluralism, 15, 30, 118, 130n156
Plutocracy, 96
Pobedonostev, Konstantin, 142n198
Police state, 62, 141n189
Political participation, 68, 103, 52, 60
"Polity of the Puritans" (John Lothrop Motley), 144n20
Polls, 2–3, 110–111
Popular participation, 15, 24, 52
Populism, 108, 114, 159–160n151
Post-communism, 101, 156n84
Progressive historians, 71
Property, 24, 155n55, 158n118
Protestantism, 40, 45, 67, 133n32
Prussia, 9, 16, 94–95, 125n56, 155n59
Pseudomorphosis, 96
Pushkin, Alexander, 52
Putin, Vladimir, 114

Ranke, Leopold von, 69
Rationality, 10, 14, 17, 25, 116; nineteenth-century Russian views of, 38–41, 43–44, 133n32, 135n71. *See also* Reason
Reactionary thought, 25, 36, 45, 114
Reagan, Ronald, 1, 107–108, 110, 159n149
Reason, 14, 16, 25, 27, 38–40, 53–54, 105, 116. *See also* Rationality
Reconstruction, 74. *See also* Gilded Age
Reform, 2, 7, 81, 150n121; Henry Adams and, 73, 75, 78, 86; nineteenth-century Germany and, 21–22; Russia and, 35–36, 42, 50, 96, 132n3, 132nn6–7; Solzhenitsyn and, 103; Tolstoy and, 51–52, 59, 141n185, 142n197
Reformation, 40, 133n32
Religion, 112, 114; Bancroft and, 69; nineteenth-century Russia and, 38–40, 49, 134n48, 135n55; Schopenhauer and, 21, 127n105; Solzhenitsyn and, 97–98, 156n95; Spengler on, 89–91, 97; Tolstoy and, 60, 62, 138n124. *See also* Christianity; Faith; Mysticism; Spirituality
Renaissance, 29, 32, 114, 131n182
Republicanism: American, 6, 67; French, 28; Kant on, 15; Roman, 86. *See also* Democracy; Parliamentarism
Republican Party, 113
Resignation, 32, 45, 83, 87, 131n177
Revolution: anti-Communist, 115–116; of 1848, 22, 25, 45; French, 22, 28, 115, 132n6; nineteenth-century Russian views of, 41, 42, 50, 133n17; October, 51, 96–97, 103; Tolstoy and, 60–62, 139n143
Revolutions of 1848, 22, 25, 45
Rights, 4, 42, 94, 154–155n55; linguistic, 101–102; property, 24, 158n118. *See also* Freedom; Liberty
Roman Catholicism, 40, 45, 100, 108, 133n27, 133n32
Rome, 100. *See also* Ancient Rome
Romney, Mitt, 113
Roosevelt, Theodore, 86
Rosenberg, Alfred, 93
Rousseau, Jean-Jacques, 58, 140n164
Rule of law, 101, 103
Russia: contemporary, 114, 157–158n110; Danilevsky and, 63–65, 113; Dostoevsky on, 48–49; eighteenth-century, 34–35, 132nn6–7; Herzen and, 45–46;

Russia (continued)
nineteenth-century, 6, 35, 36–42,
49–50, 62, 134n41, 136n93, 141–142n193;
Solzhenitsyn and, 97, 99–102, 156n84,
157n101; Spengler and, 90, 96–97; Tolstoy
and, 51–52, 54–56, 58–59, 61–63, 112,
139n141, 139n143; twentieth-century, 3, 63
Russification, 141–142n193

Sanders, Bernie, 1
Schelling, Friedrich von, 39
Schleiermacher, Friedrich, 11, 12
Schopenhauer, Arthur, 9–10, 89, 112, 117–118,
122n, 122n4, 161n20, 162n34; Henry
Adams and, 79, 82, 86–87; affinities with
Burckhardt and Nietzsche, 26–29, 31–33,
128n125, 128n127, 128n130, 129–130n151,
130n158, 131n177; biography of, 11–13;
contemporary readings of, 4–5, 24–26,
124n4; happiness and, 18–20, 123n12;
Hegel and, 19–20, 23, 124n26; Herzen
and, 45; ideology of, 24–26, 114; Indian
religions and, 123n13, 127n105; influence on later writers, 7–8, 13, 124n25;
juries and, 24, 128n123; nationalism
and, 22–23; On the Basis of Morality, 12;
On the Fourfold Root of the Principle of
Sufficient Reason, 11; Parerga and Paralipomena, 22; Spengler and, 94, 96; the
state and, 17, 19–21, 126n78, 126–127n79,
128n116; Tolstoy and, 56–57, 140n153;
the will and, 18–19, 24; The World as Will
and Representation, 11–12, 22, 27, 122n,
128n127, 128n130
Schulze, Gottlob, 12
Science, 66, 69–70, 79, 81, 83, 131n169,
135n71
Scruton, Roger, 113
Second Law of Thermodynamics, 80
Self-development, 22; Schopenhauer on, 21,
24; Solzhenitsyn on, 102–103; Tolstoy on,
61, 102, 141n186
Sermon on the Mount, 60
"Significance of the Frontier in American
History, The" (Turner), 70
Skepticism, 116
Skovoroda, Grigory, 34–35, 37
Slavophiles, 6, 36–37, 61, 96, 133n31,
134n36, 134n48; Chaadaev and, 38–41,
133n17; Danilevsky and, 63; Dostoevsky

and, 48–49; Herzen and, 45; Nicholas I,
41–42, 50, 138n122; Pan-Slavism and,
49–50; Solzhenitsyn and, 100, 102,
157n101; Tolstoy and, 52–53, 139n133;
and Westernizers, 42–43, 49
Slavs, 46, 48–49, 64–65, 138n118, 142n212
Smith, Adam, 4, 104–105
Sobornost', 133n31
Socialism, 17, 108; Herzen and, 46, 136n93;
Spengler and, 95, 154–155n55, 155n65;
Westernizers and, 42, 50, 135n55,
135–136n75
Solidarity (Solidarność), 115
Solzhenitsyn, Aleksandr, 4, 6, 112, 156n85,
156n91, 158n118, 162n34; environment
and, 99, 156n84; The Gulag Archipelago, 98;
Lasch and, 104, 109, 159–160n151; "Letter
to the Soviet Leaders," 99; One Day in the
Life of Ivan Denisovich, 97–98; religion
and, 97, 103, 117; Russian predecessors
and, 100–103; "Templeton Lecture," 98;
the West and, 98–100, 103, 157–158n110,
158n111; "A World Split Apart," 97
Soviet Union, 97–99, 101, 105, 109
Sparta, 95, 155n59
Spengler, Oswald, 4, 6, 101, 109, 153n19,
154n31, 155n56, 155n59; Brooks Adams
and, 65, 89–90, 112–114, 153n12; Burckhardt and, 154n44; Classical-Western
analogy of, 90–91, 95; Danilevsky and,
63, 65, 89–90, 112–114; The Decline of the
West, 89–90, 92–94, 96–97; Germany and,
92–96, 112, 155n65, 161n22; The Hour
of Decision, 94; Man and Technics, 94;
Nietzsche and, 33, 154n44; Prussianism
and Socialism, 95; Russia and, 96–97;
socialism and, 154–155n55, 155n65
Spirituality: Dostoevsky and, 48–49,
138n118; Lasch and, 109; nineteenth-
century Russia and, 39–41, 49, 62;
Solzhenitsyn and, 97–98, 100, 102–103;
Spengler and, 91. See also Faith; Mysticism; Religion
Spoils system, 79
Stalin, Joseph, 97
The state, 7, 118, 141n189; Henry Adams
and, 86–87; Burckhardt and, 28–30;
Danilevsky and, 65; Fichte and, 13, 16,
125n51; Hegel and, 13, 16–17; Herder and,
14, 17; Kant and, 14–15; Nietzsche and,

32, 130–131n165, 131n182; nineteenth-
century Russian views of, 41, 43–44,
50, 138n122; Schopenhauer and, 10–11,
17–26, 112, 122n4, 126n78, 126–127n79,
128n116; Solzhenitsyn and, 101, 158n118;
Spengler and, 94–95; Tolstoy and, 60–62,
112, 142n196
Statesmanship, 93–94
Statism, 25, 87, 96, 109
Stoics, 118
Suffering, 23, 27, 47, 51, 54, 138n124; Scho-
penhauer and, 18, 20, 25
Suffrage, 77
Superman, 33, 131n182
Supreme Court (U.S.), 1, 111
Surveys, 2–3, 110–111

Tea Party, 113
Technology, 3, 14, 151n133; Adams brothers
on, 79, 83–84, 151n134; Solzhenitsyn on,
97, 99; Spengler on, 90–91, 97; Tolstoy
and, 58, 62–63
Teleology, 31, 79, 157n110
Terrorism, 42, 61, 157–158n110
Theocracy, 41, 157n110
Tocqueville, Alexis de, 77–79, 97, 100,
148nn92–93, 151n140
Tolstaya, Sophia, 51
Tolstoy, Leo, 4, 6, 65, 112–113, 118, 139n133,
142n198, 142n202; anarchism and, 59–62,
112, 142n196; Anna Karenina, 53, 57,
59–60, 139n129; biography of, 51–54,
138n124, 138n126; A Confession, 52–53,
59–60, 140n151; The Kingdom of God Is
Within You, 59, 112; laws of history and,
55–58, 139n148; Nicholas I and, 36–37,
50, 62–63; "Progress and the Definition of
Education," 57; religious views of, 59–60,
62; revolution and, 62, 142n197; Rousseau
and, 58, 140n164; Schopenhauer and, 8,
56–57, 140n153; self-perfection and, 60,
141nn185–186; on war and peace, 34,
58–59, 61; War and Peace, 53–57, 59–60,
137n96, 138n127, 139n141, 143n215
Totalitarianism, 16, 24–26, 62–63, 98, 105, 109,
141–142n193. See also Authoritarianism
Trade, 85–86, 150n128
Tradition: American, 67, 69–70, 84, 108,
110, 150n121; European, 30, 155n56; German, 17, 70, 93–94, 155n56; national, 111,

160n8; Russian, 34, 39–41, 43, 49, 99–100,
134n41, 139n143; Western, 98–100
Trains, 57–58
Trump, Donald, 2, 121n7
Tsarism, 35–36, 42, 62, 101, 132n7, 134n48,
142n197. See also Autocracy; Monar-
chism; and specific tsars
Turgenev, Ivan, 45, 52, 137n106
Turgot, Anne Robert Jacques, 98, 143n3
Turner, Frederick Jackson, 68, 70–71, 73,
108, 146n44
Tyranny, 101, 131n183
Tyranny of the majority, 109, 116, 148n93

Union of Soviet Socialist Republics, 97–99,
101, 105, 109
United Kingdom, 22, 73, 78, 95, 146n56
United States, 6, 58, 88, 110; Adams
brothers and, 72–74, 77–78, 81, 83–88,
100, 112–113, 143n, 148n92; colonial
America, 69, 143n6; contemporary, 2–3,
6, 114; eighteenth-century, 6, 66–67,
143n6; Lasch and, 106–107; nineteenth-
century, 67, 69–70, 144n20, 145n28,
145n32, 148n93; Solzhenitsyn and, 97,
100, 156n91; twentieth-century, 92,
107–108, 159n149
Universalism, 7, 109, 112–114, 117,
157–158n110; American founders and, 67;
Danilevsky and, 64, 142n208; Kant and,
126n61; Russia and, 40, 48–49; Schopenhauer and, 18, 23, 56–57; Solzhenitsyn
and, 103. See also Cosmopolitanism;
Globalization
Upanishads, 123n13
Utopianism, 67, 105, 118, 136n94,
157–158n110

Van Buren, Martin, 73
Variety, 30
Vedas, 123n13
Vico, Giambattista, 113, 160–161n10
Victor Immanuel III, 93
Vietnam War, 3
Village commune, 41, 134n41, 134n48.
See also Mir
Violence, 3, 5, 44, 62, 101; Danilevsky and,
64–65; Lasch and, 105–106; Tolstoy and,
60, 142n196, 142n197. See also Nonvio-
lence; Revolution; Terrorism; War

Voltaire (François-Marie Arouet), 23–24, 35, 42, 115
Voters, 2, 76, 107, 114
Voting, 77

War, 157–158n110; Brooks Adams and, 83–86; Burckhardt and, 27–28, 129n147; Danilevsky and, 65; Dostoevsky and, 138n118; Kant and, 15, 145n28; Schopenhauer and, 21; Spengler and, 90, 94–95, 154n31, 154n35; Tolstoy and, 34, 58, 60. *See also* Civil War (U.S.); Cold War; Crimean War; Korean War, Napoleonic Wars; Vietnam War, World War I; World War II
Washington, D.C., 73–77, 87–88, 110
Weber, Max, 60
Weimar Republic, 93, 95

The West, 6, 112–113, 157–158n110, 158n111; Chaadaev and, 37–39; Russia and, 35, 61–62; Slavophiles and, 40–41, 134n48; Solzhenitsyn and, 97–102, 106; Spengler and, 90–91, 94–99, 112, 161n22
Westernization, 96–97, 132n6
Westernizers, 36–38, 42–44, 49–50, 52–53, 63, 133n17
The will (Schopenhauer term), 18–19, 23–25, 27, 56–57, 122n4
Williams, Raymond, 115
Will to power, 33
Wilson, James, 1
Women, 68, 84
Working class, 108
World War I, 3, 92–93, 95, 105, 149n106
World War II, 3, 5, 92, 105, 114, 118

Yasnaya Polyana, 51–52

## ACKNOWLEDGMENTS

Many people, more than I can acknowledge in these pages, deserve my sincere thanks for their assistance during the writing of this book. Aurelian Craiutu was my biggest champion during my time at Indiana University, advocating on my behalf before I even set foot in Bloomington. But Aurelian more than anyone else fit the mold of what I wanted in a mentor: someone with whom I shared mutual intellectual interests; someone who would push me to do better work; and someone who would invest in my future as an academic. He has continued to serve as a trusted friend even after my departure from Bloomington. Russell Hanson has also always been gracious and giving of his time. Even during the busiest and most stressful periods of his tenure as chair of the Department of Political Science, Russ provided me with much thoughtful advice. William Scheuerman, too, has more than a few times served as my sounding board. I would also like to thank Sara Stefani, who was a model teacher; I have incorporated several of Sara's practices into my own teaching. I appreciate, as well, Patrick Deneen's assistance with my project despite other demands on his time. The feedback and suggestions I received from all of these people is much appreciated; any mistakes that remain in the final product are my own.

I would like to thank several of my former colleagues at IU. Mitchell Krumm, Joe Bolinger, and Kris Rees have long been my go-to guys when it comes to commiseration; Brendon Westler has more recently joined their ranks. Katie Stewart provided useful suggestions that I incorporated into Chapter 2. Jan Campbell Peterson, Amanda Campbell, Jessica Williams, Chris McCann, and Sharon Hughes helped me with too many things to count. Professors Jack Bielasiak, William Fierman, Gregory Kasza, Marjorie Hershey, and Jacek Dalecki have provided me with sage advice.

I gratefully acknowledge past financial support from the Indiana University Department of Political Science, the Indiana University Ostrom Workshop, the Indiana University Summer Workshop on Slavic and East European

Languages, the University of Pittsburgh Summer Language Institute, and the Mercatus Center at George Mason University.

Denison University has been a congenial atmosphere in which to bring this book to fruition. I am thankful to my colleagues for their support.

Chapter 1 of this book is derived, in part, from an article published in *History of European Ideas* on January 8, 2015, available online at http://www.tandfonline.com/doi/full/10.1080/01916599.2014.991143.

Cristian Cantir read a draft of Chapter 3; I thank him for his feedback and for his friendship.

I am grateful to Damon Linker and the editorial team at Penn Press for their help with the publication process. Damon has been especially courteous and quick in his replies to my queries, and I appreciate his support for my project. Mikala Guyton at Westchester Publishing Services has been helpful during the production process. Thanks are due, as well, to Alison Anderson and the two anonymous reviewers whose suggestions have made this a stronger book.

My biggest debts are to my family. Growing up, I wanted to succeed in school like my sister, Lori, had done before me; I'd like to thank her for setting a good example (and for financial support that she and her husband, Scott, have provided). My mom, Marilyn, has been my biggest source of emotional support in happy times and when I've felt low; I'd like to thank her for talking things through with me and worrying about me. But it is my father, Ronald, especially, to whom I dedicate this work. Dad's devotion to the Sunday morning political shows could not but have had an effect on me; I might have written a work on theology or bowling or fishing if his weekend routine had been different. Dad was there every step of the way as I completed my education, helping me move to and from Nashville, to Rock Island, to Champaign, to Lawrence, and to Bloomington. While I was away from home, Dad was unfailing in his letters to me, letting me know that I was loved. I'm sorry that he was unable to see me complete my Ph.D. or the publication of this book, but I know that he was as proud of me for what I accomplished as I am of him for who he was: a great man who never, ever, even in the face of insurmountable odds, abandoned hope. You are missed, Dad, and I love you.

www.ingramcontent.com/pod-product-compliance
Lightning Source LLC
Chambersburg PA
CBHW030940150426
42812CB00064B/3084/J